Economic Growth and Societal Collapse

Wim Naudé

Economic Growth and Societal Collapse

Beyond Green Growth and Degrowth Fairy Tales

palgrave macmillan

Wim Naudé
Research Area Technology, Innovation, Marketing, Entrepreneurship
RWTH Aachen University
Aachen, Germany

ISBN 978-3-031-45581-0 ISBN 978-3-031-45582-7 (eBook)
https://doi.org/10.1007/978-3-031-45582-7

This Palgrave Macmillan imprint is published by the registered company Springer Nature Switzerland AG.
The registered company address is: Gewerbestrasse 11, 6330 Cham, Switzerland

Paper in this product is recyclable.

Books are not to teach us to live, but to make us want to live—Frédéric Gros (2011, p. 95)

Preface

In 1817, the German romantic poet Johann Mayrhofer wrote a poem "Auf der Donau"—On the Danube—that was exquisitely set to music by Franz Schubert. Roughly translated, the poem goes as follows:

> **On the Danube**
> The barge floats on the waves,
> Old castles on the cliff rise to heaven,
> The pine forests rustle like ghosts,
> And the hearts in our breasts grow weak.
>
> For all the works of humanity decline,
> Where is the tower, where the gate, where the rampart?
> Where the Mighty, protected by arms
> To war and hunt have stormed?
>
> Sad undergrowth grows wild,
> While pious illusions wither:
> And in the little barge we grow afraid,
> Waves, like time, threaten our collapse

The river of time indeed sweeps everything away—life, consciousness, and complexity. For a moment, we rage in defiance against this perceived absurdity. As in Goethe's poem *Prometheus*, wherein the protagonist defies Zeus, stealing its "fire" and demanding that the god "*Musst mir meine Erde/Doch lassen stehn/Und meine Hütte, die du nicht gebaut*" (Must let my Earth/Stand/And my hut, which you did not build"), humanity has striven to escape from, and defy, the undergrowth of harsh nature, "red in tooth and claw," as put by Alfred, Lord Tennyson. It has done so through "fire" (science, innovation, and technology) and has consequently built itself a "hut" and a "barge" (civilization). Like many civilizations before, ours has now reached a fork in the road. Which direction we take may determine whether our "hut" will remain standing and whether our "barge" continues to navigate the waves. Some argue that human civilization, and specifically the West, is extracting more than its fair share from the Earth's bounded planetary ecosystems. This "material footprint" on nature needs to shrink—and for this the road that leads to Degrowth is inevitable. Others argue that there is still much work and expansion to be done on the "hut" and that imposing limits on extraction and consumption now will do more harm than good; moreover, they argue that the path of further technological progress—the path of "Green Growth—will allow planetary ecosystems to be maintained. Some even conceive of humanity colonizing space and giving life to quintillions of future sentient beings. Perhaps, these are all illusions, or fairy tales. Maybe there is no fork in the road, only a cliff. Maybe this cliff is an existential catastrophe. Maybe it is a new beginning, a phase-transition, heralding in even greater complexity on Earth and beyond.

This short book is a modest contribution to provide a fresh perspective, largely from an economics point of view, on this Herculean choice. It is also motivated by the comparative neglect of the topic in the traditional economic growth literature. Economists, outside of ecological economics, have been rather dismissive of the importance of energy and hence of ideas that growth is subject to physical limits. Hence, economists have, largely, tended to ignore movements such as the degrowth/beyond growth movements and have only engaged reluctantly with the largely philosophical literature on existential risks and longtermism. Hopefully, this volume will stimulate work by economists in these regards, and provide those who approach the topic from an anthropological or ecology point of view with a better appreciation of the contributions that economics can make.

The book's writing has been a slow project carried out over several years, stimulated by my teaching classes on technology, innovation, and economic growth at RWTH Aachen Business School and spending a sabbatical at Saïd Business School, University of Oxford. In 2023 however, the writing was given an impetus by invitations to present some of my ideas on growth, green growth, degrowth, and on technology and the far future, at the Green European Foundation (GEF) and Wetenschappelijk Bureau GroenLinks's Meeting on *Green Growth vs Degrowth*, held in May

2023 in Utrecht, The Netherlands, and at the Global Priorities Institute at Oxford University's 12th International Workshop in June 2023. My thanks to the organizers of these meetings for the invitations, and to the participants at these meetings for their sharp questions. I am also grateful to the support from Wyndham Hacket Pain, Senior Editor at Palgrave Macmillan, during the writing and publication process, and the anonymous referees who read the initial manuscript for their helpful comments and suggestions. The usual disclaimer applies.

Aachen, Germany
September 2023

Wim Naudé

Contents

About the Author

Wim Naudé, Ph.D., is an economist and graduate of the University of Warwick (UK). He has been Lecturer and Research officer at the University of Oxford (UK), Senior Research Fellow at the World Institute for Development Economics Research (WIDER) at the United Nations University (Finland), Professor in Business and Entrepreneurship at Maastricht University (The Netherlands), and Professor in Economics at University College Cork (Ireland).

He is Fellow of the African Study Centre, University of Leiden (The Netherlands), Visiting Professor in Technology and Development at RWTH Aachen University (Germany), Distinguished Visiting Professor in Economics at the University of Johannesburg (South Africa), and an AI Expert affiliated with the OECD's AI Policy Observatory (France). In 2022–2023, he was a top ten candidate for the Dutch Green Left Party (GroenLinks) in the country's provincial parliamentary elections.

In his early career, as a member of the liberation movement in South Africa, Wim served as an elected councilor for the African National Congress (ANC) in the first democratic local government in the country (2000–2006).

His scholarly work deals with the relationships between technological innovation, entrepreneurship, trade, and economic growth and development. This work has been published widely in major peer-reviewed scientific journals, and he has been editor and coeditor and author of several academic books published by, among others, Palgrave Macmillan, Oxford University Press, Routledge, Springer and Cambridge University Press.

According to Stanford University and Elsevier's Global Ranking of Scientist (2022, 2023), Wim is among the top 2% of scientists in the world.

He lives in Maastricht, The Netherlands.

Abbreviations

°C	Degrees Celsius
AGI	Artificial General Intelligence
AI	Artificial Intelligence
AWG	Anthropocene Working Group
CBD	Conference on Biodiversity
CO_2	Carbon Dioxide
DL	Deep Learning
DMC	Domestic Material Consumption
ECB	European Central Bank
ECS	Equilibrium Climate Sensitivity
EF	Ecological Footprint
EGO	Embedded Growth Obligation
EU	European Union
ENSO	El Ninõ—Southern Oscillation
EO	Ecological Overshoot
ESB	Earth System Boundaries
FF	Fossil Fuels
GB	Gigabyte
GDP	Gross Domestic Product
gha	Global Hectares
GHG	Greenhouse Gas
GIS	Greenland Ice Sheet
GJ	Gigajoules
GMPI	Global Multidimensional Poverty Index
GMST	Global Mean Surface Temperature
GND	Green New Deal
GPT	General Purpose Technology

GWP	Global World Production
HDI	Human Development Index
ICS	International Commission on Stratigraphy
ICT	Information and Communication Technology
IMI	Innovation in the Method of Innovation
IP	Intellectual Property
IPCC	Intergovernmental Panel on Climate Change
ISM	Indian Summer Monsoon
LtG	Limits to Growth Study
MAT	Mean Annual Temperature
MF	Material Footprint
NCP	Nature's Contributions to People
PB	Planetary Boundaries
QE	Quantitative Easing
OECD	Organization for Economic Cooperation and Development
R&D	Research and Development
RMC	Raw Material Consumption
RE	Renewable Energy
SDGs	Sustainable Development Goals
SNA	System of National Accounts
SQS	Subcommission on Quaternary Stratigraphy
THC	Thermohaline Circulation
UK	United Kingdom
UN	United Nations
UNEP	United Nations Environmental Programme
USA	United States of America
WAIS	West Antarctic Ice Sheet
WAM	West African Monsoon
WEF	World Economic Forum
WID	World Inequality Database
WMO	World Meteorological Organization
ZB	Zettabyte

List of Figures

List of Tables

CHAPTER 1

Introduction

Abstract This chapter describes just how thin and precious life, and human civilization, is. It poses the questions that this book explores: has the world economy ecologically overshot planetary systems critical to our survival? What does this mean for the future trajectory of society? How can we best fix it—by stopping and reversing overshoot through technology (Green Growth) or by purposefully reducing the size of the economy (Degrowth)? Or is it best to prepare for societal collapse and a possible rebound, a phase-transition, afterwards? Is societal collapse a feature, and not a bug, of the long-run evolution of complex systems such as civilization? The chapter furthermore explains the key concepts in this book: gross domestic product (GDP), economic growth, and ecological overshoot, and describes the structure of the book.

Keywords GDP • Economic growth • Ecological overshoot • Planetary boundaries

1.1 Introduction

> *Estimates put all biomass at about 2 trillion tons (including water content), and if that were spread uniformly across the Earth's surface it would stack to a height of 4 mm; a delicate gossamer film across planet Earth. Life on this planet is indeed thin and precious* (Murphy et al., 2021, p. 3).

W. Naudé, *Economic Growth and Societal Collapse*,
https://doi.org/10.1007/978-3-031-45582-7_1

Astronomer Carl Sagan described the Earth as a "pale blue dot" reminding us that "on it everyone you love, everyone you know, everyone you ever heard of, every human being who ever was, lived out their lives [...]- on a mote of dust suspended in a sunbeam" (Sagan, 1994). So far, we have found no evidence of life anywhere else in the universe. Life is "indeed thin and precious" as the quote above points out.

This chapter describes just how thin and precious life, and human civilization, is. It poses the questions that this book explores (answer is too ambitious a word): has the world economy ecologically overshot planetary systems critical to our survival? What does this mean for the future trajectory of society? How can we best fix it—by stopping and reversing overshoot through technology (Green Growth) or by purposefully reducing the size of the economy (Degrowth)? Or is it best to prepare for societal collapse and a possible rebound, a phase-transition, afterwards? Is societal collapse a feature, and not a bug, of the long-run evolution of complex systems such as civilization?

An old English nursery rhyme is about a character called Humpty Dumpty, who, in the classic Lewis Carrol book *Through the Looking Glass*, is a giant egg.

Humpty Dumpty sat on a wall.
Humpty Dumpty had a great fall.
All the king's horses and all the king's men
Couldn't put Humpty together again.

Put another way, the questions this book explore are whether Humpty Dumpty (our outsized economy) can be prevented from falling off the (overshoot) wall, and how? Or whether after its fall, it can be put together again, perhaps even better?

1.2 Thin and Precious

Earth, the pale-blue dot which is like a mote of dust suspended in a sunbeam has the following cosmic address:[1]

Planet Earth
Solar System

[1] See: https://www.skyatnightmagazine.com/space-science/cosmic-address/

Oort Cloud
Local Interstellar Cloud
Orion Arm
Milky Way,
Local Group
Virgo Supercluster
Laniakea Supercluster
Universe[2]

The universe and planet Earth are estimated to be around 13.8 and 4.5 billion years old, respectively[3] (Lehto et al., 2013). There is no a priori reason to think that the Earth and human civilization is special. In fact, the Copernican Principle, a foundation of astronomy, holds that the Earth does not occupy a special place in the universe (Caldwell & Stebbins, 2008). We should therefore expect to find Earth-like planets with Earth-like civilizations to be common.

Indeed, galaxies with solar systems with planets orbiting stars like our galaxy, and like our solar system, seems commonplace. It is estimated that there are ~2 trillion galaxies in our universe (Conselice et al., 2016). Each galaxy has around 100 billion stars each (Cassan et al., 2012). There are even more terrestrial (rocky) planets: $\approx 2 \times 10^{19}$ around Sun-like stars and $\approx 7 \times 10^{20}$ around M-dwarf like stars (Zackrisson et al., 2016). According to one estimate, 22% of Sun-like stars may have Earth-size planets in their habitable zone—where liquid water can exist (Petigura et al., 2013). This means that if on only 1% of these planets an intelligent civilization arises, there would be *billions* of civilizations throughout the universe.

So far, however, we have found no evidence of any. Our planet, and our civilization, seems utterly unique. We may be living on a *Rare Earth* (Ward & Brownlee, 2000).

Compared to the immense time span since the beginning of the universe and the planet Earth the presence of human civilization on the planet has been of almost negligibly small duration. Modern human ancestors only separated from so-called archaic human groups between 1 million

[2] The address may be unclear, as the question is whether we live in *The* universe or *A* universe. Edwin Schrödinger proposed that we live in a multiverse to explain the quantum physical feature of superposition, where a particle exists in many positions until measured. See Deutsch (1998) on parallel universes and the multiverse.

[3] Although controversy was elicited when Gupta (2023) provided a model that suggested that the universe may be far older, in fact around 26.7 billion years.

and 300,000 years ago (Bergström et al., 2021). The expansion of humans across the globe started around 60,000 years ago (Bergström et al., 2021), and recorded history began even more recently—around 5000 years ago (Lehto et al., 2013). The universe is expected to last for another 10^{100} years, after which it will end in a "fireworks display" caused by remnants of black dwarf stars exploding as supernovae (Caplan, 2020; Mann, 2020).

Not only has the presence of humans on the planet been so far extremely short seen against geological timescales, but the ecological temperature niche where humans have flourished is very narrow. Figure 1.1 depicts the Human Climate Niche. This shows that human society has peak population densities at local climates with a mean annual temperature (MAT) of ~13 °C and a secondary peak at ~27 °C (Lenton et al., 2023). For instance, between 2000 and 2019 most humans tended to live in a niche where the the average daily mean temperature was 15.2 °C (Abrutzky et al., 2022). The niche is mediated by rainfall, with highest population densities in areas where annual rainfall is between 40 and 80 cm per year (Klinger & Ryan, 2022).

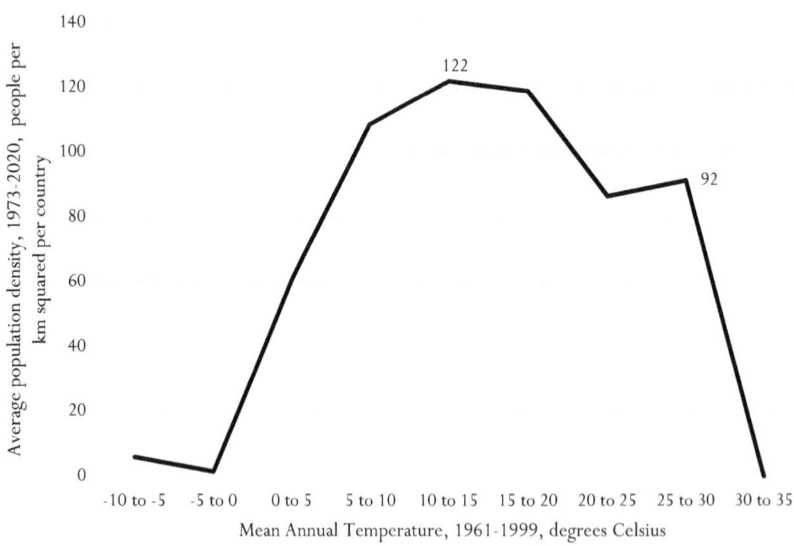

Fig. 1.1 The Human Climate Niche. (Source: Author's compilation based on population density data per country from the World Bank Development Indicators online, and Mean Annual Temperature per country from The World Bank's Climate Change Knowledge Portal: Historical Data)

Humans who are exposed to MATs outside of this niche tend to face higher mortality, morbidity, and see more migration if adaptation is not possible (Lenton et al., 2023).

It has been estimated that globally, nonoptimal temperatures are responsible for 9.43% of deaths—and around 74 out of 100,000 excess deaths (Abrutzky et al., 2022). In 2019, roughly 1.7 million deaths globally were linked to extreme temperatures—of which 356,000 were due to heat (Burkart et al., 2021). Currently, colder temperatures are indeed *more lethal* to humans: 8.52% of deaths have been ascribed to cold and 0.91% to heat (Abrutzky et al., 2022). A 2023 study found that in European cities the excess death rate from cold is ten times higher than that of heat (Masselot et al., 2023). The excess death rate from extreme heat is higher in Europe than in Africa, and conversely the excess death rate of extreme cold is higher in Africa than in Europe, suggesting adaptation to typical local temperatures (Brown, 2022).

1.3 Complex and Fragile

The economy that sustained human populations over the comparatively brief past 300,000 years was marked by different growth modes, or in other words, different ways in which society was organized and technology[4] used to ensure survival, fitness, and reproduction of the species.

Economist and economic historians have identified three such economic growth modes: humans were first foragers, then became farmers and then industrialists. This corresponds to the hunter-gatherer, agricultural and industrial eras (Hanson, 2018, 2020).

Each successive era was marked by faster economic growth: whereas economies remained stationary during the hunter-gatherer period, growth picked up during the agricultural era as food production and urbanization accelerated, from roughly 11,000 years ago. Then, during the industrial era, starting around 250 years ago, exponential, and super-exponential economic growth rates were achieved—accompanied by similar super-exponential growth in energy use and population (Johansen & Sornette, 2001).

Over the past century, the size of the economy, population, and energy consumption roughly doubled every 35 years. With it the complexity of

[4] "Technology is the sum total of instrumentally useful culturally-transmissible information" (Bostrom, 2009, p. 42).

the human enterprise—of its civilization, has increased immeasurably. This complexity is largely due to scale. Bettencourt et al. (2007, p. 7302) relate the growth in the size of human civilization (as measured for instance through GDP, energy use, materials) to population growth through a power law of the following form:

$$Y_t = Y_0 N_t^{\beta} \tag{1.1}$$

Where Υ_t is a measure of the scale or size of human civilization, N_t a measure of population and β a scaling exponent. If $\beta = 1$ there is linear scaling of human civilization, and if $\beta > 1$ there is super-linear scaling. Generally, biological systems have sub-linear scaling, that is, $\beta < 1$ and human systems based on innovation and interaction, such as cities and GDP, super-linear scaling. Bettencourt et al. (2007) report empirical estimates of super-linear scaling of GDP in cities, with $\beta \approx 1, 13 - 1, 26$. Life under super-linear scaling becomes faster and faster—what we experience as complex.

Super-linear scaling of human civilization poses the challenge of coordination of the behavior of ever- larger groups of people interacting and solving collective action problems. For this, governance systems have evolved into large hierarchies, consisting of extended bureaucrats, and manifold rules and regulations. These complex governance systems have been explained as mechanisms to solve the problems a super-linearly scaling society is facing (Tainter, 1988).

While it solves problems, it also leaves human civilization vulnerable and fragile. All previous civilizations and empires have at some point collapsed or unraveled. Turchin (2003), for instance, lists 31 polities in recent history that "rose and fell," from the seventh century Sui/Tang Empire to the British Empire's collapse in the twentieth century. None of these previous civilizations were global civilizations to the extent that ours is. We are living in the first global civilization on the planet. The question is therefore very relevant, whether such a civilization can avoid the fate of all sub-global civilizations in the past. The collective decisions of the current generation may be determining. It may turn out that we are living in perhaps the most important time in history.

1.4 The Most Important Century?

The scale and complexity of human activity is now impacting Earth Systems so substantially that a new geologic epoch is said to have begun in the 1950s: the Anthropocene[5] (Waters & Turner, 2022).

Seen against the span of 300,000 years, the economic expansion witnessed in the last 0.08% of modern human history is clearly an anomalous event. It is an "unusual" time (MacAskill, 2022). It has challenged religious scholars, philosophers, historians, and others to ask what the future holds for humanity (Bostrom, 2009). Less prosaically, it has been exclaimed that humans "live on this rocket ship that took off five seconds ago, and nobody knows where it's going" (Wiblin & Harris, 2021).

One possibility is that humanity may continue its technologically driven growth trajectory and expand into the galaxy.

Another possibility is that humanity may go extinct, or face a catastrophic disaster of such magnitude that the potential of humanity is permanently truncated (Bostrom, 2009; Ord, 2020). Since all past human civilizations have at one point collapsed and given that most life that has ever existed on the planet has gone extinct, and that there is yet no evidence of any other civilization in the universe (the Fermi Paradox), this possibility can be taken as the more probable.

There are many risks or "filters" that may truncate humanity. One risk is Ecological Overshoot: that human economic activity would overshoot planetary biophysical boundaries—to the extent that an anthropomorphic environmental disaster will make Earth uninhabitable—or create conditions too hostile for civilization to continue as is. Some warn that this may cause a civilization collapse, akin to the collapse of Easter Island's society (Diamond, 2005; Kemp et al., 2022; Steel et al., 2022). Others see it causing severe curtailment of civilization that will not cause human extinction, but rather result in a *Great Unraveling* (Heinberg & Miller, 2023) or perhaps a *Great Simplification*—an involuntary and unplanned

[5] The Subcommission on Quaternary Stratigraphy (SQS) of the International Commission on Stratigraphy has an Anthropocene Working Group (AWG) that is working on a proposal to formalize the Anthropocene as a geological epoch—see http://quaternary.stratigraphy.org/working-groups/anthropocene/. Not all scientists agree—some prefer to see the Anthropocene as an event rather that a geological epoch (Bauer et al., 2021).

reduction in "the size, complexity, and (literal) 'burn rate' of our civilization" (Hagens, 2020, p. 14). Yet others, fearing a collapse, extinction, or unraveling/simplification, want to pre-empt this by purposefully, and in a managed and controlled fashion, reduce the scale of human economic activity—they want to degrow the world economy to avoid disaster or the involuntary truncation of civilization (Kallis, 2011, 2021).

Much is therefore at stake, suggesting that the current generation of humans may live in the most important century (Karnofsky, 2021; MacAskill, 2022). Whether humans can continue, or even accelerate, economic growth without triggering an environmental collapse until such time as it can expand into the galaxy, or whether humans will impose its own, political (and possible even premature) limits on growth, will determine where the "rocket ship" that is modern civilization, will be headed. Barring some exogenous extinction event such as a large meteor impact, of course.

This book explores the destiny of this rocket ship that is modern civilization.

1.5 Key Concepts

This section explains the key concepts in this book. Although very many concepts—from economics to physics and politics and history will be introduced, for the sake of the argument the core concepts that will be helpful to explain at the outset are gross domestic output, economic growth, and ecological overshoot. The relation between these three determines the narrative.

1.5.1 Gross Domestic Product

GDP "combines in a single figure, and with no double counting, all the output (or production) carried out by all the firms, non-profit institutions, government bodies and households in a given country during a given period, regardless of the type of goods and services produced, provided that the production takes place within the country's economic territory. In most cases, it is calculated quarterly or annually, but it can also be calculated monthly" (Lequiller & Blades, 2014, pp. 14–15).

Economic growth is the change in Gross Domestic Product (GDP) of a country, region, or the world over time, where GDP is the monetary value of all final goods and services produced. It is an indicator of national income since the value of production accrues to economic agents: wages in the case of labor, rent and profits in the case of capital owners, and taxes in the case of government.

While the idea of recording national income goes back at least to the efforts of William Petty[6] and others in seventeenth-century England and France, GDP is a rather modern concept (Lepenies & Gaines, 2016). Based on contributions by, among others, Clarke (1932) Leontief (1936), Kuznets (1941), and Stone (1947), and driven by the need of the United Kingdom and United States to finance their World War II efforts, GDP was adopted as the core measure of the United Nations' System of National Accounts (SNA), first published in 1953 (Bos, 1992). For the first time, countries could track national income consistently over time and make intercountry comparisons.

In the SNA, GDP (often denoted by Y) is an accounting identity as shown in (1.2):

$$GDP_{it} \equiv Y_{it} \equiv C_{it} + I_{it} + G_{it} + X_{it} - M_{it} \tag{1.2}$$

where C_{it} is consumption expenditure in country i in year t, I_t is investment expenditure in country i in year t, G_t is government spending in country i in year t, X_t is exports in country i in year t, and M_t is imports in country i in year t. Imports are subtracted because it is not produced in country i. For a discussion of the measurement of the components of GDP and the statistical and measurement challenges these pose, see Lequiller and Blades (2014). One immediate implication from the GDP accounting identity for present purposes is that GDP does not only depend on consumption. Reducing consumption, which many advocate to reduce economic growth, will increase savings, which could increase investment (I_{it}). Moreover, reduction in one country's consumption may see more of its goods exported (X_{it}).

GDP and its measurement, as prescribed in the SNA, is a dynamic concept. From the beginning, many criticisms were levied against the

[6] William Petty was interested in measuring the government's tax base to "prove mathematically that the state could raise a much larger revenue from taxes to finance its peace and wartime needs, and that it could do so by more equitable and burdensome forms of taxation" (Bos, 1992, p. 5).

definition and measurement of GDP as prescribed in the SNA. This resulted in revisions of the SNA in 1960, 1964, 1968, 1993 and 2008.[7] The next revision is due to be published in 2025.

GDP as a single, comparable measure over time and between countries clearly has value—at least as the need to have a statistical guide to inform government planning and taxation during crises periods (such as World War II), the need to be able to empirically study the determinants of economic production over time, and the use of guiding measures in tailoring international trade and development support approaches have shown. But it does have shortcomings, as a voluminous scholarly literature has discussed—see, for instance, Stiglitz et al. (2009). As summarized by Fraumeni (2022):

> *GDP tells what is going on today but does not inform about sustainability of growth. The majority of time is spent in home production, yet the value of this time is not included in GDP. GDP does not measure happiness, so residents can be dissatisfied even when GDP is rising. In addition, GDP does not consider environmental factors, reflect what individuals do outside paid employment, or even measure the current or future potential human capital of a country.*

Further shortcomings of GDP include that it is really a subjective measure of the scale of the economy as it depends on the basis year of prices used to value production, and that it does not consider changes in the quality of products (Fix, 2015).

Criticisms against GDP as measure of national income resulted in the elaboration and use of many other measures on a country-level to complement the use of GDP as a guiding number for policy making. This recognizes that the economy is about more than money and hence that economic development is about more than can be measured by GDP alone. Accordingly, further measures that are widely used by economists to gauge society's condition include measures of absolute poverty (e.g., the share of the population that has insufficient income to afford access to sufficient caloric intake for good health), relative poverty as reflected in the distribution of income (e.g., the Gini-coefficient), subjective welfare (e.g., happiness levels), and multi-dimensional indicators of economic outcomes (e.g., the *Human Development Index*—HDI).

[7] See https://unstats.un.org/unsd/nationalaccount/hsna.asp

These also include the *Global Multidimensional Poverty Index (GMPI)* (Alkire et al., 2023). This index, which has a "less direct" relationship with economic growth and monetary measures of poverty, shows that 51 of 75 countries analyzed would achieve the UN's Sustainable Development Goal 1.2 objective of halving poverty by 2030 (Alkire et al., 2023).

1.5.2 Economic Growth

As mentioned in Sect. 5.1, ***economic growth*** refers to the change in Gross Domestic Product (GDP) of a country, region, or the world over time. If we denote GDP by Y and GDP at time t with Y_t, then economic growth can be denoted as $\Delta Y_t = Y_t - Y_{t-1}$. A good basic textbook on economic growth theory is by Acemoglu (2009). The aims of economic growth theory are to explain the cross-country differences in GDP between countries, and the evolution of GDP over time. The two major theoretical traditions are neoclassical growth theory and endogenous growth theory. To get a basic feel of the essentials of these traditions and their relevance—or irrelevance—for understanding and tracking the possible future of human civilization, Eq. (1.3) posits a very basic economic growth model, which is known as the Solow-model after Robert Solow (see Solow, 1956):

$$Y_t = K_t^{\alpha} . L_t^{\beta} \tag{1.3}$$

Here K_t stands for the capital stock and L_t for the labor force. These are the production factors that are combined into final output (GDP). The specification in (1.2) is known as a Cobb–Douglas model—after Cobb and Douglas (1928)—and is one of the most widespread production functions (mathematical functions linking outputs with inputs) used in economic growth theory. The α and β are coefficients denoting the share of capital and labor in final output (GDP). If we denote the rental income that owners of capital earn by r and the wage income that owners of labor earn by w, then we can write the shares of GDP going to the inputs as $\alpha = r\frac{K}{Y}$ and $\beta = w\frac{L}{Y}$. This assumes that capital and labor are paid their marginal contribution (marginal products) to production.

Note that land, a factor that was very important for classical economists such as David Ricardo and Thomas Malthus, is absent as production function: by the time Solow came to formulate his model, economists have taken land as essential irrelevant—its *share* was seen to be negligible.

In the Solow-model in (1.3) growth is finite: it will eventually approach zero simply because the inputs, K_t and L_t are finite and subject to diminishing returns—every additional unit of inputs would have a slightly smaller addition to output.

With the establishment of the SNA by the 1950s and 1960s, economists had sufficient time series and cross-country data on GDP and its inputs available to estimate a model such as (1.3). It transpired that capital and labor can only explain a certain share of GDP—a substantial share in the variation in GDP over time remained unexplained. This was referred to initially as a "*measure of our ignorance*" (Kuznets, 1971). The explanation was that the missing growth is due to technological progress: new ways of doing things. Technology was introduced into the Solow-model by the additive term A:

$$Y_t = A_t K_t^{\alpha} . L_t^{\beta} \tag{1.4}$$

where A_t now denotes technology. In the neoclassical tradition of growth theory, technology is assumed to come from outside the economic system—it is said to be exogenous. This was not very satisfactory. Eventually, Paul Romer and others endogenized technology by elaborating A_t as an "ideas" or knowledge production function. According to Romer (1990, 1993), the most important production factor is not the objects of capital and labor but ideas. Low GDP is not so much the result of insufficient objects (capital and labor) but insufficient ideas: an "ideas gap" will result in underdevelopment as measured by a low GDP (Romer, 1993). The ideas production function for A_t can be written following Jones (2019: 868) as:

$$\Delta A_t = \theta H_{AT} A_t \tag{1.5}$$

where Δ denotes a change, and H_{AT} the amount of human capital that is devoted to finding new ideas (i.e., to innovate) with $\theta > 0$ the productivity of human capital in coming up with new ideas (innovations). Equation (1.4) indicates that there is increasing returns to ideas: the more ideas there are, the faster will the stock of ideas grow. This property of ideas is because ideas are, in contrasts to objects such as capital and labor, nonrival in use. As Bryan (2018) explains, *give one person a hammer and they can build, say, one staircase a day. Give two people two hammers and they can build two staircases by just performing exactly the same tasks. But give two people two hammers and teach them a more efficient way to combine nail and wood, and they will be able to build more than two staircases. That 'recipe' on how to build staircases, once invented, can be passed along to every other inventor at much lower cost than what it would take to create the initial invention.*

If $s_t = \frac{H_{AT}}{\bar{H}}$ is the share of the total population devoted to innovation (to finding new ideas) then a central implication of endogenous growth theory is that growth is a function of research productivity parameter θ, the amount of human capital in the economy, $\bar{H}$, the equilibrium fraction of human capital allocated to research, s_t and the stock of knowledge, A_t. Any policies that affect these, will affect economic growth. Countries have different levels of GDP per capita because they have different technologies and innovation rates, human capital, and access to knowledge.

Moreover, because ideas are non-rival in use, entrepreneurs may not be inclined to allocate labor toward finding new ideas, as their competitors may just copy this. Hence the justification for intellectual property rights, and their protection and trade through for instance patent rights. These in effect provide the entrepreneur with monopoly power for a limited period. Seen in this way, endogenous growth theory suggests that economic growth is driven by the need for entrepreneurs to monopolize markets. It also suggests that growth, being fundamentally dependent on ideas, can in principle continue infinitely—however, there are many endogenous growth models in which economic growth is finite / bounded[8]—see for example, Sequeira et al. (2018) and Jones (2022). Later in this book—see

[8] In 2019, Swedish climate activist Greta Thunberg exclaimed at the United Nations that "all you can talk about is money and fairy tales of eternal economic growth" (Herz, 2019). As the discussion in this section and later in this book makes clear, it is not so much fairy tales of eternal economic growth that has been of global concern, but whether and how to achieve sufficient economic growth to eliminate poverty and repay debt, in the light of declining economic and productivity growth (the Great Stagnation) and zero-sum economic dynamics. Economic growth models and thinking, from the time of Thomas Malthus, David Ricardo, and Adam Smith to modern endogenous growth theories all have detailed tales of very **finite** economic growth. The fairy tales may rather be the Green Growth belief that technology will allow continued economic growth, and the Degrowth belief that downsizing the GDP of countries in the Global North will curtail ecological overshoot.

Chap. 6—we will return to these suggestions and the implicit assumptions that entrepreneurs only obtain monopoly power for a limited period and that research productivity (θ) and s_t is constant.

Just like economists have from the beginning been critical about GDP and its measurement and interpretation, so they have been critical also about the idea of economic growth and its consequences. Economic growth (and level of GDP per capita) is strongly and robustly positively correlated with a large range of desirable outcomes—from better health, education, life expectancy—which is why GDP per capita is strongly correlated with the Human Development Index (HDI). Economic growth, however, also has its downsides. Its benefits may be very unequally distributed. It may reflect increases in undesirable expenditures, such as military expenditure, rising costs of crime-fighting, and other damages. It may also, as this book discuss in more detail, cause pollution, and put undue pressure on the environment. Overall, however, economists and politicians believe that the benefit of economic growth exceeds its costs. This belief was eloquently stated by economics Nobel Laureate Simon Kuznets, in his Nobel Prize Lecture in 1971, when he said,

> *The negative effects of growth have never been viewed as so far outweighing its positive contribution as to lead to its renunciation – no matter how crude the underlying calculus may have been. Second, one may assume that once an unexpected negative result of growth emerges, the potential of material and social technology is aimed at its reduction or removal […] one may justifiably argue, in the light of the history of economic growth, in which a succession of such unexpected negative results has been overcome, that any specific problem so generated will be temporary – although we shall never be free of them, no matter what economic development is attained.*

This notion—that economic growth is net positive and that any negative effects can successfully be solved or overcome through material and social technology—continues to underlie the mainstream approach to dealing with Ecological Overshoot and its consequences, including climate change (as will be explained in more detail in Chap. 4 dealing with Green Growth).

For now, however, we can note that there is no notion of energy in either neoclassical or endogenous growth theory as formulated. For example, in his chapter in the *Handbook of Macroeconomics*, entitled "The Facts of Economic Growth," Jones (2016) does not mention the word "energy" even once. As in the case of land, economists consider the share of GDP going to energy as too small to justify inclusion. Eden and Kuruc (2023) provide estimates of the share of all natural resources to the GDP in the United States and puts it at less than 2%; they also conclude that the share of global income accruing to natural resources "is small and has remained trendless over the past few decades, despite a doubling of the global population" (Eden & Kuruc, 2023, p. 1). Neoclassical growth theory wrongly assumes that because the price or share of output going to a resource is small, it is unimportant (Fix, 2020). And if energy sources such as fossil fuels (FF) should get scarce, the assumption is that price increases would encourage innovation of new sources of energy (e.g., renewable energy—RE) for which FF could be substituted. The decline in the prices of solar PV cells and the increase of the contribution of solar energy to the energy mix is often cited as an example of this substitution mechanism at work.

1.5.3 Ecological Overshoot

To define and describe the notion of ecological overshoot, it is useful to begin by defining the Earth System. The Earth System can be defined as "the integrated biophysical and socioeconomic processes and interactions (cycles) among the atmosphere, hydrosphere, cryosphere, biosphere, geosphere, and anthroposphere (human enterprise) in both spatial—from local to global—and temporal scales, which determine the environmental state of the planet within its current position in the universe" (Rockstrom et al., 2009, p. 24).

Ecological overshoot is when the environmental state of the planet is disrupted by human consumption. Formally, Rees (2022, p. 2262) defines ecological overshoot (EO) to take place "when the consumption of bioresources and the production of wastes exceed the regenerative and assimilative capacities respectively, of supportive ecosystems."

Figure 1.2 depicts the relationships between economic growth, EO, and possible civilizational collapse. It shows that economic growth, over time, by increasing the scale of the economy, places an increasing ecological footprint on the Earth System. At some stage, where according to current estimates we already are, the carrying capacity of the Earth System will be exceeded—overshoot is said to occur. What follows? As per Fig. 1.2, the economy (civilization) will go into decline—or collapse, depending on how much it can exhaust resources. This will inevitably lead to a loss of carrying capacity. If civilization ever recovers from this, it will face a planet with a reduced carrying capacity (Rees, 2021, 2022).

Much of the current debate on the environment and sustainable development is about climate change. From the perspective EO, climate change is but one symptom of EO, which includes "plunging biodiversity, plastic pollution of the oceans, landscape and soil degradation, and tropical deforestation" (Rees, 2022, p. 2262).

1.6 Structure of the Book

The rest of the book is structured as follows.

Chapter 2 points out that the destiny of human civilization has been a topic of intense debate at least since the end of the eighteenth century. This debate has been characterized, on the one hand, by *Malthusians*, who take the position that economic growth is limited and that if it overshoots planetary boundaries, this may pose an existential risk, and on the other hand, *Cornucopians*, who trust that technological innovation and human

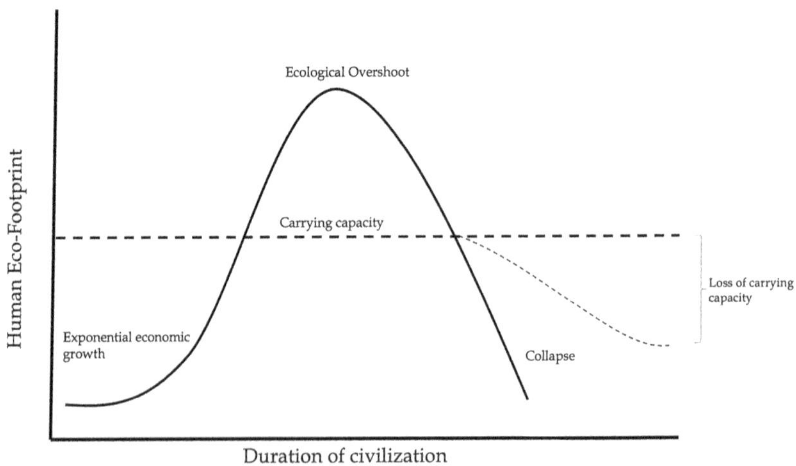

Fig. 1.2 Ecological Overshoot. (Source: Based on Fig. 1 in Rees, 2022, p. 2271)

ingenuity will be able to overcome any planetary—physical—limits to economic growth.

Chapter 3 delves deeper into the Cornucopian position given the fact that human society has become Detritovores, being greatly depended on fossil fuel energy—an input into economic growth and GDP that is, as was already mentioned, largely ignored in economic growth theory. The use of its fossil fuel bonanza, a "carbon pulse" as Nate Hagens and others have called it, and the economic growth it has enabled, has overshot planetary boundaries. The Cornucopian response is embodied in the approach of Green Growth, at the time of writing the mainstream global approach to sustainable economic growth and the mitigation of and adaptation to climate change.

Chapter 4 critically analyzes Green Growth and its foundation in technosolutionism—a correlate of the Silicon Valley Mindset as described by Douglas Rushkoff and the philosophy of the Tech-Elite of Technofeudalism, as Yanis Varoufakis calls them. The chapter concludes that Green Growth may not be able to result in complete dematerialization and absolute decoupling. It may therefore not be able to stop an ecological overshoot and the risks that this will pose to human civilization.

Chapter 5 dissects the Malthusian response to Green Growth—the Degrowth Agenda. Degrowthers reject green growth, arguing that the only way to avoid resource depletion and an existential climate crisis is to make a concerted effort to scale down GDP—to "degrow" the economy. It is argued in Chap. 5 that Degrowth will also not be likely to stop an Ecological Overshoot. It would likely worsen the environmental predicament, and on top of this it is a costly method to reduce carbon emissions and may boil down in its implementation—in top-down command fashion—to a form of austerity for the working class. For these reasons, amongst others, Degrowth as policy agenda is politically infeasible.

Chapter 6 argues that the Degrowth movement goes astray is in insisting that Degrowth would make society and the environment better. Degrowthers misses that in the West, we already live in a degrowth-type world, and that there is much about it that we do not like. The chapter, therefore, describes the Degrowth world—the Great Stagnation—that the West has been approaching since the 1970s, and its correlates: declining entrepreneurship, innovation and science, and research productivity.

Finally, Chap. 7 outlines a third approach beyond Green Growth and Degrowth: acceptance of an inevitable societal collapse (or unraveling) as a feature, and not a bug, of complexity, and managing such a collapse to minimize harm and get rid of obsolete structures. This may— and it is a big may—herald a phase-transition in economic growth and hence lay the foundation for *rebound growth*, and a transition to a new mode of "growth": which could be as qualitatively different from that characterizing the current global economy as the industrial world was different from the world of the hunter-gatherer economy (Hanson, 2018).

Chapter 8 concludes with a summary and some cautionary remarks.

References

Abrutzky, R., Osorio, S., Dang, T. N., Colistro. V., Huber, V., Lee, W., Seposo, X., Honda Y., Guo, Y. L., Bell, M. L., & Guo, Y. (2022). Global, regional, and national burden of mortality associated with short-term temperature variability from 2000–19: A three-stage modelling study. *Lancet Planet Health, 6*(5), e410–e421.

Acemoglu, D. (2009). *Introduction to Modern Economic Growth*. Princeton University Press.

Alkire, S., Nogales, R., Quinn, N. N., & Suppa, N. (2023). On Track or Not? Projecting the Global Multidimensional Poverty Index. *Journal of Development Economics*, 103150.

Bauer, A. M., Edgeworth, M., Edwards, L. E., Ellis, E. C., Gibbard, P., & Merritts, D. J. (2021). Anthropocene: Event or epoch? *Nature, 597*(7876), 332. https://doi.org/10.1038/d41586-021-02448-z. PMID: 34522014.

Bergström, A., Stringer, C., Hajdinjak, M., Scerri, E., & Skoglund, P. (2021). Origins of Modern Human Ancestry. *Nature, 590*, 229–237.

Bettencourt, L. M., Lobo, J., Helbing, D., Kühnert, C., & West, G. B. (2007). Growth, Innovation, Scaling, and the Pace of Life in Cities. *Proceedings of the National Academy of Sciences, 104*, 7301–7306.

Bos, F. (1992). *The History of National Accounting* (*MPRA Paper*). University Library of Munich. https://doi.org/10.2139/ssrn.1032598

Bostrom, N. (2003). Astronomical Waste: The Opportunity Cost of Delayed Technological Development. *Utilitas, 15*(3), 308–314.

Bostrom, N. (2009). The Future of Humanity. *Geopolitics, History, and International Relations, 1*(2), 41–78.

Brown, P. (2022, December 1). *Human Deaths from Hot and Cold Temperatures and Implications for Climate Change*. The Breakthrough Institute.

Bryan K. (2018, October 11). How We Create and Destroy Growth: The 2018 Nobel Laureates. *VoxEU CEPR*.

Burkart, K. G., Brauer, M., Aravkin, A. Y., et al. (2021). Estimating the Cause-Specific Relative Risks of Non-optimal Temperature on Daily Mortality: A

Two-Part Modelling Approach Applied to the Global Burden of Disease Study. *Lancet, 398*, 685–697.

Caldwell, R. R., & Stebbins, A. (2008). A Test of the Copernican Principle. *Physical Review Letters, 100*, 191302.

Caplan, M. E. (2020). Black dwarf supernova in the far future. *Monthly Notices of the Royal Astronomical Society, 497*(4), 4357–4362.

Cassan, A., Kubas, D., Beaulieu, J., Dominik, M., Horne, K., Greenhill, J., and et al. (2012). One or More Bound Planets per Milky Way Star from Microlensing Observations. *Nature, 481*, 167–169.

Cobb, C. W., & Douglas, P. H. (1928). A Theory of Production. *American Economic Review, 18*, 139–165.

Conselice, C., Wilkinson, A., Duncan, K., & Mortlock, A. (2016). The Evolution of Galaxy Number Density at z < 8 and its Implications. *Astrophysical Journal, 830*(2), 1–17.

Deutsch, D. (1998). *The Fabric of Reality: The Science of Parallel Universes – And Its Implications.* Penguin Books.

Diamond, J. (2005). *Collapse: How Societies Choose to Fail or Succeed.* Viking Press.

Eden, M., & Kuruc, K. (2023). *The Long-Run Relationship Between Per Capita Incomes and Population Size.* Mimeo.

Fix, B. (2015). Putting Power Back into Growth Theory. *Review of Capital as Power, 1*(2), 1–37.

Fix, B. (2020). *Can the World Get Along Without Natural Resources?* (Working Papers on Capital as Power, No. 2020/05). Forum on Capital as Power – Toward a New Cosmology of Capitalism.

Fraumeni, B. (2022). Gross Domestic Product: Are Other Measures Needed? *IZA World of Labor*, 368v2. https://doi.org/10.15185/izawol.368.v2

Gupta, R. (2023). JWST Early Universe Observations and ΛCDM Cosmology. *Monthly Notices of the Royal Astronomical Society*: stad2032.

Hagens, N. (2020). Economics for the Future – Beyond the Superorganism. *Ecological Economics, 169*, 106520.

Hanson, R. (2018). *The Age of EM: Work, Love, and Life when Robots Rule the Earth.* Oxford University Press.

Hanson, R. (2020, December 21). How Far to Grabby Aliens? Part 1. *Overcoming Bias Blog.*

Heinberg, R., & Miller, A. (2023). *Welcome to the Great Unraveling: Navigating the Polycrisis of Environmental and Social Breakdown.* Post Carbon Institute.

Herz, J. (2019, October 11). *The Fairy Tale of Eternal Economic Growth: Swedish Activist Greta Thunberg Brings Attention to the Need to Steward our Planet.* EESI (Environmental and Energy Studies Institute).

Johansen, A., & Sornette, D. (2001). Finite-Time Singularity in the Dynamics of the World Population: Economic and Financial Indices. *Physica A, 294*(3–4), 465–502.

Jones, C. I. (2016). The Facts of Economic Growth. In J. B. Taylor & H. Uhlig (Eds.), *Handbook of Macroeconomics* (Vol. 2, pp. 3–69).

Jones, C. I. (2019). Paul Romer: Ideas, Nonrivalry, and Endogenous Growth. *The Scandinavian Journal of Economics, 121*(3), 859–883.

Jones, C. I. (2022). The End of Economic Growth? Unintended Consequences of a Declining Population. *American Economic Review, 112*(11), 3489–3527.

Kallis, G. (2011). In Defence of Degrowth. *Ecological Economics, 70*(5), 873–880.

Kallis, G. (2021). Limits, Ecomodernism and Degrowth. *Political Geography, 87*, 102367.

Karnofsky, H. (2021, July 13). All Possible Views About Humanity's Future Are Wild. *Cold Takes Blog*.

Kemp, L., Xu, C., Depledge, J., Ebi, K., Gibbins, G., Kohler, T., Rockström, J., Scheffer, M., Schellnhuber, H., Steffen, W., & Lenton, T. (2022). Climate Endgame: Exploring Catastrophic Climate Change Scenarios. *Proceedings of the National Academy of Sciences, 119*(34), e2108146119.

Klinger, B. A., & Ryan, S. J. (2022). Population Distribution within the Human Climate Niche. *PLOS Climate, 1*(11), e0000086.

Kuznets, S. (1971, December 11). *Prize Lecture*. Available at: https://www.nobelprize.org/prizes/economic-sciences/1971/kuznets/lecture/

Lehto, K., Lehto, H., Brozinski, A., Gardner, E., Eklund, O., Rajala, K., & Vuorisalo, T. (2013). Time Trek: A 13.7 km Long Nature Trail Leading Through the History of the Universe and the Earth. *International Journal of Astrobiology, 12*(1), 1–7.

Lenton, T.M., Xu, C., Abrams, J.F. et al. (2023, May 22). Quantifying the Human Cost of Global Warming. *Nature Sustainability*.

Lepenies, P., & Gaines, J. (2016). *The Power of a Single Number: A Political History of GDP*. Columbia University Press.

Lequiller, F., & Blades, D. (2014). *Understanding National Accounts* (2nd ed.). OECD Publishing.

MacAskill, W. (2022). *What We Owe the Future*. Basic Books.

Mann, A. (2020, August 11). This Is the Way the Universe Ends: Not with a Whimper, But a Bang. *Science.org*.

Masselot, P., Mistry, M., Vanoli, J., Schneider, R., Iungman, T., Garcia-Leon, D., Ciscar, J. C., Feyen, L., Orru, H., Urban, A., et al. (2023). Excess Mortality Attributed to Heat and Cold: A Health Impact Assessment Study in 854 Cities in Europe. *Lancet Planet Health, 7*(4), e271–e281.

Murphy, T., Murphy, D., Love, T., LeHew, M., & McCall, B. (2021). Modernity is Incompatible with Planetary Limits: Developing a PLAN for the Future. *Energy Research & Social Science, 81*, 102239.

Ord, T. (2020). *The Precipice: Existential Risk and the Future of Humanity*. Hachette Books.

Petigura, E. A., Howard, A., & Marcya, G. (2013). Prevalence of Earth-Size Planets Orbiting Sun-Like Stars. *Proceedings of the National Academy of Sciences, 110*(48), 19273–19278.

Rees, W. E. (2021). A Note of Climate Change and Cultural Denial. *Population Matters.*

Rees, W. E. (2022). Why Large Cities Won't Survive the Twenty-First Century. In R. Brears (Ed.), *The Palgrave Encyclopedia of Urban and Regional Futures.* Palgrave Macmillan.

Rockström, J., Steffen, W., Noone, K., Persson, A., Chapin, F., Lambin, E., Lenton, T., & et al. (2009). Planetary Boundaries: Exploring the Safe Operating Space for Humanity. *Ecology and Society, 14*(2).

Romer, P. (1990). Endogenous Technical Change. *Journal of Political Economy, 98*, S71–S102.

Romer, P. (1993). Idea Gaps and Object Gaps in Economic Development. *Journal of Monetary Economics, 32*(3), 543–573.

Sagan, C. (1994). *Pale Blue Dot: A Vision of the Human Future in Space.* Ballantyne Books.

Sequeira, T., Gil, P., & Alfonso, O. (2018). Endogenous Growth and Entropy. *Journal of Economic Behavior and Organization, 15*, 100–120.

Solow, R. M. (1956). A Contribution to the Theory of Economic Growth. *The Quarterly Journal of Economics, 70*(1), 65–94.

Steel, D., DesRoches, T., & Mintz-Woo, K. (2022). Climate Change and the Threat to Civilization. *Proceedings of the National Academy of Sciences, 119*(42), e2210525119.

Stiglitz, J. E., Sen, A., & Fitoussi, J.-P. (2009). *Report by the Commission on the Measurement of Economic Performance and Social Progress.* Commission on the Measurement of Economic Performance and Social Progress.

Tainter, J. (1988). *The Collapse of Complex Societies.* Cambridge University Press.

Turchin, P. (2003). *Historical Dynamics: Why States Rise and Fall.* Princeton University Press.

Ward, P., & Brownlee, D. (2000). *Rare Earth: Why Complex Life Is Uncommon in the Universe.* Copernicus Books.

Waters, C., & Turner, S. (2022). Defining the Onset of the Anthropocene. *Science, 378*(6621), 706–708.

Wiblin, R., & Harris, K. (2021, August 19). Holden Karnofsky on the Most Important Century. *80,000 Hours Podcast.*

Zackrisson, E., Calissendor, P., González, J., Benson, A., Johansen, A., & Janson, M. (2016). Terrestrial Planets Across Space and Time. *The Astrophysical Journal, 833*(2), 1–12.

CHAPTER 2

The Malthusians and the Cornucopians

Abstract This chapter points out that the destiny of human civilization has been a topic of intense debate at least since the end of the eighteenth century. This debate has been characterized, on the one hand, by *Malthusians*, who take the position that economic growth is limited and that if it overshoots planetary boundaries, this may pose an existential risk, and, on the other hand, *Cornucopians*, who trust that technological innovation and human ingenuity will be able to overcome any planetary—physical—limits to economic growth.

Keywords Malthusian • Cornucopian • Limits to growth • Existential risk

2.1 Introduction

> *In the decades-old tensions involving environmental science, population, resource dynamics, and ecology, it's the Malthusians and the Cornucopians* (Gleick, 2020).

Whether human civilization will endure has been a topic of intense debate, at least since 1798, when the Reverend Thomas Malthus published his *Essay on the Principle of Population* warning that progress is inherently limited. Two hundred and twenty years later, Harvard psychologist Steven Pinker published *Enlightenment Now: The Case for Reason,*

W. Naudé, *Economic Growth and Societal Collapse*,
https://doi.org/10.1007/978-3-031-45582-7_2

Science, Humanism, and Progress, arguing that progress is not inherently limited, and documenting how reason, science, and humanism trumped Malthus's pessimism[1] (Pinker, 2018). He also argued that although progress is not inherently limited, it is not automatic, or guaranteed:[2] "[I]f we apply knowledge to increase human flourishing, then progress may happen. (If we don't, it won't)."

In the following subsections, the decades old tension between these positions in the intervening 220 years between Thomas Malthus and Steven Pinker, the 220 years that also saw the most substantial progress in human population and human wealth ever, are discussed. It includes the rise of neo-Malthusianism in the mid-twentieth century, and the response of Ester Boserup, Julian Simon, and other "Cornucopians" as they have been labeled, who assume the position that "people are resource creators, not resource destroyers" (Aligica, 2009, p. 73). Implications for the future of economic growth and technological development are elaborated.

2.2 The (Neo) Malthusians

In *Essay on the Principle of Population*, Malthus argued that civilization's progress is limited by fixed natural resources, such as land. Because "the power of population is so superior to the power of the earth to produce subsistence for man," it is inevitable, he argued, "that premature death must in some shape or other visit the human race" (Malthus, 1798, p. 44). In the preface to his essay, he acknowledged his deep pessimism, and referring to himself in the third person declared:

> *The view which he has given of human life has a melancholy hue, but he feels conscious that he has drawn these dark tints from a conviction that they are really in the picture, and not from a jaundiced eye or an inherent spleen of disposition* (Malthus, 1798, p. vii).

It is no coincidence that Malthus's essay was published in 1798: it was a time of strong reaction against the rationalism and secularism of the European Enlightenment. Only a few decades earlier the Enlightenment had inspired the idea that human progress is possible—as against the

[1] A well-argued criticism of Pinker's arguments is by Lent (2018). See also Robinson (2019) who describes Pinker as "the world's most annoying man." Annoying can be good.

[2] Pinker, as quoted in an interview with Cook (2018).

age-old notion to leave human fate in the hands of Providence.[3] By 1798 Enlightenment ideas had led to the 1st Industrial Revolution through a spate of institutional and technological innovations, including the steam engine (Mokyr, 2016). Progress did not come equally to all, however, and threatened vested interests. The French Revolution, which started out with high Enlightenment ideals, turned out horribly.

In 1811, the "Luddites," fearing mass job losses, turned in anger on technologies such as threshing machines and power looms, destroying many of these in public protests (Naudé & Nagler, 2015). Half a century before Karl Marx's reacted in his Communist Manifesto against the impacts of the Industrial Revolution, the Romantic Poets were amongst the first critics of capitalism (Löwy, 1987). Romantic poet John Keats lamented that scientists were "unweaving the rainbow" (Dawkins, 1998). In 1854, Henry David Thoreau wrote *Walden*, a chronicle of his two-year retreat from civilization in isolation at Walden Pond—its first chapter was entitled "Economy."[4] Malthus's melancholy hued view of human life was thus born at the dawn of Romanticism, with its skepticism of science and longing for a preindustrial age.

In the 1960s and 1970s, following two World Wars, the Great Depression, a Cold War, and the proliferation of nuclear arms, Malthus's melancholy hue would seep back into economics and the public consciousness. Neo-Malthusianism was born. In 1960, Von Foerster et al. (1960), in a paper in *Science*, predicted that Doomsday would occur on Friday, 13th November 2026, because given the up until then super-exponential growth rates in population, extrapolation indicated that global population would approach infinity by 2026. And in 1968, Paul Ehrlich (1968, p. 11) predicted that, as a result of population growth, "In the 1970s hundreds of millions of people will starve to death [...] At this late date nothing can prevent a substantial increase in the world death rate."

[3] An important contribution to the idea of progress was made by A.R.J Turgot, the French economist who was the "founder of classical economics" (Brewer, 1987). According to Nisbet (1975, p. 215), "What Turgot had to say about the advancement of human society, from its most primitive state through the long vistas of evolutionary time to the contemporary world, falls among the most impressive intellectual contributions of the whole eighteenth century."

[4] Thoreau was interested in the "true cost of things [...]" finding that "the necessities of life, the things truly precious to an individual or family, actually cost preciously little" (Kaag, 2021).

Malthus, Von Foerster, and Ehrlich underestimated the power of ideas—of innovation in technology and in governance institutions. Premature death did not visit humanity. Consider for instance that while in the 1960s, around 50 people per 100,000 died per decade due to famine: by the 2010s, it was down to 0.5. The key technological innovations that have driven food production include innovations in fertilizer production and use, and innovations that allowed international trade to expand.

Before the twentieth century, agricultural production was limited by the availability of manure—virtually the only fertilizer available. In the nineteenth century, guano from Peru became such a vital source of fertilizer for the United States and Europe, that various "guano wars" were fought in Latin America (Brazeau, 2018). With the invention and commercialization of synthetic nitrogen between 1908 and 1913 by Fritz Haber and Carl Bosch, by a process that converts nitrogen in the air into ammonia, the world obtained access to a plentiful source of fertilizer (Smil, 2004). It has been claimed that without the Haber–Bosch process, "almost half the world's population would not be alive today" (Harford, 2017). Erisman et al. (2008, p. 636) estimated[5] "by 2000, nitrogen fertilizers were responsible for feeding 44% of the world's population. Our updated estimate for 2008 is 48% – so the lives of around half of humanity are made possible by Haber-Bosch nitrogen."

As mentioned, there was a second, complementary innovation that has magnified the impact of synthetic fertilizers. This is the modern globalized economy, which is the result of process and business model innovations in the rules, institutions, and conventions underpinning trade. International trade, as Ridley (2020) described it, allows all countries and regions of the world to "specialize in production and diversify consumption." Coupled with transport innovations such as cold storage, the shipping container, modern ICT-driven logistics and port handling systems, food can move from the farm in one country to the fork in another rapidly—in a matter of hours in some cases. International trade allows countries to consume more food than their ecological systems can produce (Kissinger & Rees, 2009).

In sum, technological innovations in fertilizers and international trade have brought abundant and cheap food to households across the world, fueling economic development and population growth. This in turn generates further

[5] These estimates and conclusions have not gone unchallenged—see, for example, Benanav (2020) who has pointed out that millions of farm workers' jobs were made redundant, and urbanization fostered, because of synthetic nitrogen that made farming more productive.

innovation and economic growth. In the 1960s, while Paul Ehrlich was predicting an overpopulated planet about to starve to death, Cornucopians such as Ester Boserup and Julian Simon argued that population pressure drives innovation (Boserup, 1965, 1981; Simon, 1982, 1996). It is now accepted, also in the light of Paul Romer's elaboration of the mechanisms of growth, that population is indeed a driver of innovation (Romer, 1990). This is because innovation depends on ideas, and the more people there are, the more researchers and tinkerers there are, and the better and faster they get transmitted (Mokyr, 2007).

2.3 The Cornucopians

The consequence of escaping the Malthusian population trap, and positive feedback effects between population growth, new ideas (which lead to new technologies), and the spread of ideas through international trade resulted in historically unprecedented economic growth over the past two centuries.

2.3.1 The Great Acceleration

Figure 2.1 depicts world GDP over the past millennium, showing that GDP growth has been exponential over the past three centuries. The average annual world GDP growth rate over the past century alone was around 2%. At such a rate, the world economy doubles in size every 35 years. A graph of GDP per capita would look similar. In fact, a broad range of socioeconomic and Earth System trends follows these hockey-stick trajectories over the same period. It has been referred to as reflecting a "Great Acceleration" (Steffen et al., 2015).

As a result of this Great Acceleration, human life never had it materially so good as the current generation does (Pinker, 2018; Ridley, 2011). Barack Obama made the point that "if you had to choose any time in the course of human history to be alive, you'd choose this one" (Obama, 2016).

By 2020, world GDP per capita was, at an estimated US$5400, around 5600% higher than what it was around 10,000 years before, during the Greenlandian Age (Syvitski et al., 2020). Population and energy consumption growth closely tracked this growth in GDP: for instance, population growth accelerated from an average 0.01% per annum during the Greenlandian Age to 1.6% per year over the past 70 years, and per capita energy consumption from 6.2 to 61 GJ/year between the same periods (Syvitski et al., 2020). Humans are healthier, wealthier and safer than ever

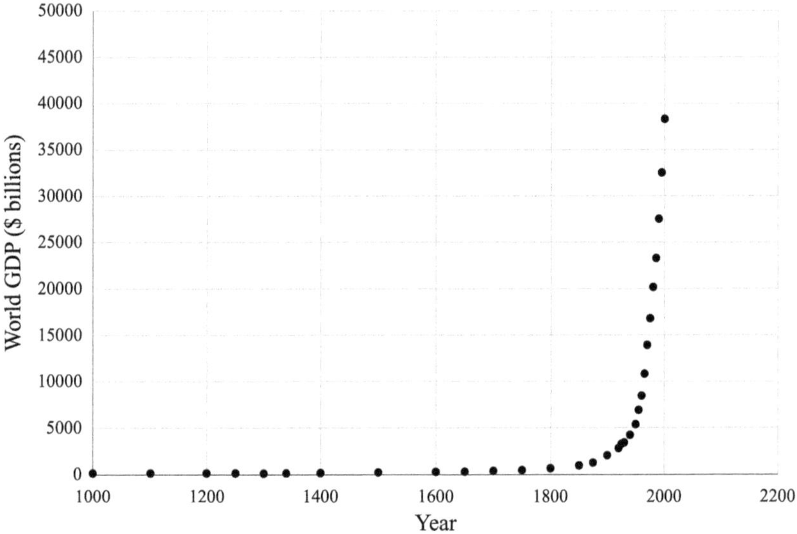

Fig. 2.1 World GDP, 1000–2000. (Source: Author's compilation based on data from DeLong, 1998, pp. 7–8)

before, on virtually all human development indicators (Alkire et al., 2023; Landes, 1999; Mokyr, 2016; Pinker, 2018; Ridley, 2011).

Closer scrutiny of Fig. 2.1 will show that the fastest acceleration occurred after 1950—the year which is roughly argued to be the start of the Anthropocene (Steffen et al., 2015; Head et al., 2021). Table 2.1 summarizes the Great Acceleration after 1950, noting the extremely large changes in a range of ecological measures between 1950 and 2015.

As Table 2.1 shows, global GDP increased by 1487% between 1950 and 2015. The impact of this increase in the scale of human economic activity has been a tremendous uptake of material resources, for instance, as reflected in the 414% increase in energy consumption, 3115% increase in cement production and 765% increase in iron and steel production, among others.

2.3.2 *The Power of Ideas*

According to endogenous growth theory, as explained in Chap. 1, the fundamental driver of economic growth is ***ideas*** (Romer, 1986, 1987,

Table 2.1 Changes in selected ecological measures, 1950–2015

Measure	*1950*	*2015*	*% Change since 1950*
World population (millions)	2499	7349	194
Global energy consumption (EJ/year)	100	514	414
Global GDP (billions 1990 international $)	4656	73,902	1487
Global reservoir capacity (km^3)	705	15,534	2103
Number of dams	7361	50,346	584
Plastic production (Mt/year)	2	381	18,950
Cement production (Mt/year)	130	4180	3115
Ammonia (NH_3) production (Mt/year)	2	175	8650
Copper production (Mt/year)	2.38	19.10	703
Iron and steel production (Mt/year)	134	1160	765
Aluminum production (Mt/year)	2	58	2800

Source: Author's compilation based on Table 1 in Head et al. (2021, p. 5)

1990). Ideas (or knowledge) are generated by people (R&D workers) and commercialized by entrepreneurs bringing new technologies to the economy—if they have the incentive to benefit from such commercialization (Jones, 1995). Because ideas are non-rival in use, entrepreneurs would only face an incentive to exploit new ideas if these could also be made excludable[6]—and there is a sufficient population to provide a large enough market (Romer, 1990).

The more people there are, the more ideas are generated, and the faster the economic growth from the technologies based on these new ideas (Davidson, 2021). The latter can sustain a larger population, creating a population–ideas feedback loop, which explains the simultaneous exponential growth in GDP and population over the past 1000 years (Lee, 1988; Kremer, 1993; Davidson, 2021). New ideas, moreover, emerge from existing ideas: a new idea can be the combination of two older ideas. This process is known as combinatorial innovation (Weitzman, 1998; Koppl et al., 2019). It is almost limitless—the world will never run out of ideas. As Romer (2019) explains:

> *The periodic table contains about a hundred different types of atoms. If a recipe is simply an indication of whether an element is included or not, there will be 100 x 99 recipes like the one for bronze or steel that involve only two elements.*

[6]This justifies the use of legal instruments such as intellectual property (IP) rights and patents (to trade these IP rights).

For recipes that can have four elements, there are 100 x 99 x 98 x 97 recipes, which is more 94 million. With up to 5 elements, more than 9 billion. [...]. Once you get to 10 elements, there are more recipes than seconds since the big bang created the universe.

Growth via ideas can follow the pattern as depicted in Fig. 2.1: a long period of slow growth, followed by a sharp, hockey-stick like upturn, into accelerating (super) exponential growth (Jones, 2001; Clancy, 2021) and mathematically if not physically, potential hyperbolic growth (Aleksander, 2019; Sandberg, 2013). What is at play here is a positive feedback loop between ideas–technology–population–ideas.

This accelerating exponential economic growth from new ideas cannot, however, be sustained and will not reach infinity, because either population growth will slow down—a demographic transition (Aleksander, 2019), and/or R&D funding will not keep up investing in commercializing each and every new idea (Weitzman, 1998), and/or research teams run out of cognitive resources (Agrawal et al., 2018). The consequence is that growth would settle into constant exponential growth, as has been the case for much of the past century (Weitzman, 1998; Clancy, 2021).

As long as total population remains constant, however, the economy can continue growing at a constant rate, albeit slower than before, as the stock of new ideas generated by that population grows at constant exponential rate (Kremer, 1993; Jones, 2022). Moreover, arguments that the world will run out of natural resources and thus limit growth have been dismissed by some, based on the argument that because ideas (technology) transform all resources, "there's really no such thing as a natural resource. All resources are artificial. They are a product of technology" (Crawford, 2022). See also Pooley and Tupy (2018).

The conclusions that the economy can continue to grow indefinitely at a constant rate and that there are no such things as natural resources have, however, been questioned: it implies an explosion in the *size* of the economy after some time and, even if growth is decoupled from most material inputs, it would still generate waste-heat. In Sect. 4.4 this limit to growth is discussed in greater detail.

For the moment however, if population growth turns *negative*, total population will decline, the flow of new ideas will stagnate, and economic growth will eventually collapse. In recent decades, with populations in more and more countries in decline (in most advanced economies, fertility rates dropped to below replacement level in the 1970s and 1980s) the prospects of a real population decline, and an eventual "Empty Planet" has arisen (Bricker & Ibbitson, 2020; Jones, 2022).

Furthermore, research productivity and innovation in advanced Western economies have also been declining—ideas have been "getting harder to find" (Bloom et al., 2020; Jones, 2009).

New ideas, as measured by patents and scientific papers have also become less disruptive over time (Park et al., 2023). Huebner (2005) finds that the global rate of innovation peaked in 1873.

As a result of declining population growth rates and declining research productivity and innovation in an increasing number of countries, economic growth in these countries has been slowing down. It has been described as the *Great Stagnation* (Cowen, 2010) and *Ossified Economy* (Naudé, 2022a). Jones (2022, p. 3), using models with both exogenous and endogenous population growth illustrates that

> *when population growth is negative, both endogenous and semi-endogenous growth models produce what we call the Empty Planet result: knowledge and living standards stagnate for a population that gradually vanishes.*

He calculates that with a 1% annual decline in population, that world GDP growth would drop to zero somewhere between 85 and 250 years (Jones, 2022, p. 9).

2.3.3 Solve Intelligence and Use It to Solve Everything Else

The "Cornucopian" position to the seemingly inevitable decline in economic growth due to a decline in population growth is that technology may make up for the decline in human population.[7] Specifically, Artificial Intelligence (AI)—hence Google DeepMind's proclamation, "solve intelligence and use it to solve everything else." Since around 2011/2012 AI systems based on Deep Learning (DL) has made rapid progress, to the extent that a growing number of scientists expect that the development of an Artificial General Intelligence (AGI), which would be an intelligence on par with or exceeding human intelligence, is imminent (Bostrom, 2014; Naudé, 2021).

Such an AGI may avert an economic growth collapse and herald in a new "mode" of economic growth, making super-exponential economic

[7] This section draws on Naudé (2022b).

growth possible, according to some (Hanson, 2001). This is because an AGI may substitute for humans—thus lack of population ceases to be a constraint—and AGI may improve R&D productivity dramatically, by being an innovation in the method of innovation (IMI). Thus, by overcoming population constraints, the burden of knowledge and the challenge of finding new ideas, AGI can unblock an ideas-lock on economic growth, causing economic growth rates to explode: these would be annual growth in Global World Production (GWP) of 30%—at this rate, the size of the world economy would double every two years, as opposed to the current doubling every 35 years (Davidson, 2021).

At the core of the expectation that an AGI will unleash a flood of growth-enhancing new ideas is the belief that AGI is not just a tool for making existing business models more efficient and competitive, but an innovation in the method of innovation (IMI) (Agrawal et al., 2019). It will be a General-Purpose Technology (GPT) that will alter the "playbook" of innovation (Cockburn et al., 2019).

What if Deep Learning does not scale up to an AGI? A modern day Cornucopian may point out that an AGI is not necessary to accelerate economic growth—other digital technologies may also bring this about. One such technology will be the creation of digital people, or *Ems*, who could possibly be the result of whole brain emulations. Hanson (2018, p. 7) defines a whole brain emulation (*em*) as resulting "from taking a particular human brain, scanning it to record its particular cell features and connections, and then building a computer model that processes signals according to those same features and connections." Once "*Ems*"—digital people—are possible, they will quickly dominate the economy. They can be (almost costless) copied and they are much faster than humans. According to Karnofsky (2021) Ems could generate "unprecedented (in history or in sci-fi movies) levels of economic growth and productivity."

Digital people—"*Ems*"—will "largely work and play in virtually reality" at subsistence levels in a hyper-fast economy to produce the computer hardware and the supporting infrastructure for the virtual reality. Economic growth is so fast—because of all the billions and billions cheap digital people and the combinations of new ideas that can generated very rapidly—that the world economy could double every month (as against the current 35 years it takes to double.[8] As described by Hanson (2018, pp. 13, 438):

> *The em world is richer, faster-growing, and it is more specialized, adaptive, urban, populous and fertile. It has weaker gender differences in personality and roles, and larger more coherent plans and designs [...] To most ems, it seems good to be an em [...] if the life of an em counts even a small fraction as much as does a typical life today, then the fact that there are so many ems could make for a big increase in total happiness and meaning relative to our world today.*

In a sense, Hanson (2018) provides the ultimate description of human society and economy in a future "Metaverse."[9] In this Em-Metaverse, humans end up as a dying-out minority "mostly enjoying a comfortable retirement on their em-economy investment" (Hanson, 2018, p. 9). According to Alexander (2016), the retired humans will

> *[B]ecome rarer, less relevant, but fantastically rich – a sort of doddering Neanderthal aristocracy spending sums on a cheeseburger that could support thousands of ems in luxury for entire lifetimes.*

In conclusion, Cornucopians are tech-optimists. They see economic growth as the beneficial outcome of growth in new ideas (technologies). Because these ideas (technologies) are unlimited, economic growth is essentially unlimited. Even if populations decline and human research and science stagnate, these could be overcome by establishing new modes of growth, just as in the past agriculture introduced a new mode of growth for foragers, and just as the industrial revolution introduced a new growth mode for farmers. Eventually in these new modes of future growth, humanity's descendants will be radically different from humans alive today—we may be transcended by digital, AI-merged sentient beings, whose eventual future population will vastly outnumber all humans that have ever lived.

[8] According to Hanson (2000, p. 18), one may think that such growth rates where the economy doubles every month—or even every two weeks are "too fantastic to consider, were it not for the fact that similar predictions before previous transitions would have seemed similarly fantastic."

[9] The label "Metaverse" comes from Neal Stephenson's 1992 science fiction novel *Snow Crash* and has come to refer to virtual and augmented realities enabled through the Internet and as found for example in multiplayer online games (Knox, 2022).

2.4 Concluding Remarks

In this chapter, the centuries-old tension between pessimists (Malthusian) and optimists (Cornucopians) regarding the prospects for economic growth were outlined. Malthus seems to have underestimated the impact of innovation—in both physical technologies (such as fertilizers) and in organizations (such as the rise of democratic, social welfare states), although his analysis inspired a next generation of neo-Malthusians to refine his insights in the twentieth century.

Malthus was not able to consider the discovery and exploitation of fossil fuels, which would super-charge economic growth after his time—from the middle of the nineteenth century to the present. How this changed, and re-asserted the Malthusian notion of limits or boundaries, is the topic of Chap. 3.

References

Agrawal, A., McHale, J., & Oettl, A. (2018). *Finding Needles in Haystacks: Artificial Intelligence and Recombinant Growth* (NBER Working Paper no. 24541). National Bureau for Economic Research.

Agrawal, A., McHale, J., & Oettl, A. (2019). *Artificial Intelligence, Scientific Discovery, and Commercial Innovation*. Mimeo.

Aleksander, S. (2019, April 22). 1960: The Year the Singularity Was Cancelled. *Slate Star Codex Blog*.

Alexander, S. (2016, May 28). Book Review: Age of EM. *Slate Star Codex Blog*.

Aligica, P. (2009). Julian Simon and the Limits to Growth Neo-Malthusianism. *The Electronic Journal of Sustainable Development, 1*(3), 73–84.

Alkire, S., Nogales, R., Quinn, N. N., & Suppa, N. (2023). On Track or Not? Projecting the Global Multidimensional Poverty Index. *Journal of Development Economics*, 103150.

Benanav, A. (2020). *Automation and the Future of Work*. Verso.

Bloom, N., Bunn, P., Chen, S., Mizen, P., & Smietanka, P. (2020, March 27). The Economic Impact of Coronavirus on UK Businesses: Early Evidence from the Decision Maker Panel. *VOX CEPR Policy Portal*.

Boserup, E. (1965). *The Conditions of Agricultural Growth: The Economics of Agrarian Change Under Population Pressure*. Routledge.

Boserup, E. (1981). *Population and Technological Change: A Study of Long-Term Trends*. Chicago University Press.

Bostrom, N. (2014). *Superintelligence: Paths, Dangers, Strategies*. Oxford University Press.

Brazeau, M. (2018, April 4). *Remember the Guano Wars: A Response to Breakthrough's Essay on the Hidden Footprint of Making All Farms Organic*. The Breakthrough Institute.

Brewer, A. (1987). Turgot: Founder of Classical Economics. *Economica, 54*(216), 417–428.

Bricker, D., & Ibbitson, J. (2020). *Empty Planet: The Shock of Global Population Decline*. Little, Brown Book Group.

Clancy, M. (2021, June 18). Combinatorial Innovation and Technological Progress in the Very Long Run. *New Things Under the Sun*.

Cockburn, I. M., Henderson, R., & Stern, S. (2019). The Impact of Artificial Intelligence on Innovation: An Exploratory Analysis. In A. Agrawal, J. Gans, & A. Goldfarb (Eds.), *The Economics of Artificial Intelligence: An Agenda* (pp. 115–148). University of Chicago Press.

Cook, G. (2018, February 15). The Secret Behind One of the Greatest Success Stories in All of History. *Scientific American*.

Cowen, T. (2010). *The Great Stagnation*. Penguin (Dutton).

Crawford, J. (2022, October 7). Can Economic Growth Continue over the Long-Term? *Longnow*.

Davidson, T. (2021, June 17). Report on Whether AI Could Drive Explosive Economic Growth. *Open Philanthropy*.

Dawkins, R. (1998). *Unweaving the Rainbow: Science, Delusion, and the Appetite for Wonder*. Houghton Mifflin.

DeLong, J. B. (1998). *Estimates of World GDP, One Million B.C. – Present*. Department of Economics, U.C. Berkeley at http://econ161.berkeley.edu/

Ehrlich, P. (1968). *The Population Bomb*. Ballantine Books.

Erisman, J., Sutton, M., Galloway, J., Klimont, Z., & Winiwarter, W. (2008). How a Century of Ammonia Synthesis Changed the World. *Nature Geoscience, 1*, 636–639.

Gleick, P. (2020, July 15). Book Review: Bad Science and Bad Arguments Abound in Apocalypse Never by Michael Shellenberger. *Yale Climate Connections*.

Hanson, R. (2000). *Long-Term Growth as a Sequence of Exponential Modes*. Mimeo/George Mason University.

Hanson, R. (2001). *Economic Growth Given Machine Intelligence*. Mimeo.

Hanson, R. (2018). *The Age of EM: Work, Love, and Life when Robots Rule the Earth*. Oxford University Press.

Harford, T. (2017, January 2). How Fertilizer Helped Feed the World. *BBC News*.

Head, M. J., Steffen, W., Fagerlind, D., Waters, C. N., Poirier, C., et al. (2021). The Great Acceleration Is Real and Provides a Quantitative Basis for the Proposed Anthropocene. *Journal of International Geoscience*. https://doi.org/10.18814/epiiugs/2021/021031

Huebner, J. (2005). A Possible Declining Trend for Worldwide Innovation. *Technological Forecasting and Social Change, 72*, 980–986.

Jones, C. (1995). R&D – Based models of Economic Growth. *Journal of Political Economy, 103*(4), 759–783.

Jones, C. I. (2001). Was an Industrial Revolution Inevitable? Economic Growth over the Very Long Run. *Advances in Macroeconomics, 1*(2), article 1.

Jones, B. (2009). The Burden of Knowledge and the Death of Renaissance Man: Is Innovation Getting Harder? *Review of Economic Studies, 76*(1), 283–317.

Jones, C. I. (2022). The End of Economic Growth? Unintended Consequences of a Declining Population. *American Economic Review, 112*(11), 3489–3527.

Kaag, J. (2021, October 20). Thoreau's Economics: The Truly Precious Costs Precious Little. *Psyche*.

Karnofsky, H. (2021, July 27). Digital People Would Be an Even Bigger Deal. *Cold Takes Blog*.

Kissinger, M., & Rees, W. (2009). Assessing Sustainability in a Globalizing World: Toward Interregional Industrial Ecology. *Journal of Industrial Ecology, 13*(3), 357–360.

Knox, J. (2022). The Metaverse, or the Serious Business of Tech Frontiers. *Postdigital Science Education, 4*, 207–215.

Koppl, R., Deveraux, A., Herriot, J., & Kauffman, S. (2019). *The Industrial Revolution as a Combinatorial Explosion*. Mimeo.

Kremer, M. (1993). The O-Ring Theory of Economic Development. *The Quarterly Journal of Economics, 108*, 551–575.

Landes, D. (1999). *The Wealth and Poverty of Nations: Why Some Are So Rich and Some So Poor*. Norton & Co.

Lee, R. (1988). Induced Population Growth and Induced Technological Progress: Their Interaction in the Accelerating Stage. *Mathematical Population Studies, 1*(3), 265–288.

Lent, J. (2018, May 21). Steven Pinker's Ideas Are Fatally Flawed. These Eight Graphs Show Why. *Open Democracy*.

Löwy, M. (1987). The Romantic and the Marxist Critique of Modern Civilization. *Theory and Society, 16*(6), 891–904.

Malthus, T. (1798). *An Essay on the Principle of Population*. Printed for J. Johnson, in St. Paul's Churchyard.

Mokyr, J. (2007). The Power of Ideas. *World Economics, 8*(3), 53–110.

Mokyr, J. (2016). *A Culture of Growth: The Origins of the Modern Economy*. Princeton University Press.

Naudé, W. (2021). Artificial Intelligence: Neither Utopian Nor Apocalyptic Impacts Soon. *Economics of Innovation and New Technology, 30*(1), 1–24.

Naudé, W. (2022a). From the Entrepreneurial to the Ossified Economy. *Cambridge Journal of Economics, 46*(1), 105–131.

Naudé, W. (2022b). The Future Economics of Artificial Intelligence: Mythical Agents, a Singleton and the Dark Forest. *IZA Discussion Paper No. 15713.*

Naudé, W., & Nagler, P. (2015). *Industrialisation, Innovation, Inclusion* (UNU-MERIT Working Paper 2015-043). United Nations University.
Nisbet, R. (1975). Turgot and the Contexts of Progress. *Proceedings of the American Philosophical Society, 119*(3), 214–222.
Obama, B. (2016, October 12). Barack Obama: Now Is the Greatest Time to Be Alive. *Wired*.
Park, M., Leahy, E., & Funk, R. (2023). Papers and Patents are Becoming Less Disruptive over Time. *Nature, 613*, 138–144.
Pinker, S. (2018). *Enlightenment Now: The Case for Reason, Science, Humanism, and Progress*. Viking.
Pooley, G., & Tupy, M. L. (2018). *The Simon Abundance Index: A New Way to Measure Availability of Resources* (Policy Analysis No. 857). Cato Institute.
Ridley, M. (2011). *The Rational Optimist: How Prosperity Evolves*. Fourth Estate.
Ridley, M. (2020). *How Innovation Works: And Why It Flourishes in Freedom*. HarperCollins.
Robinson, N. (2019, May 29). The World's Most Annoying Man. *Current Affairs*.
Romer, P. (1986). Increasing Returns and Long-Run Growth. *Journal of Political Economy, 94*(5), 1002–1037.
Romer, P. (1987). Growth Based on Increasing Returns Due to Specialization. *American Economic Review, 77*(2), 56–62.
Romer, P. (1990). Endogenous Technical Change. *Journal of Political Economy, 98*, S71–S102.
Romer, P. (2019, February 5). *The Deep Structure of Economic Growth*. Blog: https://paulromer.net
Sandberg, A. (2013). An Overview of Models of Technological Singularity. In M. More & N. Vita-More (Eds.), *The Transhumanist Reader*. Wiley.
Simon, J. (1982). Paul Ehrlich Saying It Is So Doesn't Make It So. *Social Science Quarterly, 63*(2), 381–385.
Simon, J. L. (1996). *The Ultimate Resource 2*. Princeton University Press.
Smil, V. (2004). *Enriching the Earth: Fritz Haber, Carl Bosch, and the Transformation of World Food Production*. MIT Press.
Steffen, W., Broadgate, W., Deutsch, L., Gaffney, O., & Ludwig, C. (2015). The Trajectory of the Anthropocene: The Great Acceleration. *The Anthropocene Review, 2*(1), 81–98.
Syvitski, J., Waters, C., Day, J., et al. (2020). Extraordinary Human Energy Consumption and Resultant Geological Impacts Beginning around 1950 CE Initiated the Proposed Anthropocene Epoch. *Communications Earth and Environment, 1*, 32.
Von Foerster, H., Mora, P. M., & Amio, L. (1960). Doomsday: Friday, 13 November A.D. 2026. *Science, 132*(3436), 1291–1295.
Weitzman, M. (1998). Recombinant Growth. *Quarterly Journal of Economics, 113*(2), 331–360.

CHAPTER 3

What to Do About the Detritovores?

Abstract This chapter delves deeper into the Cornucopian position given the fact that human society has become Detritovores, being greatly dependent on fossil fuel energy—an input into economic growth and GDP that is, as was already mentioned, largely ignored in economic growth theory. The use of its fossil fuel bonanza, a "carbon pulse" as Hagens and others have called it, and the economic growth it has enabled, has overshot planetary boundaries. The Cornucopian response is embodied in the approach of Green Growth, at the time of writing the mainstream global approach to sustainable economic growth and the mitigation of and adaptation to climate change.

Keywords Fossil fuels • Energy • Economic growth • EROI—energy rate of return on energy invested

3.1 Introduction

> *[...] humans have become detritovores, organisms that live off the dead remains of other organisms* (Cobb, 2015).

There are two fundamental problems with the tech-optimists' hope in never-ending economic growth described in the previous chapter. The first is that while ideas of an AGI and digital people (Ems) are not violating

W. Naudé, *Economic Growth and Societal Collapse*,
https://doi.org/10.1007/978-3-031-45582-7_3

laws of physics, they still are to be found only in the realms of science fiction. Current human civilization lacks the knowledge and the economics to realize these. The second is the assumption that there are no natural resources (or materials) scarcity, given the overriding importance of ideas (technology).

The first problem—how far humanity is from being able to develop an AGI or Ems, or whether it is at all possible given humans' intellectual and material resources, is a topic that falls outside the scope of this book.

The second problem returns the attention to the material resources needed to sustain economic growth. In this chapter, two main aspects or themes in the debate between the neo-Malthusians and the Cornucopians will be discussed. The first is the idea that human civilization is overshooting planetary boundaries, and that this poses an existential threat—threatening civilization collapse (Sect. 3.1). The second is the idea of a *Carbon Pulse* as being the main mechanism that has been driving exponential economic growth (as shown in Fig. 2.1) over the past 200 years, and what this implies for the continuation of growth (Sect. 3.2).

3.2 Ecological Overshoot

In Sect. 2.1 it was discussed how Malthus, and later neo-Malthusians, argued that land, and hence food production, was fixed and would in the face of population growth eventually result in famine. In such a Malthusian world, economic growth is limited by resources—land and food—and other material inputs. Malthus and the neo-Malthusians, we know, underestimated the role of technology and population growth (as was discussed in Sect. 2.2), and consequently made many wrong predictions of food and other resources running out.[1] The most famous of these were by the biologist Paul Ehrlich who made a bet with economist Julian Simon in 1980 that five key mineral resources—chromium, copper, nickel, tin, and tungsten—would run out, and as they do, their prices would increase. Ten years later, the prices of all five resources have fallen, and Ehrlich had lost his bet (Sabin, 2013).

As a result, and still believing that material resources are ultimately finite, much of the concern of latter-day neo-Malthusians have been on systemic scarcity—rather than scarcity of specific resources. They often

[1] See for instance Perry (2016).

refer to the finite nature of an Earth System (see Chap. 1 for a definition) that creates conditions, such as nature's contributions to people (NCP)[2] and carrying capacities—planetary boundaries (PBs)—that the world economy needs and within which the world economy must function.

While technological solutions may alleviate individual resource scarcities, and moreover improve the efficiency of resource use, the overall impact on the planet's ecosystem will inevitably increase with economic growth, to the point where continued growth would result in *ecological overshot of* the capacity of the planetary ecosystem.[3] Ecological overshoot can be defined as "the tendency of the system to generate flows larger than the carrying capacity," where carrying capacity is "the maximum flow of energy that the system can maintain for a long time" (Bardi, 2020, p. 34).

Catton (1982) was one of the first to stress the problem of *ecological overshoot*. In an imaginary interview with the Reverend Thomas Malthus, he has Malthus describe how overshoot comes from overuse by humans of the environment's supply sources, activity spaces and disposal sites:

> *Malthus: I would point out that all creatures have to use their environment in three ways – as a supply source (S), as activity space (A), and as a disposal site (D). Use the acronym, SAD, to focus on a sad fact — people depend far more than most of them realize on other (living and nonliving) components of an ecosystem, not only to supply their subsistence requirements but also to absorb and recycle everything human living gives off. Overuse of a country or a world by humans inevitably begins breaking down the system, ultimately hurting its human users* (Catton, 1998, p. 436).

Ecological overshoot thus means that the supply sources (which include ecosystem services (NCPs)) and activity spaces and disposal sites are overused (Catton, 1982, 1998).

[2] Nature's Contributions to People (NCP) are ecosystem services that are necessary for the functioning of human society. Fourteen NCPs have been identified, of which twelve are considered local and two global. Local NCPs include for example pollinator habitat sufficiency for crop production and fodder production for livestock, whereas the global NCPs are ecosystem carbon storage and atmospheric moisture recycling (Chaplin-Kramer et al., 2023).

[3] The term "ecosystem" was coined by Tansley (1935).

3.2.1 *Greenhouse Gas Emissions and Climate Change*

One example is of overuse of fossil fuels, which results in emission of *greenhouse gases* such as carbon (CO_2). The latter results in climate change—global warming[4]—which threatens to disrupt weather, agriculture, and many other parts of the planet's ecosystem. The extent of overuse of carbon, and the relation with global warming, is depicted in Fig. 3.1.

Figure 3.1 shows the steady increase in CO_2 emissions since 1850, roughly when the modern industrial era started, and close to when the first commercial oil wells were drilled in first in Enniskillen in Ontario, Canada in 1858, and then in 1859 in Titusville, Pennsylvania, United States—by the aptly named *Seneca Oil Company* (Habashi, 2000). It shows that by 2022 around 36.8 billion tons of CO_2 was emitted globally, and that global average temperatures were around 0.8 °C (almost 1 °C)

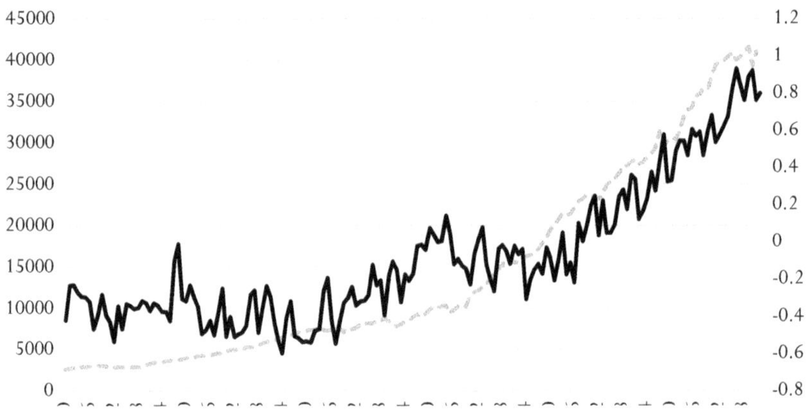

Fig. 3.1 Carbon Emission and Global Warming, 1850–2022. (Source: Author's compilation based on data from Our World in Data: https://github.com/owid/co2-data)

[4] The first "climate model", showing the greenhouse effect of carbon emissions, was published in 1896 by Svante Arrhenius (see Arrhenius, 1896).

higher that the 1961–1990 average—which was 1.15 °C above the 1850–1900 (pre-industrial) average (WMO, 2023). The bulk of the emission increase depicted in Fig. 3.1 was due to human activity, hence the conclusion by the IPCC (2018) and the scientific consensus (see Oreskes, 2004) that there is a large certainty that global warming is due to humans—hence the term *anthropogenic warming*.

By May 2023, as this book was being written, there were **424** parts per million (ppm) carbon in the atmosphere as measured by the Mauna Loa Observatory in Hawaii. This was the highest level since the Observatory started measurements in 1958.[5] It is also the highest for millennia, as Osman et al. (2021) reports that "rate and magnitude of modern warming are unusual relative to the changes of the past 24 thousand years."

To prevent catastrophic climate change it has been recommended that global warming stabilizes at not more that 1.7 °C warming before preindustrial times, which in turn implies limiting carbon in the atmosphere to not more than 350 ppm—based on assumptions about *climate sensitivity*,[6] which is the extent to which increased carbon leads to higher global mean surface temperatures (GMST) (Hansen et al., 2008). In the Paris Agreement of 2015, the EU and 194 countries of the United Nations committed themselves to limit global warming to preferably 1.5 °C above preindustrial levels (and not more than 2 °C) and that doing so would require reducing carbon emissions by around 50% by 2030.

The IPCC has produced scenarios indicating that given past trends, there would be between 2 and 3 °C of global warming above preindustrial levels by 2100 (the median is 2.2 °C), which means that the world is off-target from its Paris commitments (Pielke et al., 2022). At the time of writing, the World Meteorological Organization (WMO), using a climate

[5] See https://www.climate.gov/news-features/understanding-climate/climate-change-atmospheric-carbon-dioxide

[6] Equilibrium Climate Sensitivity (ECS) is the eventual long-run outcome on temperatures of high CO_2 ppm in the atmosphere. According to estimates, there is a 90% probability that ECS is between 2.3 and 4.7 °C (Hausfather et al., 2022).

model,[7] indicated that there was a 66% probability that GMST would exceed 1.5 °C above preindustrial levels for at least one year between 2023 and 2027 (WMO, 2023). According to Griffin (2017), if trends in fossil fuel use, the major contributor to GHG emissions, continue as in the recent past, then GMST would increase to as much as 4 °C above preindustrial levels by 2100. And Lenton et al. (2023) concludes that based on current climate mitigation policies in terms of the Paris Agreement, that GMST would still be at least 2.7 °C above preindustrial levels by 2100. As we will see in Sect. 3.2.3, this could push earth systems across critical tipping points.

Ecological Overshoot is about more than carbon emissions and climate change. According to Rees (2021) ecological overshoot is "a meta-problem, the cause of most so-called 'environmental problems' including climate change [...]. Climate change is therefore only a symptom of overshoot, implying that only reducing carbon emissions, the cause of anthropogenic global warming, will not solve all environmental problems."

3.2.2 Ecological Footprint and Earth System Boundaries

The neo-Malthusian problem has become one not of scarcity of some resource, food, or of too much carbon emissions, but of the entire human "*ecological footprint*" that is too large and causes an overshoot. The term ecological footprint (EF) was introduced by Wackernagel and Rees (1996). Hoekstra and Wiedmann (2014, p. 1114) describe an ecological footprint as an indicator

> *of human pressure on the environment and form the basis for understanding environmental changes that result from this pressure (such as land-use changes, land degradation, reduced river flows, water pollution, climate change) and resultant impacts (such as biodiversity loss or effects on human health or economy).*

[7] The are many climate models, also known as Integrated Assessment Models (IAMs), in use to forecast changes in GMST. Most prominently, the Intergovernmental Panel on Climate Change (IPCC) refers to IAMs for various climate change scenarios (Beek et al., 2020). According to Hausfather et al. (2020) "climate models published over the past five decades were skillful in predicting subsequent GMST changes, with most models examined showing warming consistent with observations." But IAMs are also subject to serious criticism and shortcomings—see, for example, Pielke and Ritchie (2021) and Hausfather et al. (2022).

They distinguish seven types of ecological or environmental footprints: land, energy, water, materials, carbon, nitrogen, and biodiversity footprints—and state that the carrying capacity of the Earth system in terms of carbon, energy, land, material, and water has been exceeded (Hoekstra & Wiedmann, 2014). EF are calculated in terms of Global Hectares (gha), which is a measure of biocapacity. Human EFs in Europe is around 4–5 gha and in the United States around 8 gha; compared to 0.5 gha in some developing countries (Rees, 2022).

Measuring the carrying capacity of Earth systems and determining whether a particular environmental footprint is exceeding this, which would signal overshoot, has resulted in the development of the concept of "*planetary boundaries*" (PB) (Rockström et al., 2009) and Earth System Boundaries (ESB) (Rockström et al., 2023).

Nine planetary boundaries (PB) have been identified. These are climate change, ocean acidification, ozone depletion, nitrogen and phosphorus cycles, global freshwater use, land systems change, rate of biodiversity loss, atmospheric aerosol loading, and chemical pollution (Rockström et al., 2009; Steffen et al., 2015).

Rockström et al. (2023) extends and links the PBs, which are only biophysical boundaries, to human well-being, by defining "safe and just" Earth System Boundaries (ESBs) "for sustaining the global commons that regulate the state of the planet, protect other species, generate NCP, reduce significant harm to humans and support inclusive human development" (p. 102). These cover the climate, biosphere, surface water, ground water, nitrogen and phosphorus nutrient cycles, and aerosol safe atmosphere.

3.2.3 Ecological Doom-Loops: Tipping Points and Existential Risks

Rockström et al. (2009, p. 1) estimated in 2009 that at least three of the planetary boundaries (PBs) had been exceeded: "*for climate change, rate of biodiversity loss, and changes to the global nitrogen cycle.*" And more recently calculated that seven of the eight of the Earth System Boundaries (ESBs) have been exceeded (Rockström et al., 2023).

While problematic, the bigger danger is that the breach of only a few planetary boundaries can potentially lead to the entire Earth system tipping, resulting in "abrupt global environmental change." This is due to the interdependence between the various planetary boundaries and nonlinear feedback effects between them, which implies that there could be potential *climate tipping points*, or thresholds, which if exceeded, may cause the tipping of the Earth system into a state which would be detrimental to civilization and life—one ecosystem's collapse feeds into that of another (Rockström et al., 2009; Lenton et al., 2019; Ritchie et al., 2021). They have been referred to as ecological doom-loops (Dearing et al., 2023).

Formally, a tipping point is "a critical threshold at which a tiny perturbation can qualitatively alter the state or development of a system" (Lenton et al., 2008, p. 1). Less formally, a tipping point is marked by sudden changes once it is crossed: "*everything's fine until it's not [...] And then everything goes to hell*" as Douglas Erwin from the Smithsonian National Museum of Natural History is quoted to have said (Truscello 2018, p. 262).

Earth systems wherein tipping points could occur to trigger abrupt climate change include the Arctic Sea-Ice, the Greenland Ice Sheet (GIS), the West Antarctic Ice Sheet (WAIS), the Atlantic Thermohaline Circulation (THC), the El Ninõ–Southern Oscillation (ENSO), the Indian Summer Monsoon (ISM), the Sahara/Sahel and West African Monsoon (WAM), the Amazon Rainforest, and the Boreal Forest (Lenton et al., 2008, 2019).

Even if the world manages to keep global warming in the range of 1.5–2 °C as per the Paris Agreement of 2015, six climate tipping points may still be triggered, such as the collapse of the Greenland and West Antarctic ice sheets, the die-off of coral reefs, and the melting of permafrost (Armstrong McKay et al., 2022). There is, to be noted, much uncertainty about tipping points, given the complexity of modeling nonlinear interdependencies in a complex system (Wunderling et al., 2020). According to Willcock et al. (2023, p. 2), "there is limited observational evidence showing that ecosystems have a record of tipping between alternate stable states."

The upshot is that crossing tipping points in the Earth System may possibly threaten societal collapse,[8] and even pose an existential risk (Richards et al., 2021; Willcock et al., 2023). It may even happen sooner than we think, given the multiple stresses on the environment (Dearing et al., 2023). "The prospect of civilization collapse has now entered the mainstream of scientific and popular discourse" (Gowdy, 2020, p. 2).

Climate change, which through a cascade of breached tipping points could cause a mega-hothouse, is considered an existential threat for several reasons (Kemp et al., 2022). One is that global warming directly threatens agriculture and food supply. According to Gowdy (2020, p. 2) some "Climate models indicate that the Earth could warm by 3°C-4 °C by the year 2100 and eventually by as much as 8 °C or more. This would return the planet to the unstable climate conditions of the Pleistocene when agriculture was impossible." He refers here to the fact that climates have been comparatively stable over the past 12,000 years (the Holocene), which allowed human societies to switch from hunting and gathering to large-scale farming.

A second reason why breaching PBs could pose an existential threat is that environmental change is implicated in all past mass extinction events (Kemp et al., 2022). Song et al. (2021, p. 1) points out that mass species extinctions[9] in the past have been associated with tipping points in climate change of >5.2 °C magnitudes. Bradshaw et al. (2021) and Dirzo et al. (2022) consider the current rate of biodiversity loss to be so significant that it signifies that humans have triggered the planet's sixth mass extinction. A growing number of authors and scientists indeed warn that a sixth mass extinction may be beginning or imminent—for example, Barnosky et al. (2011), Cowie et al. (2022), Kaiho (2022), Kolbert (2014), and McCallum (2015).

[8] There are many estimates of the economic costs of climate change, which are estimated using so-called climate damage functions (see e.g. Auffhammer, 2018). These, just like the IPCC's scenario's all assume continuing economic growth until 2100, and thus ignore the potential growth collapse from ecological overshoot (including as Sect. 3.3 discussed, fossil fuel depletion). They thus allow commentators such as Bjorn Lomborg to proclaim that despite climate change, the world will be better off economically in 2100 than at present (Lomborg, 2020). The potential economic cost, in terms of GDP, of ecological overshoot is not known.

[9] A mass extinction occurs when "the Earth loses more than three-quarters of its species in a geologically short interval" (Barnosky et al., 2011, p. 51). There have been five mass extinctions in the past—respectively 444, 372, 252, 201, and 66 million years ago (Cowie et al., 2022; Kaiho, 2022).

Other reasons that have been cited for the breaching of PBs as existential threat is that environmental collapse, say due to climate change, or water scarcity, or biodiversity loss, could cause global conflict, could increase vulnerability to other shocks, cause systemic crises, and reduce humanity's ability to recover from other catastrophes (Kemp et al., 2022).

Economic growth has therefore led humanity to overshoot the capacity of the Earth system, and this poses an existential risk. Therefore Rees (2021) has described overshoot as "ultimately a fatal condition." The extent of overshooting is increasing[10] and shows no sign of diminishing, as measured for instance by the Material Footprint (MF) / Raw Material Consumption (RMC) indicator (Fanning et al., 2022; Giljum et al., 2015; Wiedmann et al., 2015).

Despite these existential dangers, "existential risk is not a narrative or term that has been widely adopted or further developed by the climate change research community. Neither the concept of existential risks nor the term 'existential' was used in the IPCC 5th Assessment Report (AR5), nor in the IPCC Special Reports of the 6th Assessment Cycle" (Huggel et al., 2022, p. 4). And climate catastrophe remains "relatively understudied and poorly understood" (Kemp et al., 2022, p. 1).

Bradshaw et al. (2021, p. 1) concludes therefore perhaps not unsurprisingly that "future environmental conditions will be far more dangerous than currently believed. The scale of the threats to the biosphere and all its lifeforms — including humanity — is in fact so great that it is difficult to grasp for even well-informed experts." They envisage a "ghastly" future for humanity.

Others have also concluded that the collapse of global society is inevitable but that humanity should "embrace it" and not resist it (which will just make the final collapse worse) and prepare for a post-growth, simplified future (Bardi, 2017; Brozović, 2023; Hagens, 2020; Odum & Odum, 2001). For Gowdy (2020, p. 8), the other side of collapse may be something to look forward to, since "we became human as hunters and gatherers and we can regain our humanity when we return to that way of life."

The gap between the Cornucopians and the Malthusians has never been as wide: between the one group envisioning digital future humans

[10] In 2022, *Earth Overshoot Day*, "when humanity has used all the biological resources that the Earth regenerates during the entire year" fell on July 28th. In 1971, it fell on December 25th.

colonizing the galaxy and enjoying super-exponential growth, and the other envisioning collapse and a return to a foraging existence.

3.3 The Carbon Pulse

In Sect. 2.2 of this book the Cornucopian (tech-optimists) hope in never-ending economic growth and eventual transhuman future was described. One problem with this hope is that it is based on the assumptions that there are fundamentally no natural resources (or materials) scarcity, given the overriding importance of ideas (technology), which would dematerialize production and consumption, and find appropriate substitutes when materials become scarce.

3.3.1 *Dark Satanic Mills*

The blind spot in the case for unlimited growth as set out in Sect. 2.2 is that it ignores or trivializes the role of fossil fuel energy. The Industrial Revolution which started in the late eighteenth century in the UK was driven by technological and institutional innovations, including greater trade, but also by cheap (er), and easily accessible coal[11] that powered the "dark satanic mills" of industry as poet William Blake described it (Clark & Jacks, 2007; Pomeranz, 2000; Wrigley, 2010). The industrial revolution was an energy revolution (Wrigley, 2011).

Fossil fuel energy powered the industrial revolution, which started in the UK, and which propelled the UK into the world's first "industrial superpower." For instance, between 1300 and 1750 between 30% and 50% of GDP in England was needed to obtain energy, which after the introduction of fossil fuel energy dropped to around 5% (Hall, 2017). The benefits from using fossil fuels had a dark side, as

> *Britain plundered the resources of the world at the same time that it plundered the coal reserves under its belly. The results were spectacular. From an unremarkable nation in 1600, Britain accumulated so much power that by the late 1800s it was effectively the world's administrator. This rise is written in the language of energy. At the empire's peak, the typical Brit consumed about 7 times more energy than the world average* (Fix, 2020b).

[11] By 2015, more than 200 years after the start of the industrial revolution, coal was still providing 20% of energy used in the UK (Curtis, 2015).

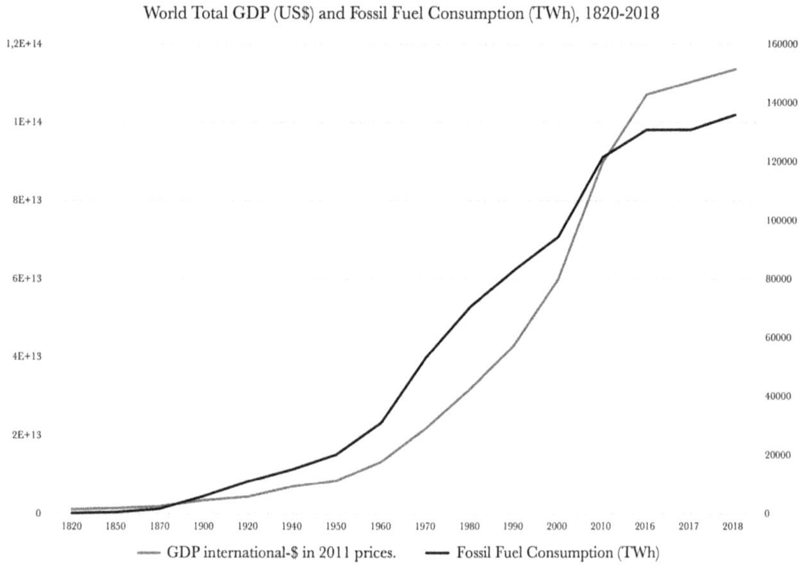

Fig. 3.2 World GDP and Fossil Fuel Consumption, 1820–2018. (Source: Author's compilation based Our World in Data and the bp Statistical Review of World Energy)

From 1861, when the first commercial oil-well was drilled in the United States by the Seneca Oil Company, crude oil was added to the fossil fuel bonanza that would facilitate exponential rates of global economic growth. By the end of the twenty-first century we had "the cheapest energy in the history of human civilization" (King, 2015, p. 12997). It would propel the United States into the next industrial superpower and contribute significantly to the economic growth in all countries in the world (even as its contribution as measured in price remained overall small).

Figure 3.2 shows the close relationship (the correlation is 0.97) between world GDP and fossil fuel consumption since 1820.

By around 2021/2022, 82% and 62% respectively of total primary energy and electricity consumption in the world were supplied by fossil fuels. This causes approximately 87% of all global GHG emissions worldwide—which drives global warming, as was discussed in Sect. 3.2.1.

A particular feature of the fossil fuel industry is that it is a powerful, concentrated industry. Around 100 fossil-fuel companies are responsible

Table 3.1 Top 21 fossil-fuel companies in the world

Company	*Country*	*Percent of global GHG emissions*
Saudi Aramco	Saudi Arabia	4,78%
ExxonMobil	USA	2,06%
Shell	UK	1,82%
BP	UK	1,65%
Chevron	USA	1,43%
Abu Dhabi	UAE	1,37%
Peabody Energy	USA	1,23%
Total Energies	France	1,05%
Kuwait Petroleum Corp	Kuwait	1,04%
ConocoPhillips	USA	0,90%
BHP	Australia	0,85%
Gazprom	Russian Federation	4,49%
Pemex	Mexico	1,65%
PetroChina	China	1,62%
Rosneft	Russian Federation	1,00%
Iraq National Oil Co	Iraq	0,94%
Petrobas	Brazil	0,87%
National Iranian Oil Co	Iran	2,60%
Coal India	India	2,33%
Petroleos De Venezuela	Venezuela	1,15%
Sonatrach	Algeria	1,07%
TOTAL		35,9%

Source: Based on Table 1 from Grasso and Heede (2023, p. 461)

for 71% of "global industrial GHG emissions" (Griffin, 2017, p. 8). The top 21 of these fossil-fuel companies, who generate close to 36% of global industrial GHG emissions (Grasso and Heede, 2023, p. 461), are listed in Table 3.1.

Thus, economic growth, which requires energy as input, and which also results in goods and services that stimulates further demand for energy is very closely associated with the exponential growth in GDP depicted in Figs. 2.1 and 3.1 and with the rise of industrial superpowers—and a highly concentrated and powerful fossil-fuel industry. The very structure and nature of global capitalism is predicated on plenty and cheap fossil fuels.

3.3.2 The Detritovores

The problem posed by the dominance of fossil fuels in economic growth and in the emergence of large, dominant oil companies, is threefold. One is the unintended consequences that the greenhouse gas emissions from using fossil fuels contributed to global warming. The potential consequences were discussed in Sect. 3.1. A second is that fossil fuels are finite resources. As explained by Hagens (2018):

> *[T]he constant growth we've experienced was correlated with human inventions and economic theories, but the cause was finding a bolus of fossil sunlight. We behave like squirrels living in a forest where a truck full of hazelnuts crashed, living off the freight and thinking it will last forever.*

Because of the "addiction" of humanity to this bolus of fossil sunlight, Catton (1982) called humans *detritovores*: "organisms that live off the dead remains of other organisms" (Cobb, 2015).

Over the very long run, the discovery of this "bolus of fossil sunlight" constitutes a one-off "carbon pulse," described by Hagens (2018) as "a one-time bolus of fossil productivity injected into the human ecosystem" and whose singular, once-off appearance over time can be depicted as in Fig. 3.3.

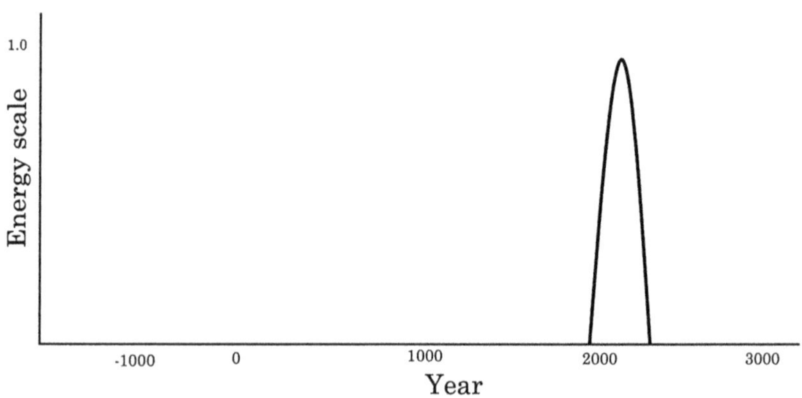

Fig. 3.3 The carbon pulse. (Source: Author's compilation based on Murphy et al. (2021, p. 2), Hagens (2018) and Hagens and White (2021, p. 260))

The bolus of fossil sunlight has provided the average inhabitant of the Earth "nearly 700 times more useful energy than their ancestors had at the beginning of the 19th century [...] it is as if 60 adults would be working non-stop, day and night, for each average person" (Smil, 2022, p. 19). Murphy et al. (2021, p. 2) observes that "it seems likely that future generations will label the past two centuries as the Fossil Fuel Age rather than the Industrial Revolution – emphasizing the critical importance of a now-depleted resource over a self- flattering celebration of human innovation."

To provide a perspective on the magnitude of the contribution of fossil fuel energy to GDP, Hagens (2020) compares its ability to do work with human labor. He calculates that the 110 billion barrels of oil that were needed in 2018 to power the world economy is equivalent to more than 500 billion human workers toiling day and night.

The problem is, oil and coal are finite stocks that took hundreds of millions of years to form, which have been since the industrial revolution being drawn down rapidly in comparison (Hagens & White, 2021). It implies two important questions: How long will the fossil fuel bonanza last? And what will happen if the world runs out of fossil fuels?

3.3.3 *Peak Oil*

The first question is often discussed with reference to the concept of **Peak Oil**—the rate of maximum production of oil after which production would decline (Campbell & Laherrere, 1998). Hubbert (1956) proposed that the rate of oil production would follow a bell-shaped curve (according to a semi-logistical curved model). Based on information at the time, he estimated that for 48 US States Peak Oil production would be reached in 1970. Figure 3.4 depicts Hubbert's prediction against actual US field production of oil data from 1900 to 2022.

Figure 3.3 shows that Hubbert was fairly accurate—US oil production peaked around 1973 and then started to decline until around 2008. But then, against the predictions of Hubbert, it increased. What happened after 2008 is the "shale-oil boom" or "shale gas revolution" (Fix, 2020a; Kapoor & Murmann, 2023). Shale oil and gas, which are unconventional fuels, are extracted from oil shale, a sedimentary rock that contains kerogen. Kerogen releases hydrocarbons when heated.[12] Shale oil and gas production is not the result of new discoveries, but of innovation in what is

[12] See, for example, https://education.nationalgeographic.org/resource/oil-shale/

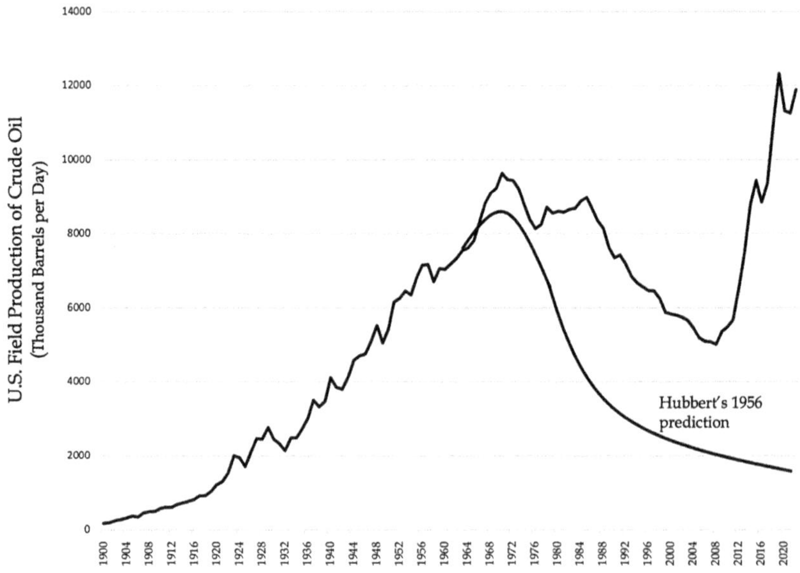

Fig. 3.4 Hubbert's 1956 prediction of peak oil in the United States vs actual production, 1900–2022. (Source: Author's compilation based on data from US Energy Information Administration and following Fix (2020a, Fig. 2)

called hydraulic fracking technology (see Speight, 2020) as well as in a range of complementary technologies including horizontal drilling, three-dimensional (3D) imaging, microseismic surveys, and "electric logging" (Kapoor & Murmann, 2023).

While Cornucopians hail the example of the shale gas revolution as indicative of the ability of technological innovation to continue to solve the challenge of energy, shale oil and gas have just postponed the timing of peak oil. The reasons are that, obviously shale oil and gas are finite resources, but also that the quality and cost of shale oil and gas extraction are subject to critical shortcomings. Hence only a fraction of the roughly 1 trillion barrels of shale oil is possibly extractable—which would add 200 billion barrels of oil to the United States's reserve (Fix, 2020a). If this is added to Hubbert's prediction, it only shifts the time of peak oil from 1970 to the mid-2020s (Fix, 2020a).

This tallies with other more recent estimates that suggest that world peak oil production will be reached in the mid-2020s—if it has in fact not yet been reached (Turner, 2014). Consistent with this, Murray and King (2012) found that there has been a "step change" in the economics of oil around 2005, after which the production of oil has become much less price elastic, with the consequence that oil prices have become much more sensitive to changes in demand. This, and the decline in oil production from existing oil fields of between 5% and 6% per year (Murray & King, 2012) together suggests that oil production may peak in the first half of the twenty-first century—see also Hall (2017), Hallock et al. (2014) and Mohr et al. (2015) -at the latest.

Cornucopians would argue that this is all too pessimistic, and that technological advances would keep increasing oil reserves, citing among others the example of nonconventional oils such as from Canada's tar sands or the United States's fracking industry. For instance, Epstein (2022, pp. 54–55) states that as far as "proven reserves" of oil are concerned, "the more we consume, the more reserves increase [...] humanity keeps getting better at using fossil fuels to power the machines that enable us to transform more of the world's massive stockpile of raw fossil fuels into usable fossil fuel reserves."

There are two weaknesses however, with this optimism. One is the belief that "the more we consume, the more reserves increase." The second is the belief that the efficiency of extraction—transforming "raw fossil fuels into usable fossil fuel reserves" is increasing. Both statements from Epstein (2022) can be critiqued.

The belief that the more oil we consume, the more reserves will increase, is commonly based on the estimates of "proven reserves" of oil, typically published in the bp Statistical Review of World Energy. Indeed, according to the data, "proven" reserves of oil against production, expressed in the Oil Reserves to Production Ratio (R/P)[13] has been increasing over time—as Fig. 3.5 show.

Figure 3.5 suggests that, based on estimates of "proven" oil reserves, by 1980 there were 31 years of existing estimated oil stocks left.[14] By 2020, this had risen to 53 years! Thus, indeed it seems, as Epstein (2022) claims, the more the world consumes oil, the more reserves increase. How

[13] The Reserves to Production ratio (R/P) is the ratio of total estimated oil reserves to the annual production (extraction) of usable fuel. It indicates how many years of oil supply are left.

[14] This does not include the possibility that in future new reserves will be discovered. Most of this will have to come from opening new oil fields and exploiting nonconventional oil. Estimates of the extent of such possible future oil discoveries are however contentious and subject to much uncertainties (McGlade, 2012; Murray & King, 2012).

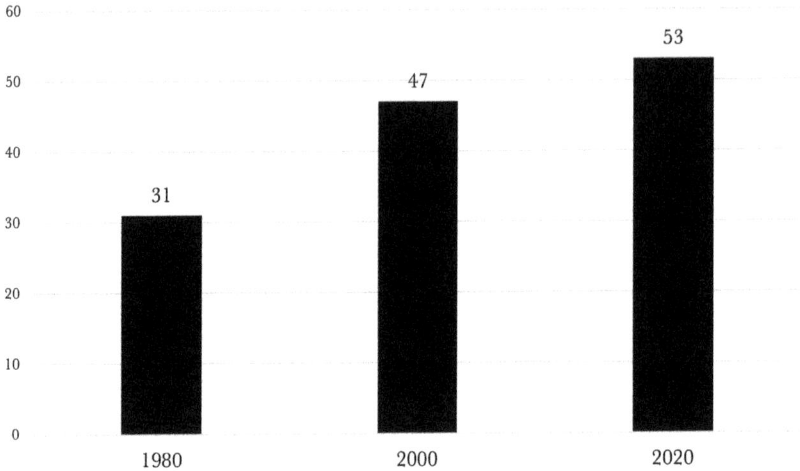

Fig. 3.5 "Proven" oil reserves to production ratio (R/P), 1980–2020. (Source: Author's compilation based on data from the bp Statistical Review of World Energy)

very extraordinary this is, has been criticized by Bardi (2020, p. 126), who compared the world's use of oil like eating a cake and "as long as you have some cake left, there is nothing to be worried about. The peculiar cake that is crude oil has the characteristic that it becomes bigger as you eat it (!)"

Naturally, this cake that gets bigger as you eat it, has led several scientists and journalists to attempt to scrutinize how estimates of proven reserves are obtained. Just how proven are these (politically welcome) estimates? Estimates of oil reserves cannot be done directly and rely on many assumptions on technology, economics, and geology; moreover, how these assumptions are combined with other information is not transparent as "probably half to three-quarters of the world's oil is in countries where the oil sector is a state monopoly and whose governments do not feel the need to explain the basis of their reserves estimates (Mitchell, 2004, p. 1). As a result, and because they face economic incentives to do so (it influences their share prices), oil companies tend to significantly overstate[15] their reserves (Jefferson, 2016). In the case of nonconventional oil from

[15] For example, in 2004 Shell admitted to overstating its reserves by 4.47 billion barrels, see https: //www.sec.gov/news/press/2004-116.htm

fracking, Olson et al. (2019) reported on several methods that oil companies use to inflate their reserves and expected output, including cherry picking data and understating depreciation expenses.

3.3.4 EROI: Energy Return to Energy Invested

The second response of Cornucopians to the question of how long the oil bonanza will last, is the belief that the efficiency of extraction—transforming "raw fossil fuels into usable fossil fuel reserves" is increasing, as Epstein (2022) claims. Such greater efficiency would lengthen the curation of the bonanza—"kick the can down the road." It seems, however, contrary to Epstein (2022)'s claim, that it is getting more and more difficult and expensive to extract and use oil. Usable oil, a flow, is more and more costly to obtain. Even if one would assume that provable oil reserves are not overstated, a higher cost of extraction would in effect deflate the value of the available stocks. As put by Murray and King (2012, p. 434) "we are not running out of oil, but we are running out of oil that can be produced easily and cheaply."

It takes energy to extract and make oil usable. Taking the cost and energy of extracting raw oil to use-able oil therefore raises the importance of making a distinction between energy and *net* energy. This is the energy available for use "after the energy costs of getting and concentrating that energy are subtracted" (Odum, 1973, p. 220). The ratio between the energy and costs in producing net energy (usable oil) is known as the Energy Return to Energy Invested (EROI) ratio An EROI of ">5 to 7 is required for modern society to function" (Mearns, 2016). With EROI = 1, we use all available energy to produce energy, leaving none spare for use elsewhere in the economy.

In the case of resource (oil) depletion, the EROI would be declining (Bardi & Lavacchi, 2009). This is indeed what has been happening (Brockway et al., 2019; Court & Fizaine, 2017; Jackson, 2021). For fossil fuels at the primary energy stage, the EROI is typically more than 25 (it peaked in the 1930s–1940s at 50); however, after turning this into end-stage energy for example petrol or electricity, the EROI drops to around 6—and this has been seemingly declining further in recent years (Brockway et al., 2019; Court & Fizaine, 2017). We seem to be on course for an EROI of 2–3, like that in England between 1300 and 1750, when between 30% and 50% of England's GDP was spent on energy (Hall, 2017). According to Fizaine and Court (2016), if the United States would spend more than 11% of its GDP on energy, it would not be able to grow anymore.

The EROI of renewables (the great hope of Green Growth proponents) have so far been much lower than that of fossil fuels.[16] Mearns (2016) for instance reported an EROI of between 1 and 2 for corn ethanol and 1–5 for solar photovoltaic (PV) cells, lamenting that "new Green technologies designed to save humanity from CO_2 may kill humanity through energy starvation instead." To this low EROI of renewables, one may add the ecological impact of manufacturing renewables, which still extensively requires fossil fuels. Singer (2023) documents some of the ecological demands from scaling up renewables, in being heavily depended on minerals and resulting in waste. For example, copper (1 kg of kilogram of mined copper leads to at least 210 kg of waste); cobalt and coltan (the mining of which is associated with deforestation, child labor and conflict); lithium (filtering a ton of lithium requires two million liters of water).

Thus, the problem as formulated above remains. Oil and coal are finite stocks that took hundreds of millions of years to form, which are since the industrial revolution being drawn down in a comparatively brief period, with the fossil fuel bonanza likely ending in the first half of the twenty-first century. The next big question then is, as raised above, is what will happen if the world runs out of fossil fuels?

The answer is that it will spell —eventually—the end of economic growth. As already pointed out in 1973 by Odum (1973, p. 225), "During periods when expansion of energy sources is not possible, then the many high density and growth promoting policies and structures become an energy liability because their high energy cost is no longer accelerating energy yields."

Because the world will not run out of fossil fuels abruptly, but rather follow the more gradual decline along the contours of a semi-logistical curve, as fossil fuels become scarcer and the only the most difficult reserves remain to be extracted, with the EROI continuing to decline, the impact will be, paradoxically, continued and even temporarily higher economic

[16] Murphy et al. (2022) compared the EROI of difference energy sources concluding that PV, wind, and hydropower have EROIs > 10 and petroleum < 10. According to Berman (2023), who elaborates the methodological flaws in this paper, one should "stop trying to make renewables look like something that are not and cannot be, and just learn to live with them as they are [...] Substituting renewables for fossil fuels is not a solution without greatly curtailing our total energy consumption."

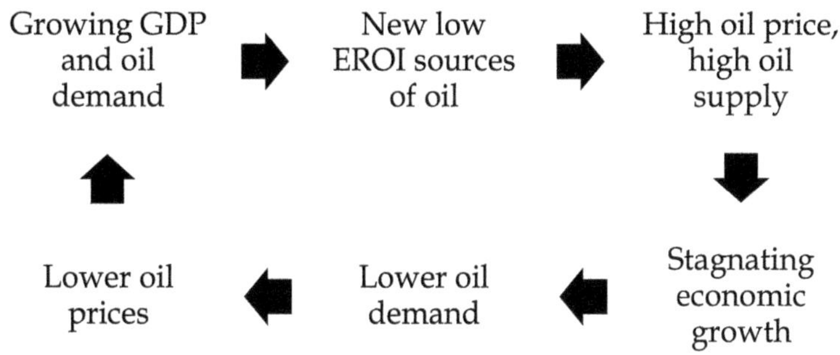

Diagram 3.1 Growth paradox during peak oil and declining EROI. (Source: Author's adaptation of Murphy & Hall, 2011, p. 70)

growth during as the EROI declines. Diagram 3.1 describes how this growth paradox can occur.

As Diagram 3.1 shows, a high oil price stimulates high oil supply, which reduces economic growth rates. Reduced economic growth rates (and even degrowth or recession) results in lower demand for oil, which reduces pressure on oil prices. The lower oil prices lead to higher use of oil, which stimulates higher economic growth. Which in turn leads to the search for new sources of oil, including unconventional oil and gas and RE with a lower EROI, which results in higher oil prices—and the cycle continues (Murphy & Hall, 2011).

Eventually though, the supply of new low EROI sources will run out. This will leave the economy with "an increase in energy prices, the general rate of price inflation, and the unemployment rate, and negatively impacts the functional income distribution. Combined, these effects cause a recession followed by a period of below trend output growth" (Jackson, 2021).

It has been argued that the secular decline in economic growth experienced in the West since the 1970s reflects the growing cost of energy (as reflected in EROI declines) (Naudé, 2022; Heinberg, 2011).

3.4 The Dataome

We must enlarge our approach to encompass the formation, taking place before our eyes ... outside and above the biosphere, of an added planetary layer, an envelope of thinking substance, to which, for the sake of convenience and sym-

metry, I have given the name of the Noosphere. – Pierre Teilhard de Chardin, 1947, quoted in Wright (2023).

So far, we have discussed ecological overshoot only in relation to the traditional biosphere or traditional Earth System very much as it would exist before the Anthropocene. It has been argued that this traditional Earth system or biosphere has evolved into a "Noosphere" (also spelled Noösphere) because of the revolution in data and artificial intelligence that has been one of the most remarkable features of technological change over the past century. Not only has our civilization been transformed by the carbon pulse but has been experiencing in recent years an unprecedented "information pulse." It is establishing a planetary mind. This planetary mind is changing the very geological nature of the planet. Christian (2017) refers to one of the earliest proponents of the Noösphere, the geologist Vernadsky who pointed out that "mineralogical rarity, native iron, is now being produced by the billions of tons. Native aluminum, which never before existed on our planet, is now produced in any quantity."

Is this planetary mind now coming to grips with its basis in biophysical reality?

According to Wright (2023) "Artificial intelligence is the crystallization of the Noosphere." This is because artificial intelligence (AI), being based on ubiquitous and cloud computing, the Internet, big data and software code, can be described as a form of *collective intelligence* that is arising (Lanier, 2023).

The Noösphere has been called the *Dataome* by Scharf (2021a) to emphasize the key role played by information in the collective intelligence or extended mind that is being overlaid on the biophysical planet. He defines the Dataome as "all of the non-genetic data we carry internally and externally" (p. 6). It is related to the concept of the Global Datasphere. This data can be expressed digitally, in binary digits (bits) that has, following Claude Shannon's path-breaking paper of 1948, driven the ICT revolution—see Shannon (1948). Eight bits is a byte of information, in which all storage of data is measured. A CD-ROM typically stores 5 gigabytes (5 GB = 10^9 bytes). Currently, global annual data growth, collected for instance in data centers, or through the Internet, or mobile phones, is measured in zettabytes (ZB), where 1 ZB = 10^{21} bytes. The amount of data that is generated and stored is growing super-exponentially: it has been predicted that this volume will grow from 33 ZB in 2018 to 175 ZB in 2025 (Reinsel et al., 2018). In 2011 one needed 1000 datacentres, which would fill 20% of the size of Manhattan, to store one zettabyte (Jackson, 2011).

The Dataome is heavily energy-intensive. ICT cannot function without transistors—the key components of a computer. As Singer (2023) notes, "manufacturers produce 1000 times more transistors than farmers grow grains of wheat and rice combined." Moreover, the silicon from which transistors are made requires production in "toxic waste-emitting smelters and refineries" that requires heating in smelters of almost 1700 °C running for many years uninterruptedly. Rinsing a single silicon wafer requires around 8000 liters of ultra-pure water. And connecting computers and smartphones via the Internet and mobile networks scale up the energy demands dramatically.

For example, building and operating 5G networks needs the energy equivalent to that of 36 nuclear reactors (Singer, 2023). Ubiquitous computing through the cloud to store the huge volumes of data generated and downloaded every second requires energy-and-water (for cooling) demanding data storage facilities—some of which are so big they can be seen from outer space (Singer, 2023).

Growing information demands further energy in transmission and storage. As Scharf (2021b) prosaically explain:

> *It's possible that altogether the simple act of human arms raising and lowering copies of Shakespeare's writings has expended well over 4 trillion Joules of energy. That's equivalent to combusting several hundred thousand kilograms of coal. Additional energy has been utilized every time a human has read some of those 835,997 words and had their neurons fire. [...] Add in the energy expenditure of the manufacture of paper, books, and their transport and the numbers only grow and grow. It may be impossible to fully gauge the energetic burden that William Shakespeare unwittingly dumped on the human species, but it is substantial. Of course, we can easily forgive him. He wrote some good stuff.*

In other words, humans are spending huge amounts of energy to create the Dataome Using the Dataome to solve problems facing human society (and for entertainment and virtual signaling and other ways to obtain dopamine rushes) in turn creates new information, with further demands on energy. The Dataome is energy-hungry, and its coming into being is hard to imagine without the Carbon Pulse.

Our need to capture and transmit information also changes the physical landscape—through the need to mine minerals and create physical copies of information—such as the book you are reading, the Fairy Tales of the Brothers Grimm, compact discs, photographs, paintings, and other paper records. According to Scharf (2021b), every page of paper we produce to store and transmit information is equivalent to burning 5 grams of coal.

The question that the growth of the Dataome poses is whether it still is in a healthy human–Dataome symbiosis? Scharf (2021a, b) speculate that the benefit from the large Dataome may perhaps not be worth the expenditure in terms of energy anymore. He refers to the proliferation of low-quality data ("energy-wasting junk") and misinformation, disinformation, and data delusions, all that add up to a cost, reducing the value of the Dataome. It may even establish a digital dystopia. The collective intelligence that the Dataome represents will, in such a case, perhaps not be able to enable humanity to steer its future evolution past the challenge of ecological overshoot.

3.5 Concluding Remarks

Chapter 2 outlined the basic debate between the Malthusians and the Cornucopians. It was shown that the failures of Malthus's predictions of resource scarcity and famine to materialize, and the powerful impacts that technological innovation had on human society following the Enlightenment and the first Industrial Revolution, buoyed the belief of the Cornucopians in never-ending economic growth.

In this chapter, this belief was critically examined and shown to be hard to maintain once the strong relationship between GDP growth and broad systemic material resource use (ecological footprint) and its relation to planetary boundaries are recognized—including the rise of the Noösphere or Dataome.

Moreover, once the significant role that fossil fuels played in enabling exponential economic growth from the mid-twentieth century onward is acknowledged (something that Malthus could not foresee and which is neglected by economic growth theory), then this chapter can conclude on somewhat pessimistic note, by sharing the likely consequences of the decline in oil as aptly described by (Bardi, 2020, p. 122):

> *Without liquid fuels, everything would stop in the world [....] No fuels, no trucks, no food, no civilization. Could it really happen? It could. Something similar already happened with the great "oil crisis" of the 1970s that for a period seemed to destroy the very foundations of the Western civilization. If you experienced that crisis, you cannot forget what happened: gas prices suddenly*

skyrocketing, long lines at the gas stations, governments enacting all sorts of measures: lower speed limits on highways, "odd-even rationing" schemes, support to the production of small cars, and more. The shock on the financial system was even worse: recession and two-digit inflation. It was a disaster for a world that had experienced, up to then, more than 2 decades of uninterrupted economic growth.

Chapter 4 asks whether Green Growth can realistically bring about an energy transition away from fossil fuels in a manner that will allow economic growth to continue.

References

Armstrong McKay, D., Staal, A., Abrams, J., Winkelmann, R., Sakschewski, B., Loriani, S., Fetzer, I., Cornell, S., Rockström, J., & Lenton, T. (2022). Exceeding 1.5°C Global Warming Could Trigger Multiple Climate Tipping Points. *Science, 377*(6611), eabn7950.

Arrhenius, S. (1896). On the Influence of Carbonic Acid in the Air upon the Temperature of the Ground. *Philosophical Magazine and Journal of Science, 5*(41), 237–276.

Auffhammer, M. (2018). Quantifying Economic Damages from Climate Change. *Journal of Economic Perspectives, 32*(4), 33–52.

Bardi, U. (2017). *The Seneca Effect: Why Growth Is Slow, But Collapse Is Rapid*. Springer.

Bardi, U. (2020). *Before the Collapse: A Guide to the Other Side of Growth*. Springer.

Bardi, U., & Lavacchi, A. (2009). A Simple Interpretation of Hubbert's Model of Resource Exploitation. *Energies, 2*, 646–661.

Barnosky, A., Matzke, N., Tomiya, S., et al. (2011). Has the Earth's Sixth Mass Extinction Already Arrived? *Nature, 471*, 51–57.

Beek, L. v., Hajer, M., Pelzer, P., van Vuuren, D., & Cassen, C. (2020). Anticipating Futures Through Models: The Rise of Integrated Assessment Modelling in the Climate Science-Policy Interface Since 1970. *Global Environmental Change, 65*, 102191.

Berman, A. (2023, May 27). Does Renewable Energy Have a Higher EROI than Fossil Fuels? *The Petroleum Truth Report*.

Bradshaw, C., Ehrlich, P., Beattie, A., Ceballos, G., Crist, E., Diamond, J., Dirzo, R., Ehrlich, A., Harte, J., Pyke, G., Raven, P., Ripple, W., Saltré, F., Turnbull, C., Wackernagel, M., & Blumstein, D. (2021). Underestimating the Challenges of Avoiding a Ghastly Future. *Frontiers in Conservation Science, 1*, 615–641.

Brockway, P., Owen, A., Brand-Correa, L., & Hardt, L. (2019). Estimation of Global Final-Stage Energy-Return-On-Investment for Fossil Fuels with Comparison to Renewable Energy Sources. *Nature Energy, 4*, 612–621.

Brozović, D. (2023). Societal Collapse: A Literature Review. *Futures, 145*, 103–175.
Campbell, C., & Laherrere, J. (1998). The End of Cheap Oil. *Scientific American, 278*(3), 80–86.
Catton, W. (1982). *Overshoot: The Ecological Basis of Revolutionary Change*. University of Illinois Press.
Catton, W. (1998). What If Malthus Were Writing Today? *Organization & Environment, 11*(4), 434–437.
Chaplin-Kramer, R., Neugarten, R. A., Sharp, R. P., et al. (2023). Mapping the Planet's Critical Natural Assets. *Nature Ecology and Evolution, 7*, 51–61.
Christian, D. (2017). *The Noösphere. Edge: What Scientific Term or Concept Ought to Be More Widely Known?* Edge.Org.
Clark, G., & Jacks, D. (2007). Coal and the Industrial Revolution, 1700–1869. *European Review of Economic History, 11*(1), 39–72.
Cobb, K. (2015, February 15). William Catton's Warning. *Resource Insights*.
Court, V., & Fizaine, F. (2017). Long-Term Estimates of the Energy-Return-On-Investment (EROI) of Coal, Oil, and Gas Global Productions. *Ecological Economics, 138*, 145–159.
Cowie, R. H., Bouchet, P., & Fontaine, B. (2022). The Sixth Mass Extinction: Fact, Fiction or Speculation? *Biological Reviews, 97*(April 2022), 640–663.
Curtis, B. (2015, December 23). The Life and Death of King Coal. *The Conversation*.
Dearing, J., Cooper, G., & Willcock, S. (2023, June 25). Ecological Doom-Loops: Why Ecosystem Collapses may Occur Much Sooner than Expected, *The Conversation*.
Dirzo, R., Ceballos, G., & Ehrlich, P. (2022). Circling the Drain: The Extinction Crisis and the Future of Humanity. *Philosophical Transactions of the Royal Society of London Biological Sciences, 377*(1857), 20210378.
Epstein, A. (2022). *Fossil Future: Why Global Human Flourishing Requires More Oil, Coal, and Natural Gas – Not Less*. Penguin Books.
Fanning, A., O'Neill, D., Hickel, J., & Roux, N. (2022). The Social Shortfall and Ecological Overshoot of Nations. *Nature Sustainability, 5*, 26–36.
Fix, B. (2020a, November 16). Peak Oil Never Went Away. *Economics from the Top Down*.
Fix, B. (2020b, July 11). Why America Won't Be 'Great' Again. *Economics from the Top Down*.
Fizaine, F., & Court, V. (2016). Energy Expenditure, Economic Growth, and the Minimum EROI of Society. *Energy Policy, 95*, 172–186.
Giljum, S., Bruckner, M., & Martinez, A. (2015). Material Footprint Assessment in a Global Input-Output Framework. *Journal of Industrial Ecology, 19*, 792–804.
Gowdy, J. (2020). Our Hunter-Gatherer Future: Climate Change, Agriculture and Uncivilization. *Futures, 115*, 102488.

Grasso, M., & Heede, R. (2023). Time to Pay the Piper: Fossil Fuel Companies' Reparations for Climate Damages. *One Earth, 6*(5), 459–463.

Habashi, F. (2000). The First Oil Well in the World. *Bulletin for History of Chemistry, 25*(1), 64–66.

Hagens, N. (2018, April 23). Where are We Going? *Resilience.*

Hagens, N. (2020). Economics for the Future – Beyond the Superorganism. *Ecological Economics, 169*, 106520.

Hagens, N., & White, D. (2021). *Reality Blind: Integrating the Systems Science Under- pinning Our Collective Futures Vol. 1.* Independently Published.

Hall, C. (2017). Will EROI Be the Primary Determinant of Our Economic Future? The View of the Natural Scientist Versus the Economist. *Joule, 1*, 635–638.

Hallock, J. L., Wu, W., Hall, C. A. S., & Jefferson, M. (2014). Forecasting the Limits to the Availability and Diversity of Global Conventional Oil Supply: Validation. *Energy, 64*, 130–153.

Hansen, J., Sato, M., Kharecha, P., Beerling, D., Berner, R., Masson-Delmotte, V., Pagani, M., Raymo, M., Royer, D. L., & Zachos, J. C. (2008). Target Atmospheric CO_2: Where Should Humanity Aim? *The Open Atmospheric Science Journal, 2*, 217–231.

Hausfather, Z., Drake, H. F., Abbott, T., & Schmidt, G. A. (2020). Evaluating the Performance of Past Climate Model Projections. *Geophysical Research Letters, 47*, e2019GL085378.

Hausfather, Z., Marvel, K., Schmidt, G. A., Nielsen-Gammon, J. W., & Zelinka, M. (2022). Climate Simulations: Recognize the 'Hot Model' Problem. *Nature, 605*, 26–20.

Heinberg, R. (2011). *The End of Growth: Adapting to Our New Economic Reality.* New Society Publishers.

Hoekstra, A., & Wiedmann, T. (2014). Humanity's Unsustainable Environmental Foot- print. *Science, 344*(6188), 1114–1117.

Hubbert, M. (1956). *Nuclear Energy and the Fossil Fuels.* Presented before the Spring Meeting of the Southern District, American Petroleum Institute, Plaza Hotel, San Antonio, Texas, March 7–9.

Huggel, C., Bouwer, L., Juhola, S., et al. (2022). The Existential Risk Space of Climate Change. *Climatic Change, 174*(8).

IPCC. (2018). Global *Warming of 1.5°C.* Intergovernmental Panel on Climate Change.

Jackson, N. (2011, May 17). Infographic: How Big Is a Yottabyte? *The Atlantic.*

Jackson, T. (2021). *Post Growth – Life After Capitalism.* Policy Press.

Jefferson, M. (2016). A Global Energy Assessment. *WIREs Energy and Environment, 5*(1), 7–15.

Kaiho, K. (2022). Relationship Between Extinction Magnitude and Climate Change During Major Marine and Terrestrial Animal Crises. *Biogeosciences, 19*(14), 3369–2022.

Kapoor, R., & Murmann, J. P. (2023). The Organizational and Technological Origins of the U.S. Shale Gas Revolution, 1947 to 2012. *Industrial and Corporate Change*, dtad021.

Kemp, L., Xu, C., Depledge, J., Ebi, K., Gibbins, G., Kohler, T., Rockström, J., Scheffer, M., Schellnhuber, H., Steffen, W., & Lenton, T. (2022). Climate Endgame: Exploring Catastrophic Climate Change Scenarios. *Proceedings of the National Academy of Sciences, 119*(34), e2108146119.

King, C. W. (2015). Comparing World Economic and Net Energy Metrics, Part 3: Macroeconomic Historical and Future Perspectives. *Energies, 8*, 12997–13020.

Kolbert, E. (2014). *The Sixth Extinction: An Unnatural History.* Henry Holt and Company.

Lanier, J. (2023, April 20). There is no A.I. *The New Yorker.*

Lenton, T. M., Held, H., Kriegler, E., & Schellnhuber, H. (2008). Tipping Elements in the Earth's Climate System. *Proceedings of the National Academy of Sciences, 105*(6), 1786–1793.

Lenton, T., Rockström, J., Gaffney, O., Rahmstorf, S., Richardson, K., Steffen, W., & Schellnhuber, H. (2019, November 27). Climate Tipping Points – Too Risky to Bet Against. *Nature.*

Lenton, T.M., Xu, C., Abrams, J.F. et al. (2023, May 22). Quantifying the Human Cost of Global Warming. *Nature Sustainability.*

Lomborg, B. (2020). Welfare in the 21st Century: Increasing Development, Reducing Inequality, the Impact of Climate Change, and the Cost of Climate Policies. *Technological Forecasting and Social Change, 156.*

McCallum, M. (2015). Vertebrate Biodiversity Losses Point to a Sixth Mass Extinction. *Biodiversity and Conservation, 24*, 2497–2519.

McGlade, C. (2012). A Review of the Uncertainties in Estimates of Global Oil Resources. *Energy, 47*(1), 262–270.

Mearns, E. (2016, May 25). ERoEI for Beginners. *Energy Matters.*

Mitchell, J. (2004). Petroleum Reserves in Question. *Chatham House Paper SDP BP 04/03.*

Mohr, S., Wang, J., Ellem, G., Ward, J., & Giurco, D. (2015). Projection of World Fossil Fuels by Country. *Fuel, 1*, 120–135.

Murphy, D. J., & Hall, C. A. (2011). Energy Return on Investment, Peak Oil, and the End of Economic Growth. *Annals of the New York Academy of Sciences, 1219*, 52–72.

Murphy, T., Murphy, D., Love, T., LeHew, M., & McCall, B. (2021). Modernity is Incompatible with Planetary Limits: Developing a PLAN for the Future. *Energy Research & Social Science, 81*, 102239.

Murphy, D. J., Raugei, M., Carbajales-Dale, M., & Rubio Estrada, B. (2022). Energy Return on Investment of Major Energy Carriers: Review and Harmonization. *Sustainability, 14*(12), 7098.

Murray, J., & King, D. (2012). Oil's Tipping Point Has Passed. *Nature, 481*, 433–435.

Naudé, W. (2022). From the Entrepreneurial to the Ossified Economy. *Cambridge Journal of Economics, 46*(1), 105–131.
Odum, H. (1973). Energy, Ecology, and Economics. *Ambio, 2*(6), 220–227.
Odum, H., & Odum, E. (2001). *A Prosperous Way Down: Principles and Policies.* University Press of Colorado.
Olson, B., Elliott, R., & Matthews, C. M. (2019, January 2). Fracking's Secret Problem – Oil Wells Aren't Producing as Much as Forecast. *The Wall Street Journal.*
Oreskes, N. (2004). The Scientific Consensus on Climate Change. *Science, 30*, 1686–1686.
Osman, M. B., Tierney, J., Zhu, J., Tardif, R., Hakim, G. J., King, J., & Poulsen, C. J. (2021). Globally Resolved Surface Temperatures Since the Last Glacial Maximum. *Nature, 599*(7884), 239–244.
Perry, M. (2016, April 21). 18 Spectacularly Wrong Predictions Made Around the Time of the First Earth Day in 1970, Expect More This Year. *AEIdeas.*
Pielke, R., & Ritchie. (2021). How Climate Scenarios Lost Touch with Reality. *Issues in Science and Technology, 37*(4).
Pielke, R., Burgess, M. G., & Ritchie, J. (2022). Plausible 2005–2050 Emissions Scenarios Project Between 2 °C and 3 °C of Warming by 2100. *Environmental Research Letters, 17*, 024027.
Pomeranz, K. (2000). *The Great Divergence: China, Europe, and the Making of the Modern World Economy.* Princeton University Press.
Rees, W. E. (2021). A Note of Climate Change and Cultural Denial. *Population Matters.*
Rees, W. E. (2022). Why Large Cities Won't Survive the Twenty-First Century. In R. Brears (Ed.), *The Palgrave Encyclopedia of Urban and Regional Futures.* Palgrave Macmillan.
Reinsel, D., Gantz, J., & Rydning, J. (2018, November). The Digitization of the World from Edge to Core. *IDC White Paper.*
Richards, C., Lupton, R., & Allwood, J. (2021). Re-Framing the Threat of Global Warming: An Empirical Causal Loop Diagram of Climate Change, Food Insecurity and Societal Collapse. *Climatic Change, 164*(49).
Ritchie, P., Clarke, J., Cox, P., & Huntingford, C. (2021). Overshooting Tipping Point Thresholds in a Changing Climate. *Nature, 592*, 517–523.
Rockström, J., Steffen, W., Noone, K., Persson, A., Chapin, F., Lambin, E., Lenton, T., et al. (2009). Planetary Boundaries: Exploring the Safe Operating Space for Humanity. *Ecology and Society, 14*(2).
Rockström, J., Gupta, J., Qin, D., et al. (2023). Safe and Just Earth System Boundaries. *Nature, 619*, 102–111.
Sabin, P. (2013). *The Bet: Paul Ehrlich, Julian Simon, and Our Gamble over Earth's Future.* Yale University Press.
Scharf, C. (2021a). *The Ascent of Information: Books, Bits, Genes, Machines and Life's Unending Algorithm.* Riverhead Books.

Scharf, C. (2021b, October 24). The Selfish Dataome: Does the Data We Produce Serve Us, or Vice Versa? *Nautilus.*

Shannon, C. (1948). A Mathematical Theory of Communication. *The Bell System Technical Journal, 27*, 379–423.

Singer, K. (2023, June 7). Policies for More Ecologically-Sound Tech. *Katie Singer's Substack.*

Smil, V. (2022). *How the World Really Works.* Penguin Books.

Song, H., Kemp, D., Tian, L., Chu, D., Song, H., & Dai, X. (2021). Thresholds of Temperature Change for Mass Extinctions. *Nature Communications, 12*(4694).

Speight, J. (2020). Chapter 5 – Hydraulic Fracturing. In J. Speight (Ed.), *Shale Oil and Gas Production Processes.* Gulf Professional Publishing.

Steffen, W., Richardson, K., Rockström, J., Cornell, S., Fetzer, I., et al. (2015). Planetary Boundaries: Guiding Human Development on a Changing Planet. *Science, 347*(6223), 1259855.

Tansley, A. (1935). The Use and Abuse of Vegetational Concepts. *Ecology, 16*, 284–307.

Truscello, M. (2018). Catastrophism and Its Critics: On the New Genre of Environmentalist Documentary Film. In J. Jagodzinski (Ed.), *Interrogating the Anthropocene* (Palgrave Studies in Educational Futures). Palgrave Macmillan.

Turner, G. (2014). Is Global Collapse Imminent? An Updated Comparison of the Limits to Growth with Historical Data. *Melbourne Sustainable Society Institute, Research Paper No. 4.*

Wackernagel, M., & Rees, W. (1996). *Our Ecological Footprint: Reducing Human Impact on the Earth.* New Society Publishers.

Wiedmann, T., Schandl, H., Lenzen, M., Moran, D., Suh, S., West, J., & Kanemoto, K. (2015). The Material Footprint of Nations. *Proceedings of the National Academy of Sciences, 112*(20), 6271–6276.

Willcock, S., Cooper, G. S., Addy, J., & Dearing, J. A. (2023, June). Earlier Collapse of Anthropocene Ecosystems driven by Multiple Faster and Noisier Drivers. *Nature Sustainability.*

WMO (2023). *WMO Global Annual to Decadal Climate Update (Target years: 2023–2027).* World Meteorological Society.

Wright, R. (2023, June 29). Artificial Intelligence and the Noosphere: Seeing the age of AI in cosmic perspective can help us navigate it. *Nonzero Newsletter.*

Wrigley, E. (2010). *Energy and the English Industrial Revolution.* Cambridge University Press.

Wrigley, E. (2011, July 22). Opening Pandoras Box: A New Look at the Industrial Revolution. *VOXEU.*

Wunderling, N., Donges, J., Kurths, J., & Winkelmann, R. (2020). Interacting Tipping Elements Increase Risk of Climate Domino Effects Under Global Warming. *Earth Systems Dynamics, 18*, 1–21.

CHAPTER 4

Green Growth

Abstract This chapter critically analyzes Green Growth and its foundation in technosolutionism—a correlate of the Silicon Valley Mindset as described by Douglas Rushkoff and the philosophy of the Tech-Elite of Technofeudalism, as Yanis Varoufakis calls them. The chapter concludes that Green Growth may not be able to result in complete dematerialization and absolute decoupling. It may therefore not be able to stop an ecological overshoot.

Keywords Green growth • Technofeudalism • Decoupling • Dematerialization • Eco-modernism

4.1 Introduction

In this book so far, the question of whether the exponential economic growth that had brought humanity unprecedented incomes, wealth, and consumption in the comparatively short time span of a few centuries can be sustained indefinitely was discussed from the perspectives of the (neo)-Malthusians and Cornucopians—two opposite positions.

It was explained that the Cornucopians are tech-optimists who reject the Malthusian belief in limits to growth—see Chap. 2. The conclusion was drawn, however, that if the Cornucopians are to present a convincing

W. Naudé, *Economic Growth and Societal Collapse*,
https://doi.org/10.1007/978-3-031-45582-7_4

narrative in favor of unlimited economic growth, they need to be able to provide a case that technological innovations will be able to mitigate climate change and steer around possible existential threats from ecological overshoot (EO), and moreover in doing so, they would need to argue a convincing case that technological innovation can make up for the energy loss implied by the end of the carbon pulse (cheap and abundant fossil fuels)—see Chap. 3.

Cornucopians have made their case largely through advocating for the notion of Green Growth. Through Green Growth, the trust is that economic growth can be decoupled from the environment—that economic growth can continue without exhausting resources or contributing to global warming, and that alternative, renewable, and non-carbon energy sources can be found to substitute for the phasing out of fossil fuels.

In the remainder of this chapter, the Green Growth approach is critically evaluated.

4.2 Defining Green Growth

To prevent a "ghastly future" from existentially risky climate change and the running out of the oil bonanza, the mainstream or central approach adopted across international organizations and in many countries is that of Green Growth (D'Alessandro et al., 2020). The Green Growth approach underpins among others the 2015 Paris Climate Agreement to reduce carbon emissions by 2050 to keep global warming to less than 1.5 degrees above preindustrial levels, the 2015 Sustainable Development Goals (SDGs) of the UN, the European Green Deal of 2020 to achieve net-zero emissions of greenhouse gases by 2050, the United States's Green New Deal (GND) of 2019, and the 2022 UN Biodiversity Conference (CBD) to at least 30% of terrestrial, inland water, and marine areas by 2030 (Chaplin-Kramer et al., 2023).

The OECD (2011, p. 9) defines green growth[1] as "fostering economic growth and development while ensuring that natural assets continue to provide the resources and environmental services on which our well-being relies." It sees this as a subset of the older concept of sustainable development. The World Bank defines green growth as "growth that is efficient in

[1] Green growth as catalyst of economic growth is described as "strong" green growth, to contrast it with green growth that may entail short-term costs, but deliver longer-term benefits (Jakob & Edenhofer, 2014).

its use of natural resources, clean in that it minimizes pollution and environmental impacts, and resilient in that it accounts for natural hazards and the role of environmental management and natural capital in preventing physical disasters" (World Bank, 2012, p. 2).

In practice, policies to promote green growth result in attempts to decarbonize the global economy, transition economic growth into growth that will be decoupled from resource use and carbon emissions, promote as much as possible circularity in production and consumption, regulate the protection of biodiversity and other natural assets, and ban pollution. The steering of technological innovation—and stimulation of eco-innovation—together with "getting the prices rights," for example, carbon taxes are crucial aspects of the approach (Capasso et al., 2019).

There is, however, a political dimension to green growth. In essence, green growth is an attempt to overcome the collective action problem of addressing climate change by framing it in a positive light: countries can have their cake and eat it, that is, grow and reduce their environmental footprints. Moreover, pursuing green growth is often painted as offering many opportunities to enhance growth and job creation—and moreover to have "the shift to a low-emissions economy pay for itself" (Zysman & Huberty, 2012, p. 140). The European Commission (EC, 2011, p. 8) moreover noted that many believe that "environmental technology/resource efficiency [is] one of the drivers of profound global structural change that will bring in the next long-term period of growth."

The green growth-as-business opportunity strategy has understandably led many to reject green growth as viable, and to conclude that green growth is likely to ultimately make the EO problem worse. Owen (2011, p. 4), for instance, sees green growth justifying the continuation of conspicuous consumption, writing that

> One of our favorite green tricks is reframing luxury consumption preferences as gifts to humanity. A new car, a solar-powered swimming-pool heater, a two-hundred mile-an-hour train that makes intercity travel more pleasant and less expensive, better tasting tomatoes – these are the sacrifices we're prepared to make for the future of civilization.

Based on the belief and business strategy of green growth as paying for itself and offering many new opportunities to inaugurate a new period of long-term (consumption) growth, there has been a proliferation in recent years of "green" finance and "green" industrialization plans. Next to "smart," "green" has become the big buzzword in business plans. It also offers the opportunity of "greenwashing"—business-as-usual camouflaged as consistent with green growth (Supran & Hickey, 2022).

4.3 Eco-Innovation

At the core of green growth is the Cornucopian assumption that the right kind of technological innovation and correctly pricing externalities, to change behavior, will allow for a decoupling between economic growth and material inputs and between economic growth and its ecological impacts (such as carbon emissions). Technological innovations, for example in the form of digitalization have been touted as causing the dematerialization of the economy. McAfee (2019), a proponent of dematerialization, argues that "we invented the computer, the network, and a host of other digital tools that let us swap atoms for bits [think, for example, of how many different devices and media have vanished into the smartphone]. Quite literally, these inventions have changed the world."

One way in which decoupling is concretely envisaged is through an energy transition: phasing out fossil fuel energy and replacing these with renewable and low-carbon-emitting sources of energy, such as nuclear power. The premise of most Green New Deal type of plans is that fossil fuels can be completely replaced by renewable sources of energy. This premise is, as the rest of this chapter will show, false. More likely, the world will have to deal with an "energy descent"—making do with substantially less energy (Floyd et al., 2020; Friedemann, 2021). The problem is that Green Growth and its concept of net zero by 2050 may ultimately be "an illusion or dangerous trap that at best, unnecessarily extends the FF era" (Rees, 2022, p. 2269).

As far as the notions of decoupling is concerned, there are two types of decoupling: *relative decoupling*, when growth in material inputs or carbon emissions grow slower than GDP, and *absolute decoupling*, when material inputs and carbon emissions decline when GDP grows (Ward et al., 2016; Jackson & Victor, 2019).

4.4 Critical Analysis: Can Green Growth Decouple GDP?

In Sect. 4.3, the issue of an energy descent was mentioned. As such, the challenge of decoupling is whether energy use can be decoupled—at least relatively—from GDP? Green growth advocates would state that it can, and perhaps refer to the efficiency gains in energy use over the last decades—as is shown in Fig. 4.1. This shows a significant increase in the efficiency of sign energy in production of GDP. The question is to what extent can this continue?

As the EROI continues to decline, it will require even faster acceleration in the technologies to ensure that efficiency gains continue, a rather unlikely outcome given that diminishing returns to R&D is increasingly experienced across myriads of fields (see the discussion in Chap. 6, Sect. 6.3.2).

Moreover, as GDP grows, the growth in energy consumption will not decline—it will continue in aggregate to increase. Hence, when one plots the relationship between GDP growth and energy consumption growth

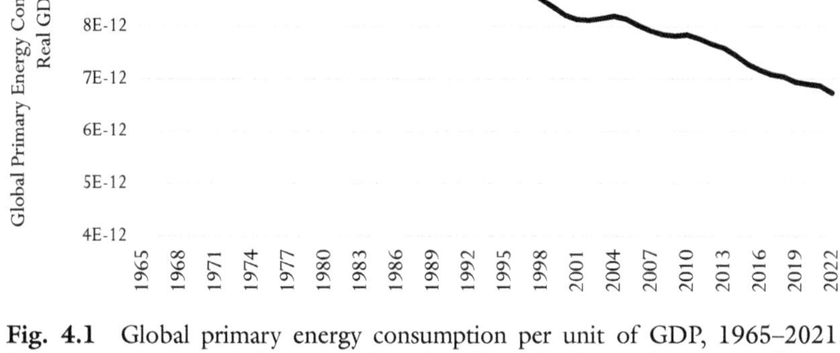

Fig. 4.1 Global primary energy consumption per unit of GDP, 1965–2021. (Source: Author's compilation based on data World Bank Development Indicators Online (GDP) and BP Energy Institute Statistical Review of World Energy (Primary Energy))

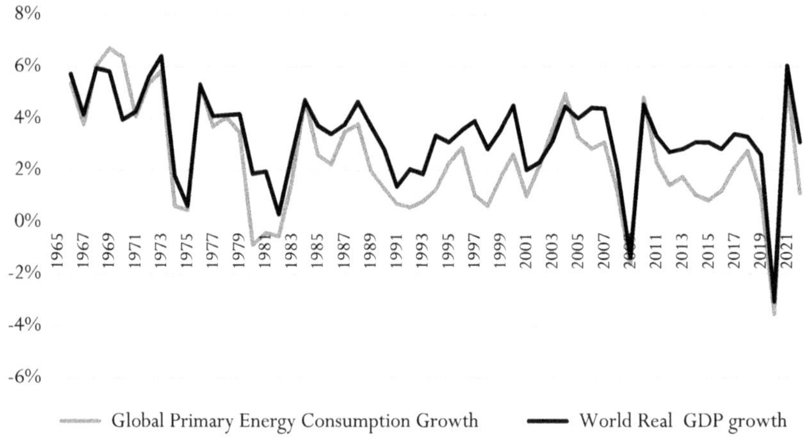

Fig. 4.2 Global growth in GDP and primary energy consumption, 1965–2021. (Source: Author's compilation based on data World Bank Development Indicators Online (GDP) and BP Energy Institute Statistical Review of World Energy (Primary Energy))

(see Fig. 4.2), any suggestion of potential decoupling that is implied in Fig. 4.1 disappears.

Earth systems are being overshot by economic growth not only in terms of energy demands, but many other resources, as Chap. 2 explained. Therefore, ecologists have been considering the relationship between economic growth and broader measures of material inputs. One such measure used by the European Commission, OECD, UNEP, and other global organizations to measure decoupling between GDP growth and material through-put is Domestic Material Consumption (DMC) (OECD, 2014).

According to Eurostat,[2] the DMC "measures the total amount of materials directly used by an economy and is defined as the annual quantity of raw materials extracted from the domestic territory, plus all physical imports minus all physical exports." The ratio between DMC and GDP expresses DMC as the kilograms of materials used to produce a unit value of inflation-adjusted GDP. It is a resource

[2] See https://ec.europa.eu/eurostat/statistics-explained/index.php?title=Glossary:Domestic_material_consumption_(DMC)

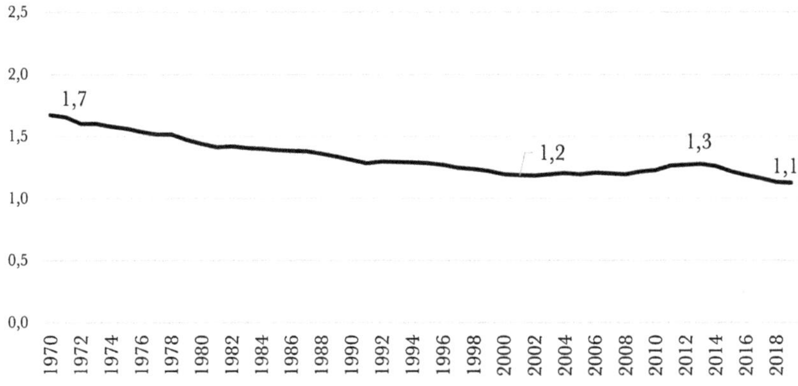

Fig. 4.3 Green Growth? Domestic Material Consumption per unit of constant GDP—per kg. (Source: Author's compilation based on data from the UNEP IRP Global Material Flows Database)

efficiency measure: if it declines it would indicate more efficient resource use,[3] which would be consistent with green growth.

Figure 4.3 shows the DMC to GDP ratio for the world economy between 1970 and 2019. It shows that resource efficiency in the world economy did improve between 1970 and 2019—from around 1.7 kg per unit of GDP value produced in 1970 to around 1.1 kg per unit of GDP by 2019. Moreover, most of the resource efficiency gains seem to have been achieved before 2000, since when DMC has remained around the 1.1 kg level for the world and even increased between 2001 and 2013. It is not consistent with global green growth—at least not in the last two decades.

As opposed to the global lack of green growth, several mainly high-income Western countries have been able to achieve more significant resource efficiency as measured by the DMC:GDP ratio. For example, in the Netherlands, the DMC to produce a unit of constant GDP fell from 0.7 kg in 1970 to 0.3 kg in 2019, which is indicative of green growth. However, a shortcoming of the DMC on a country level is that, as Eurostat

[3] The limitations of the DMC-GDP ratio, such as that it measures resources by weight while impacts of resource use may not always depend on weight, and that if used on a country level it ignored consumption impacts taking place outside of that country's borders, is recognized by the European Commission that advocates also using additional measures of environmental impact (EC, 2011).

points out,[4] it "does not include upstream 'hidden' flows related to imports and exports of raw materials and products."

A measure that includes these upstream flow effects is the Material Footprint (MF) measure, proposed by Wiedmann et al. (2015), who define it as "the global allocation of used raw material extraction to the final demand of an economy" (Wiedmann et al., 2015). If for example the MF for the Netherlands is calculated, it shows an MF to GDP ratio in 2019 much higher than the DMC:GDP ratio, namely 0.7—thus twice as high as the DMC:GDP measure. This indicates that the global resource use impact of the Netherlands is much larger than its domestic resource impact—its demand for resources raised resource use in other countries. Moreover, over time the MF:GDP ratio in the Netherlands has not declined much and has at least until 2008 tended to follow GDP closely.

Figure 4.4 depicts DMC, MF, and GDP (in constant prices) in the Netherlands between 1970 and 2019 to illustrate this point. It shows that while DMC in absolute use (in tons) have remained constant over the period, the MF has increased in absolute values quite significantly between 1970 and 2008. It briefly declined during the global financial crisis and its immediate aftermath (2008–2012) but thereafter, in line with GDP growth, continued its upward trajectory.

In sum, what Fig. 4.4 indicates is that in a country such as the Netherlands, while there has been evidence of relative decoupling at best, there is little evidence of absolute decoupling. Neither DMC nor MF is declining in absolute terms over time. And, as Fig. 4.5 has shown, on a global level there is little evidence of absolute decoupling as GDP and DMC seems to have a relatively stable 1:1 relationship.

Figure 4.5 plots global GDP in comparison to global MF of all countries: it shows no indication of absolute decoupling: GDP growth implies more resource use. The relationship between GDP and the MF is like the relationship between GDP and fossil fuel use (see Fig. 3.2). The apparent decline in the slopes of fossil fuel use and MF suggests some degree of relative decoupling.

The conclusion that can be made from the foregoing figures is that there is no absolute decoupling between fossil fuel use and the material footprint (MF), on the one hand, and global GDP growth, on the other hand. Similarly, whereas many countries have been decoupling GDP

[4] See https://ec.europa.eu/eurostat/statistics-explained/index.php?title=Glossary:Domestic_material_consumption_(DMC)

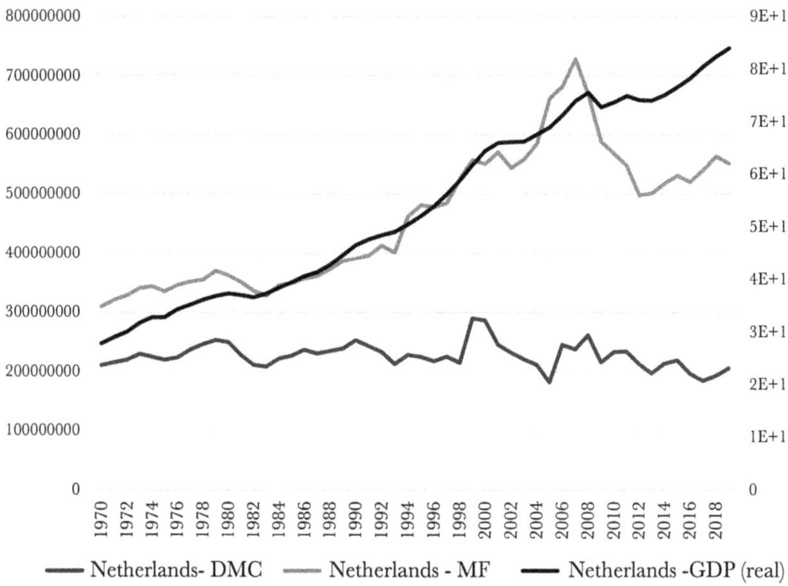

Fig. 4.4 The Netherlands: DMC and MT (per ton) and GDP in constant 2015 US$, 1970–2019. (Source: Author's compilation based on data from the UNEP IRP Global Material Flows Database)

growth in relative terms from CO_2 emissions (among others, but not exclusively, by shifting some production overseas), in absolute terms, CO_2 emissions have not declined—as Fig. 4.6 indicates.

The lack of absolute decoupling but evidence of relative decoupling is found in several rigorous studies. For example, Wiedmann et al. (2015) finds that there has been improvements in resource use in the EU-27, the OECD, the United States, Japan, and the United Kingdom—consistent with relative decoupling—but no absolute decoupling. Ward et al. (2016) concludes that "while relative decoupling has been observed in multiple countries, absolute decoupling remains elusive [...] no country has achieved absolute decoupling during the past 50 years." Haberl et al. (2020), surveying the empirical literature on decoupling, concludes that there is evidence of relative decoupling between GDP growth and carbon emissions, but not for decoupling between GDP growth and energy use. They conclude that "large rapid absolute reductions of resource use and

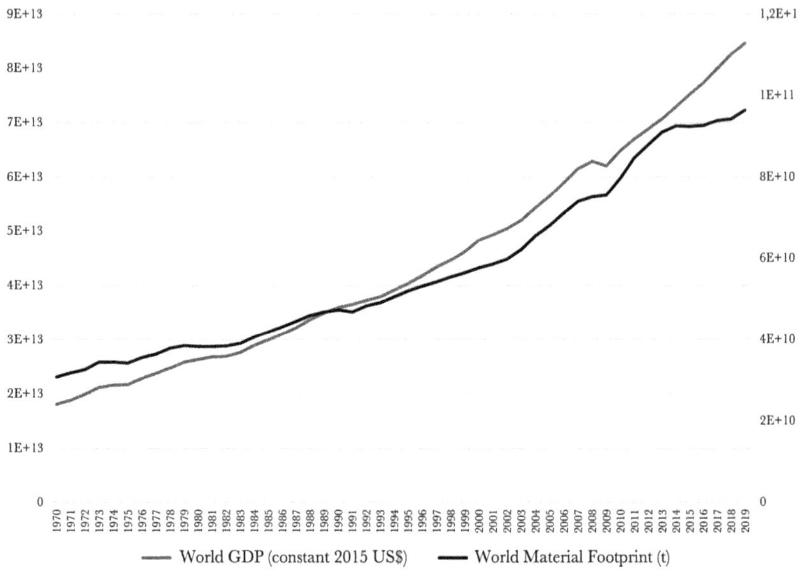

Fig. 4.5 World material footprint and GDP in constant 2015 US$, 1970–2019. (Source: Author's compilation based on data from the UNEP IRP Global Material Flows Database)

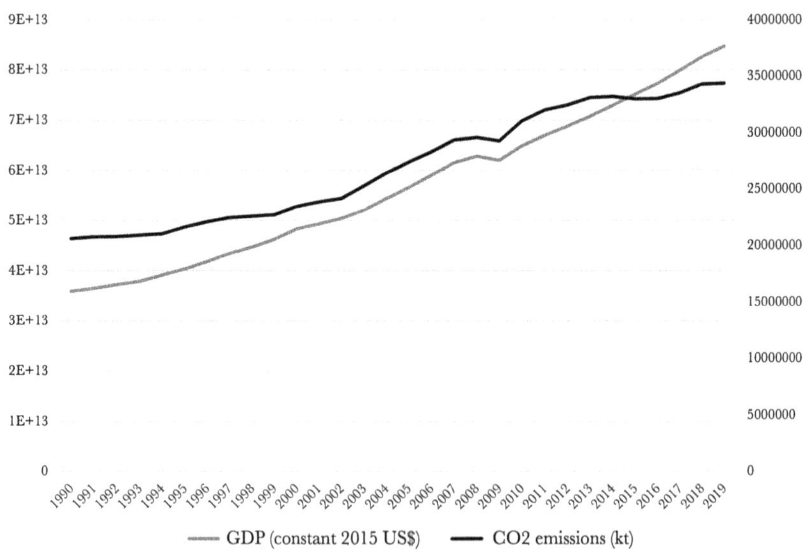

Fig. 4.6 Carbon emissions (tons) and World GDP in constant 2015 US$, 1990–2019. (Source: Author's compilation based on data from World Bank's World Development Indicators Online)

GHG emissions cannot be achieved through observed decoupling rates" (Haberl et al., 2020).

Jackson and Victor (2019) similarly cite examples of relative decoupling but conclude that there is no evidence for absolute decoupling on the global level. Moreover, Jackson and Victor (2019) argues that even if absolute decoupling could be achieved under green growth policies, it would not be sufficient to prevent a climate breakdown because the extent of absolute decoupling that would be required to sufficiently reduce carbon emissions to limit global warming in line with the Paris Agreement, would not be attainable. They calculate this as to require a decline in the carbon intensity of global GDP of 14% per year for at least three decades, which they conclude is too great a requirement (Jackson & Victor, 2019).

Not only is there little evidence of absolute decoupling, but the magnitude required also seems to be impossible to achieve given what is required to limit global warming. Furthermore, even relative decoupling may have little aggregate advantages in terms of reducing resource use due to the Jevons paradox,[5] also described as a rebound effect. Increased resource efficiency, resulting in productivity gains and price declines, will result in higher aggregate demand, which in turn stimulates further absolute resource use (Bardi, 2020; Bowen & Hepburn, 2014; Magee & Devezas, 2017).

In addition to this devastating criticism, there are also other criticisms of green growth. These will be briefly mentioned. The reader is also referred to Friedemann (2021) and Ketcham (2023).

One further criticism is that green growth is economically costly, and may make poverty reduction more difficult (Resnick et al., 2012; Dercon, 2014). This has raised the issue of climate justice as an ancillary to global green growth initiatives, reflecting concerns that developing countries which may suffer the worse impacts of climate change, have contributed the least to the current stocks of human emitted CO_2 in the atmosphere. In exchange for subscribing to green growth, developing countries are therefore demanding substantial financial[6] and know-how transfers from advanced economies—that have pledged US$ 100 billion in financial

[5] Jevons (1866) noted that technological progress in the efficiency of coal-driven locomotives lead not to the decline in the demand for coal, but in an increase, due to productivity and cost effects.

[6] According to the IPCC between $1.6 and $3.8 trillion is required annually to achieve climate targets in line with keeping global warming below 1.5 °C (Timperley, 2021).

resources for developing countries to fight climate change, but have failed to live up to this commitment (Diffenbaugh & Burke, 2019; Ehresman & Okereke, 2015; Robinson & Shine, 2018; Timperley, 2021).

Another criticism of green growth is that green growth places undue hope in the energy transition, that is, the phasing out of fossil fuels, and replacing these with renewable energy sources. The first problem is that replacing fossil fuels with renewable energy is not feasible: all renewable energy technologies need fossil fuel energy to be manufactured and renewable energy systems need backup from fossil fuel or nuclear energy (Hagens, 2020; Rees, 2021). And second problem is that promotion of renewable energy will stimulate the re-materialization of world production—due to the need for various mineral resources as inputs for renewable energy systems. Bleischwitz (2010) and Zeihan (2022) lists some of the critical mineral resources needed for renewable energies, which include copper, lithium, gallium, aluminum, tantalum, nickel, cobalt, silicon, chromium, graphite, zinc, manganese, molybdenum, gold, silver, and platinum.

In addition to the re-materialization of the world economy that this would stimulate, many of these minerals are found in countries with poor institutional development, meaning that the exploitation of these resources could lead to significant human rights abuses.[7] Kara (2023) documents such human rights abuses, which he calls a ***human rights and environmental catastrophe***, in cobalt[8] mines in the Democratic Republic of Congo.

A final and further devastating criticism of the hope that green economic growth is possible, and could moreover be sustained indefinitely, is provided by the laws of physics. This suggests that even if in a science fiction world full absolute decoupling from physical inputs could be obtained, there would still be the waste heat, an outcome of the 2nd Law of Thermodynamics, that will eventually stop growth. For instance, if the world GDP continues to expand at its current rate of around 2% per annum, it will double in size every 35 years. By 2037, the world GDP would be US$500 trillion after which would "explode" to $30.7 quadrillion in

[7] Zeihan (2022) considers the complications surrounding integrating the mineral extraction and supply chains for green technologies to be significantly more daunting than that faced in the oil industry: "*In 'moving on from oil' we would be walking away from a complex and often-violent and always critical supply and transport system, only to replace it with at least ten more.*"

[8] Cobalt is an essential requirement in rechargeable lithium-ion batteries that are found in every smartphone, electric vehicle, and laptop.

2046 and to \$1.9 quintillion a year later (Roodman, 2020). In just over 8000 years, it would be 3×10^{70} its current size, which would be a physical impossibility (Karnofsky, 2021).

Even if growth slowed and the world economy doubled in size only every 100 years, then after a million years (a very brief period on cosmic timescale) the economy would be 10^{3010} times larger, which implies that if there are around 10^{80} atoms in the galaxy,[9] "each atom would have to support an average of around 10^{2950} people" (Hanson, 2009).

A brake on growth long before these timescales is energy. Even if the global economy would be able to increase energy efficiency and be able to decouple much growth from physical resources, it would still need significant amounts of energy to run its soft- and hardware. The share of the economy that can be nonphysical (and that can thus be de-materialized) is ultimately bounded. The economic growth implied in Fig. 2.1 has been due to an annual average growth in energy consumption of around 2.3% per annum (Murphy, 2022). If one assumes that a Cornucopian economy would eventually be able to generate economic growth that doubles the world economy every month, as discussed in Sect. 2.2 (see also Hanson (2018)), with such energy efficiency that energy use continues to grow at only 2.3%, then energy use on the planet will grow from its current (2019) level of 18 Terawatt (TW) to 100 TW in 2100 and 1000 TW in 2200. Murphy (2022) calculates that at such a rate, the economy would use up all the solar power that reaches the earth in 400 years and in 1700 years all the energy of the sun.

The use of so much energy would generate tremendous waste heat independent of any future smart green-energy technology. It would be so hot as to boil the surface of the Earth in about 400 years (Murphy, 2022).

4.5 Doomsday Bunkers

The belief that technology will save the day by allowing decoupling between energy and material use and GDP that underpins Green Growth, and the selling of Green Growth as a growth-accelerating business opportunity is fundamentally driven by dominant corporate giants of our time: the tech-industry and big finance.

[9] It is estimated that there are between 10^{78} and 10^{82} atoms in the observable universe, see https: //www.universetoday.com/36302/atoms-in-the-universe/

In the run-up to the global financial crisis (2008–2009), many of the big financial institutions were selling collateralized debt obligations (CDOs) backed by subprime mortgages based on promoting a view of continued increases in house prices, whilst at the same time taking in positions to hedge against the eventual collapse of the housing market.[10]

Today, the tech-giants and their billionaire owners and CEOs are similarly hedging themselves. While they are proclaiming technology as the savior, they are building doomsday bunkers and planning their escape from what they see as the inevitable, and even desired, coming collapse of human civilization.

4.5.1 Davos Man and the Rise of Technofeudalism

The economic growth of the past fifty years, the resulting scaling up of the world economy, and the evolution of the Dataome (as was discussed in Chap. 2 and Sect. 3.4) have been accompanied by rising income and wealth disparities—and in the creation of a small global elite or oligarchy that has been described as Davos Man (Goodman, 2022). The reference is to Davos, the home of the World Economic Forum (WEF), which is "ground zero of global capitalism" (Rushkoff, 2022). Goodman (2022, p. 5) explains that

> *Davos Man has grown into a catchall used by journalists and academics as shorthand for those who occupy the stratosphere of the globe-trotting class, the billionaire – predominantly white and male – who wield unsurpassed influence over the political realm while promoting the notion that [...] when the rules are organized around the greater prosperity for those who already enjoy most of it, everyone's the winner.*

Davos Man owns a huge and increasing share of global income and wealth. As Oxfam (2022) notes, by 2022 there were around 2755 billionaires worldwide, of whom the top ten men (yes, they are all men) had more wealth than the bottom .3.1 billion people on the planet. In the United States, wealth disparities are at historical highs: The PEW Research

[10] See, for example, the coverage of the Wall Street Firm Goldman Sachs paying a fine for "deceiving investors" in the LA Times at https://www.latimes.com/archives/la-xpm-2011-apr-14-la-fi-crisis-probe-20110414-story.html

Centre[11] reports that the wealth gap between rich and poor households in the country "more than doubled from 1989 to 2016" and that the wealthiest 5% of households had 248 more wealth than households in the second quintile of the income distribution. The middle class has been contracting.

One indicator of the extent of wealth inequality is the extent of wealth growth, that is, the ratio of wealth to income. Recall in Chap. 1 that the share of capital in GDP was denoted as $\alpha = r\frac{K}{Y}$. Piketty (2013) has stressed that if GDP growth ($g = \Delta Y$) is smaller than the rent accruing to capital, that is, if $g < r$, then the share of capital in GDP will increase. If in addition the economy becomes more capital-intensive, that is, the ratio $\frac{K}{L}$ increases, then this will drive the share of capital (α) even higher, creating a positive feedback loop between α and $\frac{K}{L}$. In such a situation wealth inequality would become quite pronounced. This seems to be the situation many countries are in at the time of writing. In the United States, the wealth to income ratio is the highest in more than a century—at 628% in 2021, as shown in Fig. 4.7. It suggests that the share of income going to the owners of capital has increased—which is contrary to a basic assumption (or "stylized facts") in neoclassical growth theory (see Chap. 1) that the shares of capital and labor (α and β) are constant over time—the assumption of "balanced growth" (Kaldor, 1961). Under balanced growth—or fixed shares of capital and labor—income distribution and redistribution have no effect on economic growth, and vice versa (Fix, 2015).

However, a substantial literature has in recent years been documenting the decline in the share of GDP going to labor, and the fact that this has been a major driver of overall inequality, and of inequality influencing economic growth (see, e.g., Autor et al., 2020; Gollin, 2002; Karabarbounis & Neiman, 2013; Jacobson & Occhino, 2012). According to Piketty and Zucman (2014), the share of GDP going to capital has increased in advanced economies from around 15% to 25% in the 1970s, to a range of 25% to 35% by 2010.

[11] See https://www.pewresearch.org/social-trends/2020/01/09/trends-in-income-and-wealth-inequality/

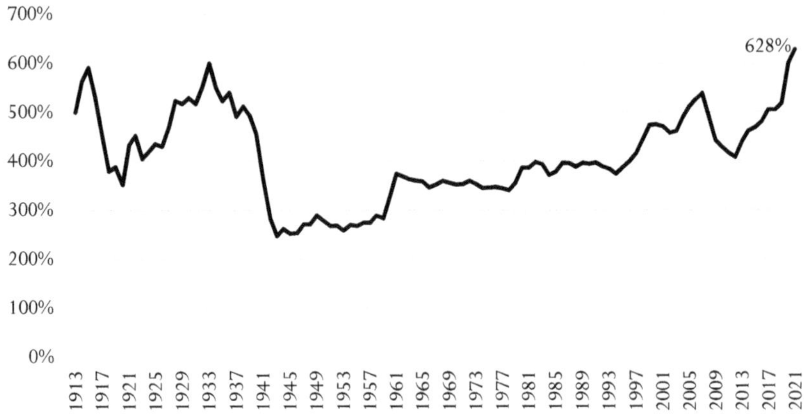

Fig. 4.7 Net National Wealth to Net National Income Ration in the USA, 1913–2021. (Source: Author's compilation based on data from the World Inequality Database (WID) at https://wid.world)

Not only does the growing wealth gap undermine social cohesion and trust and contribute to social rot and political disintegration (Turchin, 2023), but the wealth gap also means that a small elite disproportionately appropriates energy and mineral inputs and disproportionately pollutes. For example, the 20 richest billionaires have been estimated to emit on average 8000 times more CO_2 than the poorest 1 billion people on the planet (Oxfam, 2022). High wealth–income ratios have also been associated with financial instability—such as housing and financial bubbles and crises (Piketty & Zucman, 2014).

The 2009 global financial crisis, the 2020 pandemic[12] and the 2022 war in Ukraine have swelled the fortunes of Davos Man. They are wielding increasing power over international affairs. The capital accumulation that they have been engaging in, as shown in Fig. 4.5 allows them to build large corporate hierarchies of firms, which centralizes their power (Fix, 2015). We live in a new (neo-) feudal with tech billionaires increasingly assuming the mantle of our new overlords. These overlords "do not wear chain mail or top hats, but instead direct our future in jeans and hoodies" and their power "is enabled by technologies that once were widely seen as

[12] According to Oxfam (2022), during the COVID-19 pandemic the fortunes of the world's richest ten men have doubled.

holding great promise for grassroots democracy and decision making but have become tools for surveillance and consolidation of power" (Kotkin, 2020, p. 7). Varoufakis (2023) calls these mainly Silicon Valley-based tech billionaires and the digital platform capitalism that their tech industry has enabled, *Technofeudalism*.

Varoufakis (2023) remarks that "value extraction has increasingly shifted away from markets and onto digital platforms, like Facebook and Amazon, which no longer operate like oligopolistic firms, but rather like private fiefdoms or estates [...] digital platforms have replaced markets as the locus of private wealth extraction."

4.5.2 Embedded Growth Obligations

At the time of writing, seven of the top ten most-valued corporates in the world (measured by value of market capitalization) were digital platform firms / ICT companies. Apple and Microsoft top the list, with each being valued more than US$ 2 trillion in 2023. The global economy on which they are perched are supported, especially following the global financial crisis of 2008–2009 and the COVID-19 pandemic by massive quantitative easing (QE)—the injection of large amounts of central bank money into the economy.

This injection of money and subsequent credit into the economy creates an embedded growth obligation (EGO) (Weinstein, 2021). This is because debt requires future growth (and growth in turn enables debt) (Tverberg, 2012), which in turn requires future energy use (Hagens, 2020). For almost a decade, the European Central Bank (ECB) kept interest rates artificially low and pumped unimaginable amounts of money into the economy through QE. This allowed debts, which are claims on future energy consumption, to continue growing. Furthermore, in July 2022, the European Central Bank implemented a "Transmission Protection Instrument" to buy government bonds from member countries—who may face pressure from the inevitable rise in interest rates as of 2022. This moral hazard will allow even fiscally poorly managed countries in the EU to build up government debt even more, raising the EGO.

The problem from an EO point of view is that with ever-accumulating levels of money and debt, it obligates future consumption and growth. In the EU, government debt is supposed to remain below 60% of GDP. Thus, when debt approaches this level, raising GDP is one way for governments to continue borrowing. The ECB's July 2022 step has, in one fell swoop, incentivized debt and, through these, claims on future energy and on GDP growth. A move for which it is, by the way, not democratically accountable—and probably in breach of its rules (GIS, 2022).

As pressure on energy and materials (and deforestation) continues to increase, one result will be inflation. Inflation will not only be due to excess consumption: as the input prices of energy and materials rise, the corporate sector, to protect its profits, will raise prices—at least 83% of 2022–2023 inflation in Spain was estimated to be due to corporations trying to maintain profits (Oxfam, 2023).

High wealth-income ratios as shown in Fig. 4.5 have, as has been remarked, been associated with financial instability. But so are the interventions of Central Banks through QE—following a review of central bank QE practices over 400 years and 17 economies, Ferguson et al. (2023, p. 1) concludes that "hthe provision of central bank liquidity to financial markets raises the probability of future boom-bust episodes."

The EO crisis is accompanied by deep underlying social (inequality) and financial (monetary) instability. To this, Turchin (2023) has argued that political disintegration threatens the West, suffering from increased elite overproduction and worker immiseration. This "destabilized status quo" has been described as the polycrisis (Heinberg, 2023).

4.5.3 The Silicon Valley Mindset

At the core of Green Growth is the belief in eco-innovation; that there is a tech solution to the EO crisis. This *Technosolutionist Belief* is closely aligned, and largely originates from, what Rushkoff (2022) calls the Silicon Valley Mindset. The Silicon Valley Mindset is the attitude of many tech billionaires that sees the world as a game that is being played and where "winning means earning enough money to insulate themselves from the damage they are creating by earning money in that way. It is as if they want to build a car that goes fast enough to escape from its own exhaust" (Rushkoff, 2022, p. 10).

What Rushkoff (2022) is referring to, is the attempts by Silicon Valley's Technofeudalists to escape what they call "The Event"—the ecological collapse of the planet. These attempts include Elon Musk and Jeff Bezo's plans to emigrate to space, Mark Zuckerberg's development of a virtual reality metaverse, and Peter Thiel's reportedly planned doomsday bunker in New Zealand. These are based, as Green Growth, on that technology is the ultimate solution. However, whereas Green Growth wants to save the planet for all, for the tech billionaires the collapse is real, and the only role for technology is to save themselves. Hence, even as EO intensifies, the tech companies are aiming to accelerate economic growth and introduce even more disruptive technologies with huge carbon footprints—in effect it would seem, almost deliberately courting disaster.

As Rushkoff (2022) explains, the Silicon Valley Mindset relishes in doomsday scenarios—it implies the endgame in which they can be victorious, and they "actively seek the endgame" (p. 11). "Actual, imminent catastrophes from the climate emergency to mass migrations support the mythology, offering these would-be superheroes the opportunity to play out the finale in their own lifetimes" (Rushkoff, 2022, pp. 11–12).

They have even developed their own philosophy and ethical framework for justifying their escape plans. This is known as Longtermism, which is an outflow from the Effective Altruism (EA) Movement. It may become the new "ethics of plunder."

4.5.4 *The New Ethics of Plunder?*

Longtermism is the view that if we want to be maximally altruistic, we should serve the interest of the vast numbers of future people who may yet live. These may include possible sentient digital people (Shulman & Bostrom, 2021). Any existential risk must be eliminated at all costs—even if it means neglecting current problems such as EO, climate change, and poverty (Torres, 2021; Crary, 2023).

Longtermism is subscribed to and financially, royally, supported by Technofeudalists—including Elon Musk, Peter Thiel, and Jaan Tallin. The disgraced CEO of FTX, Sam Bankman-Fried has apparently donated millions to promote Longtermism (Hyatt, 2022). Cremer and Kemp (2021) lists hundreds of millions of dollars in philanthropic funding from tech billionaires to institutes to study and promote Longtermism. For instance, the *Future of Life Institute*, which regularly publishes "Open Letters" by scientists, including warning against the existential threats posed by AI, was started by a US$ 10 million donation from Musk. Other institutes funded by tech billionaires include the *Centre for Security and Emerging Technology* (CSET), and the Future of Humanity Institute. Indeed, the enthusiasm with which Technofeudalists embrace Longtermism has led to it being described by Torres (2021) as a disturbing secular religion that looks like it addresses humanity's deepest problems, but actually justifies pursuing the social preferences of elites.

These social preferences may have nothing to do with current global challenges such as poverty, inequality, conflict, migration, and EO. Greaves and MacAskill (2021), for example, recommended that "for the purposes of evaluating actions, we can in the first instance often simply ignore all the effects contained in the first 100 (or even 1,000) years, focusing primarily on the further-future effects." Nick Bostrom, Oxford philosopher and an intellectual father of Longtermism, argues that "the expected value of reducing existential risk by a mere one billionth of one billionth of one percentage point is worth a hundred billion times as much as a billion human lives" (Bostrom, 2013, p. 19).

This type of reasoning could lead some to the contestable conclusion that sacrificing a billion human lives now, to achieve the very slightly probable existence of a trillion beings in the very far future, is morally correct. Using this reasoning, Bostrom further argues that few things are as crucial as galactic expansion. This belief is of course philosophical fuel for the current billionaire space-race, which has seen among others Elon Musk launching a Tesla Roadster into space. Longtermists have argued that not investing considerable sums in space exploration now (e.g., colonizing Mars as Musk wants to do) is an "astronomical waste" of opportunity (Bostrom, 2003).

No wonder the response to this has been warnings that

> *Longtermism could be a justification for some outright ghoulish behaviour. Should we put any regulatory limits on the new billionaire space race? A Longtermist could easily conclude that any government standing in the way of Elon Musk's interstellar ambitions is a moral abomination – directly harming the potential wellbeing of trillions of future humans* (Karpf, 2022).

In sum, Davos Man, who increasingly is led by Silicon Valley's Technofeudalists, is the beneficiary of capturing and thwarting the digital revolution that held great promise at the beginning of the 1990s. Instead of digital technologies that furthers the decoupling of economic activity from material inputs and pollution, these technologies were pushed in a direction of fueling further consumption, driving corporate concentration, the power of superstar firms and oligopolies, and consolidate regulatory capture. At the same time as driving their wealth, the Technofeudalists have been claiming that the very system through which they are subjecting the economy is in the planet's interest, and that technology will save the planet. Meanwhile, planning their own escape from a planet which they consider doomed—or even worse, need to be doomed.

4.6 Concluding Remarks

The most important shortcoming of Green Growth strategies that emerges from this chapter is that they have not yet, and does not seem able in future, to achieve absolute decoupling between GDP growth and material inputs (resource uses) and carbon emissions (growth impacts). There is little possibility of green-tech saviorism being real. The narrative of technology-as-savior is one that is deeply embedded in the rise of Silicon Valley's tech giants and its class of Technofeudalists—billionaire tech elites, who, with emboldened by their own ethical foundation of Longtermism—are touting the benefits of technology whilst at the same time planning their escape strategies to avoid what they see as the coming apocalypse. Indeed, given their belief in such an "Event" and their preparations for it, they may very well welcome such an eventuality as a desired "endgame" of their worldview.

Green Growth will therefore not be able to prevent the ecological overshooting of planetary systems. Relative decoupling is possible, can extend the availability of resources, and reduce the impact of emissions by a small magnitude, but even these efficiency gains may end up increasing total energy use due to rebound (Jevons Paradox) effects. Hence, Green Growth has been called an oxymoron (Rees, 2022).

In addition to this shortcoming, there were also other criticisms of green growth discussed in this chapter. In light of these shortcomings, it is no surprise that Ketcham (2023) asked why an idea such as green growth persists given that it "has so little substance behind it?" He quotes Steinberger's explanation, which is that "growth aligns with currently powerful forces and structures in our economies: profit-oriented corporations, wealth accumulation and the power that comes with wealth." The discussion in this chapter of the rise of Davos Man and Technofeudalism support this explanation.

The conclusion from this chapter is that even if the optimistic Cornucopian green economy scenarios could be realized, any acceleration in economic growth may ultimately be transient event—if it ever happens.

As Murphy (2022, p. 847) has warned, "we would be wise to plan for a post-growth world."

The Degrowth Movement is one movement that aspires to move the planet toward such a post-growth world. Its proposed solutions to the overshoot crisis are critically examined in Chap. 5.

References

Autor, D., Dorn, D., Katz, L., Patterson, C., & Reenen, J. V. (2020). The Fall of the Labor Share and the Rise of Superstar Firms. *The Quarterly Journal of Economics, 135*(2), 645–709.

Bardi, U. (2020). *Before the Collapse: A Guide to the Other Side of Growth.* Springer.

Bleischwitz, R. (2010). International Economics of Resource Productivity Relevance, Measurement, Empirical Trends, Innovation, Resource Policies. *International Economics and Economic Policy, 7*, 227–244.

Bostrom, N. (2003). Astronomical Waste: The Opportunity Cost of Delayed Technological Development. *Utilitas, 15*(3), 308–314.

Bostrom, N. (2013). Existential Risk Prevention as Global Priority. *Global Policy, 4*, 15–31.

Bowen, A., & Hepburn, C. (2014). Green Growth: An Assessment. *Oxford Review of Economic Policy, 30*(3), 407–422.

Capasso, M., Hansen, T., Heiberg, J., Klitkou, A., & Steen, M. (2019). Green Growth – A Synthesis of Scientific Findings. *Technological Forecasting and Social Change, 146*, 390–402.

Chaplin-Kramer, R., Neugarten, R. A., Sharp, R. P., et al. (2023). Mapping the Planet's Critical Natural Assets. *Nature Ecology and Evolution, 7*, 51–61.

Crary, A. (2023). The Toxic Ideology of Longtermism. *Radical Philosophy,* 214, 49–57.

Cremer, C. Z., & Kemp, L. (2021). *Democratising Risk: In Search of a Methodology to Study Existential Risk.* The Future of Humanity Institute (FHI), University of Oxford.

D'Alessandro, S., Cieplinski, A., Distefano, T., et al. (2020). Feasible Alternatives to Green Growth. *Nature Sustainability, 3*, 329–335.

Dercon, S. (2014). Is Green Growth Good for the Poor? *World Bank Research Observer, 29*(2), 163–185.

Diffenbaugh, N., & Burke, M. (2019). Global Warming has Increased Global Economic Inequality. *Proceedings of the National Academy of Sciences, 116*(20), 9808–9813.

EC. (2011, September 20). *Analysis Associated with the Roadmap to a Resource Efficient Europe Part I.* European Commission Staff Working Paper SEC (2011) 1067 final.

Ehresman, T., & Okereke, C. (2015). Environmental Justice and Conceptions of the Green Economy. *International Environmental Agreements: Politics, Law and Economics, 15*, 13–27.

Ferguson, N., Kornejew, M., Schmelzing, P., & Schularick, M. (2023). *The Safety Net: Central Bank Balance Sheets and Financial Crises, 1587-2020* (Economics Working Paper 23102). Hoover Institution.

Fix, B. (2015). Putting Power Back into Growth Theory. *Review of Capital as Power, 1*(2), 1–37.

Floyd, J., Alexander, S., Lenzen, M., Moriarty, P., Palmer, G., Chandra-Shekeran, S., Foran, B., & Keysser, L. (2020). Energy Descent as a Post-Carbon Transition Scenario: How 'Knowledge Humility' Reshapes Energy Futures for Post-normal Times. *Futures, 122*, 102565.

Friedemann, A. J. (2021). *Life After Fossil Fuels: A Reality Check on Alternative Energy*. Springer.

GIS. (2022, August 1). *The ECB: Broken Rules, Frivolous Policy.* Comment by Prince Michael of Liechtenstein.

Gollin, D. (2002). Getting Income Shares Right. *Journal of Political Economy, 110*, 458–474.

Goodman, P. S. (2022). *Davos Man: How the Billionaires Devoured the World.* Custom House.

Greaves, H., & MacAskill, W. (2021). *The Case for Strong Longtermism* (GPI Working Paper No. 5-2021). Global Priorities Institute, University of Oxford.

Haberl, H., Wiedenhofer, D., Virág, D., Kalt, G., Plank, B., Brockway, P., Fishman, T., Hausknost, D., Krausmann, F., Leon-Gruchalski, B., et al. (2020). A Systematic Review of the Evidence on Decoupling of GDP, Resource Use and GHG Emissions, Part II: Synthesizing the Insights. *Environmental Research Letters, 15*, 065003.

Hagens, N. (2020). Economics for the Future – Beyond the Superorganism. *Ecological Economics, 169*, 106520.

Hanson, R. (2009). Limits to Growth. *Overcoming Bias Blog.*

Hanson, R. (2018). *The Age of EM: Work, Love, and Life when Robots Rule the Earth.* Oxford University Press.

Heinberg, R. (2023, June 15). Polycrisis, Unraveling, Simplification, or Collapse: Coming Soon to a Planet Near You? *Resilience.*

Hyatt, J. (2022, November 17). Sam Bankman-Fried's Donations to Effective Altruism Nonprofits Tied to An Oxford Professor Are at Risk Of Being Clawed Back. *Forbes.*

Jackson, T., & Victor, P. (2019). Unraveling the Claims For (and Against) Green Growth. *Science, 366*(6468), 950–951.

Jacobson, M., & Occhino, F. (2012). Labor's Declining Share of Income and Rising Inequality. *Federal Reserve Bank of Cleveland Economic Commentary*, pp. 1–5.

Jakob, M., & Edenhofer, O. (2014). Green Growth, Degrowth, and the Commons. *Oxford Review of Economic Policy, 30*(3), 447–468.
Jevons, W. (1866). *The Coal Question* (2nd ed.). Macmillan.
Kaldor, N. (1961). Capital Accumulation and Economic Growth. In F. A. Lutz & D. C. Hague (Eds.), *The Theory of Capital* (pp. 177–222). St. Martin's Press.
Kara, S. (2023). *Cobalt Red: How the Blood of the Congo Powers Our Lives.* Macmillan.
Karabarbounis, L., & Neiman, B. (2013). The Global Decline of the Labor Share. *Quarterly Journal of Economics, 129*, 61–103.
Karnofsky, H. (2021, August 3). This Can't Go On. *Effective Altruism Forum.*
Karpf. D. (2022, August 13). Against Jackpot-Longtermism: Examining the Stories Tech Billionaires Tell Themselves. *The Future, Then and Now.*
Ketcham, C. (2023, April 4). The Green Growth Delusion. *TruthDig.*
Kotkin, J. (2020). *The Coming of Neo Feudalism: A Warning to the Global Middle Class.* Encounter Books.
Magee, C., & Devezas, T. C. (2017). A Simple Extension of Dematerialization Theory: Incorporation of Technical Progress and the Rebound Effect. *Technological Forecasting and Social Change, 117*, 196–205.
McAfee, A. (2019). *More from Less: The Surprising Story of How We Learned to Prosper Using Fewer Resources – And What Happens Next.* Scribner.
Murphy, T. (2022). Limits to Economic Growth. *Nature Physics, 18*, 844–847.
OECD. (2011). *Towards Green Growth* (OECD Green Growth Studies). OECD Publishing.
OECD. (2014). *Green Growth Indicators 2014* (OECD Green Growth Studies). OECD.
Owen, D. (2011). *The Conundrum: How Scientific Innovation, Increased Efficiency, and Good Intentions Can Make Our Energy and Climate Problems Worse.* Riverhead Books.
Oxfam. (2022, January). Inequality Kills. *Oxfam Briefing Paper.*
Oxfam. (2023, January 16). Richest 1% Bag Nearly Twice as Much Wealth as the Rest of the World Put Together over the Past Two Years. *Press Briefing.*
Pikkety, T. (2013). *Capital in the 21st Century.* Harvard University Press.
Pikkety, T., & Zucman, G. (2014). Capital is Back: Wealth-Income Ratios in Rich Countries 1700–2010. *The Quarterly Journal of Economics, 129*(3), 1255–1310.
Rees, W. E. (2021). A Note of Climate Change and Cultural Denial. *Population Matters.*
Rees, W. E. (2022). Why Large Cities Won't Survive the Twenty-First Century. In R. Brears (Ed.), *The Palgrave Encyclopedia of Urban and Regional Futures.* Palgrave Macmillan.
Resnick, D., Tarp, F., & Thurlow, J. (2012). The Political Economy of Green Growth: Cases from Southern Africa. *Public Administration & Development, 32*(3), 215–228.

Robinson, M., & Shine, T. (2018). Achieving a Climate Justice Pathway to 1.5 °C. *Nature Climate Change, 8*, 564–569.

Roodman, D. (2020, June 15). Modelling the Human Trajectory. *Open Philanthropy.*

Rushkoff, D. (2022). *Survival of the Richest: Escape Fantasies of the Tech Billionaires.* W.W. Norton.

Shulman, C., & Bostrom, N. (2021). Sharing the World with Digital Minds. In S. Clarke, H. Zohny, & J. Savulescu (Eds.), *Rethinking Moral Status.* Oxford University Press.

Supran, G., & Hickey, C. (2022). *Three Shades of Green (washing): Content Analysis of Social Media Discourse by European Oil, Car, and Airline Companies.* Available at https://ati.io/three-shades-of-greenwashing/

Timperley, J. (2021). The Broken $100-Billion Promise of Climate Finance – And How to Fix It. *Nature, 5982*, 400–402.

Torres, E. (2021, July 28). The Dangerous Ideas of Longtermism and Existential Risk. *Current Affairs.*

Turchin, P. (2023). *End Times: Elites, Counter-Elites, and the Path of Political Disintegration*. Penguin.

Tverberg, G. E. (2012). Oil Supply Limits and the Continuing Financial Crisis. *Energy, 37*, 27–34.

Varoufakis, Y. (2023). *Technofeudalism: What Killed Capitalism.* Penguin.

Ward, J., Sutton, P., Werner, A., Costanza, R., Mohr, S., & Simmons, C. (2016). Is Decoupling GDP Growth from Environmental Impact Possible? *PLoS One, 11*(10), e0164733.

Weinstein, E. (2021). *Embedded Growth Obligations.* The Portal Group.

Wiedmann, T., Schandl, H., Lenzen, M., Moran, D., Suh, S., West, J., & Kanemoto, K. (2015). The Material Footprint of Nations. *Proceedings of the National Academy of Sciences, 112*(20), 6271–6276.

World Bank. (2012). *Inclusive Green Growth: The Pathway to Sustainable Development.* The World Bank.

Zeihan, P. (2022, April 27). Greentech and the End of the World. *Zeihan on Geopolitics* (Blog).

Zysman, J., & Huberty, M. (2012). Religion and Reality in the Search for Green Growth. *Intereconomics, 3*, 140–163.

CHAPTER 5

The Degrowth Movement

Abstract This chapter dissects the Malthusian response to Green Growth—the Degrowth Agenda. Degrowthers reject green growth, arguing that the only way to avoid resource depletion and an existential climate crisis is to make a concerted effort to scale down GDP—to "degrow" the economy. It is argued in this chapter that Degrowth will not stop ecological overshoot. It would likely worsen the environmental predicament, and on top of this, it is a costly method to reduce carbon emissions and may boil down in its implementation—in top-down command fashion—to a form of austerity for the working class. For these reasons, among others, Degrowth as policy agenda is politically infeasible, and ecological iatrogenics.

Keywords Degrowth • Post-growth • Doughnut economics • Ecological iatrogenics • Eco-Marxism

5.1 Introduction

Chapter 4 described the mainstream approach known as Green Growth and noted that although it will contribute to resource efficiency, this is insufficient to keep economic growth from overshooting planetary boundaries. There is a 1:1 relationship between GDP and material inputs. Even if GDP could be completely and absolutely

W. Naudé, *Economic Growth and Societal Collapse*,
https://doi.org/10.1007/978-3-031-45582-7_5

dematerialized and decoupled from material inputs, it will still need energy and the waste heat that even a relatively modest 2% growth in energy demand would entail would imply an end to economic growth within a few centuries.

Because of the ultimate futility of Green Growth, the have been arguments for deliberate and planned "degrowth"—in other words, economic downsizing. Pro-actively downsizing the economy is considered the only way to avoid a catastrophic environmental overshoot. As put by Murphy et al. (2021, p. 4), "It is time [to] admit that growth is not only temporary, but ultimately may constitute an existential threat to human wellbeing." And to achieve climate justice, the proposal is for advanced economies to downsize while allowing developing countries to reach a better level of per capita income.

This chapter introduces Degrowth and provides, together with the next chapter, Chap. 6, a critique of the movement's idea to downsize the economy. Section 5.2 defines and describes degrowth as a movement or agenda. Section 5.3 provides four points of common criticism against the proposal to degrow the West. Section 5.4 concludes.

5.2 What Is Degrowth?

"It seems very pretty," she said when she had finished it, "but it's rather hard to understand!" […]"Somehow it seems to fill my head with ideas—only I don't exactly know what they are! However, somebody killed something: that's clear, at any rate." – Alice, in Through the Looking-Glass by Lewis Carrol.

Hickel (2021, p. 1105) defines degrowth as "a planned reduction of energy and resource use designed to bring the economy back into balance with the living world in a way that reduces inequality and improves human well-being." The Degrowth Movement, from which it arises, is about more than reducing energy and resource use. According to Akbulut (2021, p. 98) "degrowth denotes a far more encompassing transformation: a break with the ideology of growth, the repoliticization of the economy, and a reorientation of economic relations along different principles."

The encompassing transformation referred to include "decolonialization" through reducing inequalities between the Global North and Global South. Hence, the reduction in energy and resource use necessary according to the Degrowth Movement is only applicable to the countries of the Global North; the developing world, the Global

South, is exempt. The Degrowth Movement, which so far has been a "marginal left-wing position" whose "discourse is shaped by authors from high-income, mainly Mediterranean, countries" (Weiss & Cattaneo, 2017, pp. 227; 200) has recognized that "without actively addressing dependencies in the world system and repairing the harm of centuries of uneven growth, degrowth could be one additional instrument in kicking away the ladder" (Schmelzer & Nowshin, 2023, p. 3). Thus, not only should the Global South be excluded from degrowth, but the Global North should pay it climate reparations for having misappropriated more than its fair share of carbon emissions (Schmelzer & Nowshin, 2023; Fanning & Hickel, 2023; Grasso & Heede, 2023; Hickel, 2020).

This exemption for the Global South is an implicit acknowledgment that Degrowth's proposals entail possible harm—harm in the sense of reduced economic and human development. Degrowth boils down to, as its proponents Schmelzer and Nowshin (2023) state, kicking away the ladder that is economic growth. The movement considers it appropriate that the Global North abandons this ladder. As Jason Hickel proclaimed, it is "time to de-develop" the West (Hickel, 2015).

The idea of degrowth agenda is related to concepts of post-growth (e.g., Jackson (2009), steady-state economics (e.g., Daly (1992), and "Doughnut" economics[1] (e.g., Raworth (2017)), which also considers GDP growth unsustainable, and moreover not meaningful after a certain level of income has been attained.[2]

[1] Most criticisms against degrowth are also applicable to Kate Raworth's Doughnut Economics. Economic scholars have been rather dismissive of Doughnut Economics. Schokkaert (2019, p. 131), for instance, concludes that Kate Raworth "discards all insights from modern mainstream economics—in fact, it simply does not mention any of these insights [...] it becomes more of a sermon than an analysis." And according to Maxwell (2017), "It was surprising to find, given Kate's history at UNDP, with the Human Development Report, and at Oxfam, how little there was in the book of development economics [....]. The omissions are so numerous and so startling that they really stand out."

[2] Degrowth, post-growth, and Doughnut Economics share the view, based on the Easterlin Paradox (see Easterlin et al. (2010)) that after a certain level of income, more money does not buy happiness. This view has been criticized, among others on the grounds that the Easterlin Paradox refers to changes in income and changes in happiness, not levels (Easterlin & O'Connor, 2020); and that Easterlin's original research was subject to measurement errors, which if corrected shows "no evidence of a saturation point" for happiness (Stevenson & Wolfers, 2013).

Degrowth is Malthusian in that it recognizes limits to growth (planetary boundaries) and it rejects the tech-optimism of Cornucopians. It does not offer a coherent theory of sustainable economic growth; rather, it is better described as a movement or agenda, with its intellectual roots in the 1970s views of Marxist philosopher André Gorz and economist Nicolas Georgescu-Roegen (Georgescu-Roegen, 1971, 1975).

As described by Kallis and March (2015, p. 360), "Degrowth is an advanced reincarnation of the radical environmentalism of the 1970s and speaks to pertinent debates within geography [...] degrowth is on purpose subversive [...] it embraces conflict as its constitutive element." In a similar vein it has been hailed as "a powerful oppositional Marxist[3] ecology that represents a path to a truly sustainable Earth" (Boettcher, 2021, p. vi).

The Degrowth Movement's agenda is thus a radical one (Kallis, 2011). Its deep-seated belief is that GDP growth, Green Growth, and the sustainable development goals (SDGs) are futile because these approaches are rooted in democratic capitalism, the ultimate problem. Therefore, "radical political project" is advocated (Kallis, 2011, p. 873) that would displace capitalism and in that way force a reduction of overconsumption of consumer goods, and material inputs into production, and of fossil fuels.

5.3 Deconstructing Degrowth

5.3.1 *Degrowth May Be De-effective*

Ultimately, the proposal for degrowth as proposed by the Degrowth movement turns out, much like that of green growth, not to be a solution. Most importantly, degrowth has been criticized that its proposal to reduce the GDP of advanced economies will have no significant impact on reducing the world's Material Footprint (MF), or carbon emissions, significantly enough to avoid an ecological overshoot. This is because most (63%) of current carbon emissions come from developing countries—where it will only continue to increase in the foreseeable future.[4] The 2022 *Emissions*

[3] According to Harvard psychologist Steven Pinker, proponents of degrowth have an "obvious" agenda: "it's humiliating to their world view that the data show massive improvements due to markets and globalization rather than an overthrow of capitalism and global redistribution"—as quoted in Coyne (2019).

[4] Thus, it is the case that "the planet's future will be determined in large part by the arc of growth in the developing world – that's where most of the people are, in China and India and, increasingly, sub-Saharan Africa" (Wallace-Wells, 2019).

Gap Report notes UNEP (2022, p. 67) that "virtually the entire future increase in global primary energy demand is expected to occur in these [developing] economies."

And after the GDP of rich economies are downsized—say by a hypothetical significant 40%, there would still remain a footprint of 60% and 60% of their economies to de-carbonize (Hickel & Hallegatte, 2022). van den Bergh (2011, p. 885) concluded that "Even if we would man-age to 'scale the economy down' to 50% [....] we still only would have reduced the size of the environmental problems by half. But this is by far insufficient for most environmental problems." It is clearly insufficient to halt the growth in material footprints and carbon emissions and not reduce these "tout court." Phillips (2019) uses the example of the successful reduction in the hole in the ozone layer to illustrate the shortcoming of the Degrowth proposal, explaining that:

> *we embraced degrowth with respect to ozone depletion by attempting to arrest growth in, say, the number of fridges in the world—or even reduce the total number—instead of regulation to enforce technology-switching, disaster would have befallen us. Saying" this many fridges and no more" would only have arrested the growth in emissions, not emissions tout court* (Phillips, 2019).

Moreover, even if the GDP growth of all countries, not only that of the developed countries, could be curtailed, it may still not be effective to reduce carbon emissions and MF sufficiently to achieve climate goals. This can easily be seen using the so-called IPAT identity, used to gauge the drivers of the environmental impact of the economy (Bretschger, 2021; Bruers, 2021). The IPAT identity decomposes the environmental impact (I) of an economy into the consequences of population (P), affluence (A), and technology (T) (Holdren, 1993). It can be written as follows (where a 'hat' over a variable indicates a rate of change):

$$I = \hat{P} + \frac{\hat{A}}{P} + \frac{\hat{T}}{A} \tag{5.1}$$

If affluence (A)—s measured in GDP—is reduced as per Degrowthers' proposal, it will lead to a reduction in impact (I). This is the basis of degrowth. However, if $\hat{P}$ continues to grow, and if technological innovation ($\hat{T}$) declines or remains slow, then the reduction in impact caused by

GDP degrowth would be offset. The important point to note is that both offset mechanisms *are more likely to apply at lower levels of GDP*.

Furthermore, if reduced GDP led to a reduction in technological innovation in the richer countries, the environmental impact may be even worse. Holdren (1993, p. 5) shows in this regard that "a change for the worse in the technology of production is more serious environmentally if it occurs in a populous, affluent society than if it occurs in a small, poor one"—which are precisely the type of societies that the Degrowth movement wants to downsize.

5.3.2 Degrowth May Be Dirty

Worse even, not only is downsizing the economies of rich countries not likely to be effective, but it may worsen ecological overshoot in several ways. "Degrowth might turn out to be dirty" (van den Bergh, 2011, p. 882). It amounts to ecological iatrogenics (Naudé, 2023c).

One way is that countries will have less resources to invest in climate change mitigation and adaptation technologies, and hence they will be more vulnerable to the impacts of ecological deterioration (Phillips, 2019).

A second is that firms may substitute more expensive cleaner production techniques for cheaper, but more polluting, technologies.

Third, government revenues will drop—an inevitable consequence of economic shrinkage. Governments would not be able to borrow further to spend on social and basic needs or environmental protection. They would need to repay their existing debt in the EU, the rule that government debt cannot exceed 60% of GDP implies that, if GDP declined, debt would also need to fall (Bruers, 2021).

Fourth, poorer households in (after degrowth) rich countries are likely to revert to deforestation and environmental destruction as they did during the 2021/2022 winters in Europe when faced with rising energy prices following the Ukraine war (Moloney, 2022; Rankin, 2021; Kauppi et al., 2006).

Fifth, the redistribution that the Degrowth Movement envisaged, from the Global North to the Global South, not only through downsizing the Global North but also through reparation payments to the Global South, is likely to stimulate global economic growth. This growth-through-redistribution mechanism is well known. In fact, if the Degrowth Movement wants to believe that its redistribution will not stimulate economic growth, they must believe in the basic neoclassical growth theory assumption that the shares of capital and labor in GDP are constant (see Chap. 1).

Downsizing the economies of developed countries in the global north should not be assumed to lead to less environmental destruction. Pre-industrial societies, which were less numerous and wealthy than modern society, were quite capable of significant ecological impact. For example, it has been estimated that "roughly three quarters of deforestation in temperate forests occurred before the industrial revolution" (Nordhaus, 2020). In contrast, Europe's forests have increased by a third between 1900 and 2010 (Fuchs et al., 2013). Higher GDP is associated with reforestation across the world, not deforestation (Kauppi et al., 2006).

5.3.3 *Degrowth May Be Expensive and Worsen Global Inequality*

A further shortcoming of degrowth is that if one considers degrowth as a method to decreasing carbon emissions, it is a much more expensive method than any currently comparable technological investments as green growth is pushing for. According to calculations by Jakob and Edenhofer (2014), if the world shrinks GDP per capita by 10% (around US$7000 billion), it will reduce carbon emissions by about 3.3 gigatons, meaning a cost of US$ 2100 per ton of emissions. In comparison, the social cost of carbon dioxide (SC-CO2) has been estimated at US$ 185 per ton of emissions (Rennert et al., 2022).

In addition to being likely ineffective, to worsen the environmental challenge, and a very expensive way to reduce carbon emissions, degrowth may disproportionately hurt the poorest of the poor—and make global inequality worse. One mechanism through which this could occur is that degrowth in the Global North will severely curtail development in the Global South because of the intertwined nature of the global economy (and there is no time for the Global South to successfully "decouple" if at all that is possible). The COVID-19 crisis emphasized this interdependency—poverty rose more sharply in the Global South than the Global North—and indicated how difficult it would be for the Global South to decouple from the Global North. Hence it may be indeed the case that, "the degrowth people are living a fantasy where they assume that if you bake a smaller cake, then for some reason, the poorest will get a bigger share of it [...] that has never happened in history" (Horowitz, 2022).

Ultimately, degrowth will make global inequality worse because it will be the poor who will pay the price, and not the rich, who have the means and connections to find shelter[5]—and who have arguably the most wasteful consumption. Hence, "Degrowth is, in essence, a form of ecological austerity for working-class people" (Chambers, 2021).

Finally, in the words of Bruers (2021) degrowth is not only ineffective, likely to worsen the environment, very expensive and a form of austerity for the working class, but redundant:

> *Economic degrowth is not necessary, because it targets the wrong enemy. GDP is not the enemy; environmental impact is the enemy. Environmental scientists are able to determine upper bounds on environmental impacts such as pollution. For example, climatologists have determined the carbon budget: how much greenhouse gases can still be emitted that keep the atmospheric temperature increase below 1.5°C. But GDP is measured in dollars, a totally different quantity than kg CO_2. Hence, none of the economic degrowthers are able to say what is the upper bound or true limit on affluence. There are no scientific studies that estimate the maximum level of GDP that is still permissible.*

5.4 Concluding Remarks

Degrowth, as a response to the overshoot crisis, is politically infeasible[5] (Piper, 2021). Because of the endowment (loss aversion) effect, people attach high value to their current levels of GDP per capita wherever they live. They would be unlikely to vote for politicians who propose lowering their levels of GDP per capita. And politicians, being generally subject to a status quo bias, would be reluctant to propose such a radical policy. As degrowth proponents themselves acknowledge, "political parties that have put forward degrowth ideas have received limited support in elections" (Hickel et al., 2022, p. 402).

In 2023 in the Netherlands, the political party (BBB) that strongly opposed government policies to degrow the agricultural sector, to reduce nitrogen and other emissions scored a massive election victory. Indeed, democracy and degrowth are inherently uncomfortable bedfellows. The only example in history of a sustainable and thriving stationary

[5] The empirical evidence is unanimous that environmental change has had and will likely have a much greater negative economic impact on developing countries than on advanced economies—see for instance Dell et al. (2012), Diffenbaugh and Burke (2019), Raddatz (2009), and Noy (2009).

(non-growing) society was Japan during the Edo (Tokugawa) period (1603–1868). It was, however, "a brutal dictatorship" (Bardi, 2020, p. 221).

Given that a democracy is unlikely to choose degrowth voluntarily, the Degrowth Movement may set the world on the dangerous path toward rejecting democracy, and reverting to an authoritarian collective, to enforce its agenda. After all, so their proponents may argue, given that their lofty goal is to save the entire planet from destruction, no price—including sacrificing democracy and liberty—may be too high a price to pay.

Chapter 6 provides a further critical analysis of the Degrowth Movement—namely, of its confidence that degrowing and de-developing Western economies will not negatively affect the innovative capabilities of the world to deliver technologies to reduce material use, and that political and social stability can be maintained in a degrowth world. It does so by pointing out that we basically already live in a degrowth world, and that we do not like it.

References

Akbulut, B. (2021). Degrowth. *Rethinking Marxism, 33*(1), 98–110.

Bardi, U. (2020). *Before the Collapse: A Guide to the Other Side of Growth.* Springer.

Boettcher, K. (2021). *Seeing Red over the Climate Crisis: Ecosocialism as Emergency Brake.* Thesis Presented to the Faculty of California State University, Stanislaus.

Bretschger, L. (2021). Getting the Costs of Environmental Protection Right: Why Climate Policy Is Inexpensive in the End. *Ecological Economics, 188*, 10711.

Bruers, S. (2021, December 30). The Case Against Degrowth. *Effective Altruism Forum Blog.*

Chambers, C. (2021, July 20). *Degrowth: An Environmental Ideology with Good Intentions, Bad Politics.* Liberation School.

Coyne, J. (2019, January 31). Is the World Really Getting Poorer? A Response by Steve Pinker. *Why Evolution Is True Blog.*

Daly, H. (1992). *Steady- State Economics* (2nd ed.). Earthscan.

Dell, M., Jones, B., & Olken, B. (2012). Climate Change and Economic Growth: Evidence from the Last Half Century. *American Economic Journal: Macroeconomics, 4*(3), 66–95.

Diffenbaugh, N., & Burke, M. (2019). Global Warming has Increased Global Economic Inequality. *Proceedings of the National Academy of Sciences, 116*(20), 9808–9813.

Easterlin, R., & O'Connor, K. J. (2020). The Easterlin Paradox. *IZA DP No. 13923.*

Easterlin, R., McVey, L., Switek, M., Sawangfa, O., & Zweig, J. (2010). The Happiness- Income Paradox Revisited. *Proceedings of the National Academy of Sciences, 107*, 2246322468.

Fanning, A. L., & Hickel, J. (2023, June 5). Compensation for Atmospheric Appropriation. *Nature Sustainability.*

Fuchs, R., Herold, M., Verburg, P., & Clevers, J. (2013). A High-Resolution and Harmonized Model Approach for Reconstructing and Analysing Historic Land Changes in Europe. *Biogeosciences, Biogeosciences, 10*, 15431559.

Georgescu-Roegen, M. (1971). *The Entropy Law and the Economic process.* Harvard University Press.

Georgescu-Roegen, N. (1975). Energy and Economic Myths. *Southern Economic Journal, 41*(3), 347–381.

Grasso, M., & Heede, R. (2023). Time to Pay the Piper: Fossil Fuel Companies' Reparations for Climate Damages. *One Earth, 6*(5), 459–463.

Hickel, J. (2015, September 23). Forget Developing Poor Countries, It's Time to De-develop Rich Countries. *The Guardian.*

Hickel, J. (2020). Quantifying National Responsibility for Climate Breakdown: An Equality-Based Attribution Approach for Carbon Dioxide Emissions in Excess of the Planetary Boundary. *Lancet Planet Health, 4*, e399–e404.

Hickel, J. (2021). What Does Degrowth Mean? A Few Points of Clarification. *Globalizations, 18*(7), 1105–1111.

Hickel, J., & Hallegatte, S. (2022). Can we Live within Environmental Limits and Still Reduce Poverty? Degrowth or Decoupling? *Development Policy Review, 40*, e12584.

Hickel, J., Kallis, G., Jackson, T., O'Neill, D. W., Schor, J., Steinberger, J. K., Victor, P., & Ürge-Vorsatz, D. (2022). Degrowth Can Work – Here's How Science Can Help. *Nature, 612*, 400–403.

Holdren, J. (1993, September 7). A Brief History of IPAT (Impact= Population x Affluence x Technology). *MAHB.*

Horowitz, J. (2022, November 15). Degrowth: A Dangerous Idea or the Answer to the World's Biggest Crisis? *CNN Business.*

Jackson, T. (2009). *Prosperity Without Growth? The Transition to a Sustainable Economy.* Sustainable Development Commission.

Jakob, M., & Edenhofer, O. (2014). Green Growth, Degrowth, and the Commons. *Oxford Review of Economic Policy, 30*(3), 447–468.

Kallis, G. (2011). In Defence of Degrowth. *Ecological Economics, 70*(5), 873–880.

Kallis, G., & March, H. (2015). Imaginaries of Hope: The Utopianism of Degrowth. *Annals of the Association of American Geographers, 105*(2), 360–336.

Kauppi, P. E., Ausubel, J., Fang, J., Mather, A., Sedjo, R., & Waggoner, P. (2006). Returning Forests Analyzed with the Forest Identity. *Proceedings of the National Academy of Sciences, 103*(46), 17574–17579.

Maxwell, S. (2017, April 24). Review of Kate Raworth's Doughnut Economics. *Simon Maxwell Blog*.
Moloney, E. (2022, March 10). Call to Restart Irish Peat Harvesting Amid Energy Crisis and Russia's War on Ukraine. *Independent.Ie*.
Murphy, T., Murphy, D., Love, T., LeHew, M., & McCall, B. (2021). Modernity is Incompatible with Planetary Limits: Developing a PLAN for the Future. *Energy Research & Social Science, 81*, 102239.
Naudé, W. (2023c). No, Degrowth Won't Save Us. *BMJ (British Medical Journal), 382*, 2245. https://doi.org/10.1136/bmj.p2245.
Nordhaus, T. (2020). Must Growth Doom the Planet? [Review of Growth: From Microorganisms to Megacities, by V. Smil]. *The New Atlantis, 61*, 76–86.
Noy, I. (2009). The Macroeconomic Consequences of Disasters. *Journal of Development Economics, 88*, 221–231.
Phillips, L. (2019, August 30). The Degrowth Delusion. *Open Democracy*.
Piper, K. (2021, August 3). Can We Save the Planet by Shrinking the Economy? *Vox*.
Raddatz, C. (2009). *The Wrath of God: Macroeconomic Costs of Natural Disasters* (Policy Research Working Paper Series WPS 5039). World Bank, Policy Research Department.
Rankin, J. (2021, July 16). Enough with the Burning: EU Executive Accused of Sacrificing Forests. *The Guardian*.
Raworth, K. (2017). *Doughnut Economics: Seven Ways to Think Like a 21st-Century Economist*. Random House.
Rennert, K., Errickson, F., Prest, B., Rennels, L., Newell, R., Pizer, W., Kingdon, C., et al. (2022). Comprehensive Evidence Implies a Higher Social Cost of CO2. *Nature, 610*(7933), 687–692.
Schmelzer, M., & Nowshin, T. (2023, June 27). Ecological Reparations and Degrowth: Towards a Convergence of Alternatives Around World-making After Growth. *Development*.
Schokkaert, E. (2019). Review of Kate Raworth's Doughnut Economics. London: Random House. *Erasmus Journal for Philosophy and Economics, 12*(1), 125–132.
Stevenson, B., & Wolfers, J. (2013). Subjective Well-Being and Income: Is There Any Evidence of Satiation? *The American Economic Review, 103*(3), 598–604.
UNEP. (2022). *The Closing Window: Emissions Gap Report 2022*. United Nations Environmental Programme.
van den Bergh, J. (2011). Environment versus Growth – A Criticism of Degrowth and a Plea for A-growth. *Ecological Economics, 70*(5), 881–890.
Wallace-Wells, D. (2019, February 2). 'The Devastation of Human Life Is in View': What a Burning World Tells Us About Climate Change. *The Guardian*.
Weiss, M., & Claudio Cattaneo, C. (2017). Degrowth – Taking Stock and Reviewing an Emerging Academic Paradigm. *Ecological Economics, 137*, 220–230.

CHAPTER 6

Living in a Degrowth World

Abstract This chapter argues that the Degrowth movement goes astray in insisting that Degrowth would make society and the environment better. Degrowthers miss that in the West, we already live in a degrowth-type world, and that there is much about it that we do not like. The chapter, therefore, describes the Degrowth world—the Great Stagnation—that the West has been approaching since the 1970s, and its correlates: declining entrepreneurship, innovation and science, and research productivity.

Keywords Degrowth • Stagnation • Zero-sum society • Conflict

6.1 Introduction

This is a good moment to recap. The narrative in this book so far has been that there are two broad approaches in the debate on tackling the ecological crisis. One is Green Growth, according to which there are essentially no limits to economic growth, and which promotes (eco-) innovation to reduce the impacts of growth on the environment, both in terms of resource use and emissions. The Green Growth approach is the mainstream global economic policy approach to the ecological crisis, as promoted for instance, by the European Commission (EC (2011)), OECD (2009, 2011, 2014), and World Bank (2012). This approach was discussed in Chap. 3.

W. Naudé, *Economic Growth and Societal Collapse*,
https://doi.org/10.1007/978-3-031-45582-7_6

Another approach is that of the Degrowth Movement, which identifies strict limits to economic growth, which, if breached, would lead to an environmental catastrophe and "ghastly future" (Kallis, 2011; Kallis & March, 2015; Hickel, 2019, 2021; Bradshaw et al., 2021). A rallying cry is "you can't have infinite growth on a finite planet" (Phillips, 2019). As such, economic growth needs to be curtailed, and indeed GDP in advanced economies needs to be reduced—it is time to "de-develop rich countries" as called for by Hickel (2015). This follows from Degrowth's belief that Green Growth will not be able to decouple resource use and emissions from GDP (Hickel, 2019)—and that "growth is not working" to make the world a better place (Hickel, 2015). This approach was outlined in Chap. 5.

As was explained in Chap. 5, in the Degrowth Movement's narrative, policymakers are "obsessed" with maximizing economic growth, because of the nature of global capitalism, which also produces large inequalities between the Global North and the Global South—degrowth is a "demand for decolonization" (Hickel, 2021). The Degrowth movement therefore wants to reduce GDP in advanced economies and not the Global South, and do so via a "radical political project" of reconfiguration of the entire global socioeconomic system, starting in the rich, decadent, and consumption-driven West (Kallis, 2011, p. 873). The Degrowth Movement believes this is consistent with abundance and happiness, and that the extent of GDP and consumption in the West can be significantly reduced without making people worse off—at least this is what they claim (Hickel & Hallegatte, 2022). Moreover, they believe that limits and boundaries to GDP, consumption and resource use will stimulate innovation and creativity—leading to a better society all-round (Raworth, 2017; Kendrick, 2023).

The Degrowth movement is largely accurate[1] in its analysis of the shortcomings of Green Growth in terms of the latter's ability to decouple growth from material use (Naudé, 2023a). This paper argues that where the Degrowth movement, however, goes astray, is in insisting on degrowth, and in claiming that this would make society and the environment better. Degrowthers misses that in the West, we already live in a degrowth-type world, and that there is much about it that we do not like.

[1] As is argued elsewhere, the Degrowth Movement is less accurate in analyzing the links between economic growth, poverty reduction, and subjective welfare. See, for example, Naudé (2023b), Coyne (2019), or Bruers (2021).

This chapter, therefore, describes the degrowth world—the Great Stagnation as it has been called by Cowen (2010)—that the West has been approaching since the 1970s, and its correlates: declining entrepreneurship, innovation and science, and research productivity. The declines in these suggest that the hope that a degrowth economy can generate the technological progress and the social cohesion necessary to tackle ecological and social crises is far-fetched and naive. Moreover, as recent decades of suffering under economic stagnation have illustrated, the consequence of degrowth is a zero-sum society. With the size of the economic cake essentially fixed or shrinking, the economy is a theater of conflict. One group, or one country, can only make itself better off at the expense of another. Redistribution, instead of production, is the basis of the economy.

Thus, in a context of a curtailed ability to generate technological innovations and a zero-sum economy, even more degrowth, as proposed by the Degrowth Movement, will only make problems worse.

Hence, in Chap. 7 this book concludes by making some suggestions for moving beyond Degrowth—pointing to two divergent views of humanity's future, the one expecting societal collapse, the other expecting that breakthrough technology, such as an Artificial General Intelligence (AGI) and/or whole brain emulations may result in a Singularity. Whether collapse or an unimaginably prosperous future enabled by breakthrough technological progress will be the future, these scenarios suggest that there is more to humanity's future than envisaged by the Degrowth Movement.

The rest of the chapter proceeds as follows. Section 6.2 asks: Can economic growth continue forever? In this section, it is shown that if one wants to believe in indefinite growth, strong assumptions are needed concerning entrepreneurship, innovation, science, population, and R&D productivity—and that the experience of the West over the past fifty years shows that these assumptions do not seem to hold. Section 6.3 lays out the empirical evidence in this regard, briefly analyzing the decline in the West of entrepreneurship, innovation and science, and research productivity. These sections are brief, as more details are available elsewhere, for instance, in Bhaskar (2021), Erixon and Weigl (2016), Gordon (2018), and Naudé (2022) among others. Section 6.4 argues that the declines in economic growth and its correlates have resulted in an economy increasingly characterized by zero-sum outcomes. Then, Sect. 6.5 examines the Degrowth Movement's agenda against the context of an already degrowing economy in the West. It is argued that the Degrowth Movement itself can be seen as a social reaction against degrowth. Section 6.6 concludes.

6.2 Can Economic Growth Continue Forever?

As a result of the takeoff in economic growth since around the end of the eighteenth century, world GDP per capita today, around US$5400, is 5600% higher than what it was 10,000 years before, when we lived as foragers and hunter-gatherers (Syvitski et al., 2020) as pointed out in Chap. 2—see also Fig. 2.1.

Growth not only transformed the nature of the economy, but also of society, including its values. Democracy, tolerance, human rights, freedom, social justice—these were all enabled, and in turn contributed to, an expanding economy. As historian Ian Morris reminds us, "Most people in the world today think democracy and gender equality are good, and that violence and wealth inequality are bad. But most people who lived during the 10,000 years before the nineteenth century thought just the opposite" (Morris, 2015).

But can this continue? The field of economics, in the time of Adam Smith, David Ricardo and Thomas Malthus started considering economic growth bounded by the finiteness of resources, such as land, labor, and capital. Robert Solow's 1956 Nobel Prize-winning contribution suggested that economic growth will over time decline to zero, unless technology "rains down" exogenously to keep growth positive (Solow, 1956). In 2018, Paul Romer received the Nobel Prize in economics for showing how technological innovation can emerge endogenously from within the economic system, and so long as there is technological innovation, economic growth can continue indefinitely (Romer, 1986, 1987, 1990).

Romer's central contribution was to argue that innovation is unbounded because it is based on ideas (recipes) that are non-rival in use and can have increasing returns to scale—the more people there are, the more ideas there will be, and with a larger stock of ideas more new ideas can arise by combination of existing ideas (Romer, 1993). As Romer (2016) explains:

> *For recipes that can have four elements, there are 100 x 99 x 98 x 97 recipes, which is more 94 million. With up to 5 elements, more than 9 billion. Mathematicians call this increase in the number of combinations "combinato-*

rial explosion." Once you get to 10 elements [ideas], there are more recipes than seconds since the big bang created the universe.

If economic growth therefore depends on ideas/recipes (technology), then, if one believes in unlimited economic growth, one must believe that (1) entrepreneurs will face sufficient incentives to continue to search for new ideas; (2) the population, from which ideas spring, will continue to grow; and (3) that research productivity (the search for new ideas) will not decline. Hence, if entrepreneurship, population and research productivity decline, there would not be increasing returns to scale in ideas, and indefinite economic growth would not be possible. Economic growth would be decreasing over time and eventually stop.

If we look at economic growth rates in the advanced economies, of say Western Europe, then we see that it indeed has been declining since the 1950s and 1960s, which were in a historical context the golden years of economic growth (see Fig. 6.1). Average economic growth rates in Western Europe today are historically low and resemble those of the 1860s (which saw the rise of Marxism and the founding of the First International),

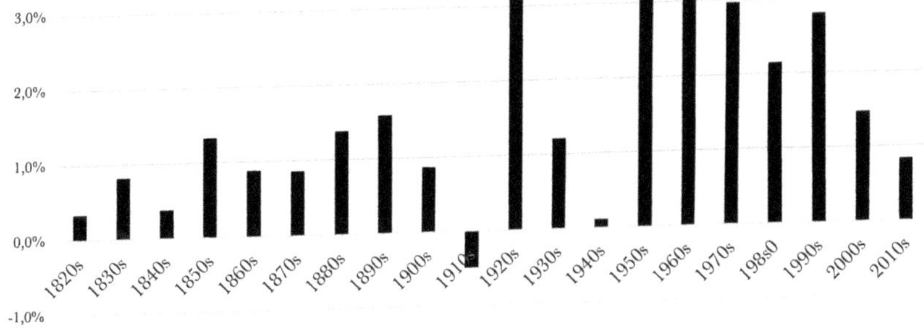

Fig. 6.1 GDP per capita growth rates per decade in Western Europe, 1820s to 2010s. (Source: Author's compilation based on data from the Maddison Project Database 2020, see Bolt and van Zanden (2020))

the 1870s (which saw the rise of the New Imperialism), and 1900s (a period of rising nationalism and militarism).

The decline in growth since the 1950s, which looks similar in the United States, has been described as the Great Stagnation (Cowen, 2010). No respite is in sight; indeed not only growth in the West, but in the rest of the world is according to a World Bank study set to fall further in coming decades, concluding that "Today nearly all the economic forces that drove economic progress are in retreat" (Kose & Ohnsorge, 2023, p. xix).

The Great Stagnation has been accompanied by declines in entrepreneurship, population growth, innovation, and research productivity. These are, in terms of Romer's theoretical framework, causal mechanisms for slowing growth down. But, because these are endogenous to the economy, slower economic growth will also in turn depress entrepreneurship, innovation, and research productivity (Romer, 1994).

Sequeira et al. (2018) developed an endogenous economic growth model with a "complexity index'" in which economic growth is finite. Their model dynamics predict that the current economic slowdown (also reflected in the slowdown in TFP and entrepreneurship) will continue until economic growth collapses completely around the year 2450.

Let us consider some empirical trends in entrepreneurship, innovation, and research productivity in the West. Not everybody realizes that behind the fascination with the digital world's shiny objects, the economy has lost its innovative luster. We do not really live in such a fast-changing technological world as it is often made out to be. It is not that we have too many technological disruptions: it is rather that we may not have enough.

6.3 The Great Decline

6.3.1 Entrepreneurship

We live in an ossified, and not an entrepreneurial economy (Naudé, 2022). A growing volume of research has confirmed that entrepreneurship, according to many measures, has been declining since around the 1970s in the United States and other Western economies, including the UK, Belgium, and Germany. For example, the share of new to old firms in the United States has dropped by 50% between 1978 and 2011 (Hopenhayn et al., 2018, 2022). The share of entrepreneurs in the country's working population has declined from 7.8% in 1985 to 3.9% in 2014 (Salgado, 2020). In Belgium, the new business formation rate declined from 12% in

1986 to –1% in 2014 (Bijnens & Konings, 2018), and in the UK start-up rates declined between 1998 and 2012 from 6.5% to 0.8% between 1998 and 2012 (Ugur et al., 2016). And evidence from Germany suggests that start-up activity declined by 50% between 1990 and 2013 (Naudé & Nagler, 2018).

These declines in entrepreneurship measures have been across sectors—including high-tech (Haltiwanger, 2022)—and has seen the share of young firms (that tend to be more innovative) dropping (Decker et al., 2014). It has been accompanied by declines in labor mobility, as the opportunities that firm dynamism creates dries up (Konczal & Steinbaum, 2016). Historically, entrepreneurship has been a vehicle for social mobility (Connor & Storper, 2020), and accordingly, as this vehicle has been running out of steam, inequality has increased (Pikkety, 2013). Declining entrepreneurship leads to slower growth and higher inequality, but it is just as much the case that slower economic growth and degrowth lead in turn to declining entrepreneurship (Naudé, 2008).

6.3.2 Innovation and Science

As entrepreneur Peter Thiel lamented, "We wanted flying cars, instead we got 140 characters." This reflects disappointment that predictions of the 2020s made back in the 1950s and 1960s turned out overoptimistic. According to Huebner (2005, p. 980), "The rate of innovation peaked in the year 1873 and is now rapidly declining. We are at an estimated 85% of the economic limit of technology, and it is projected that we will reach 90% in 2018 and 95% in 2038."

Other measures are consistent with such a bleak conclusion. For instance, in the UK, labor productivity growth is the lowest in 200 years (Tenreyro, 2018); in Germany, total factor productivity growth (an indirect measure of innovation) averaged 2.73% in the 1960s but declined to -0.26% between 2000 and 2010 (Naudé & Nagler, 2018). Increasingly, patent registrations (another measure of innovation) have been getting narrower in scope and less original (Akcigit & Ates, 2019).

Kelly et al. (2021) constructed, using patent data, an aggregate innovation index for the United States covering 1840–2020. This shows that origin of breakthrough-patents has shifted over time, from engineering and manufacturing in the nineteenth century, to transport and chemistry in the first half of the twentieth century, eventually to ICT (e.g., microchips) in the late twentieth century. Indeed, outside of the computer industry, there have been historically few breakthrough-patents the past three decades.

The slowdown in innovation is part of the broader slowdown in scientific progress and discovery. In particular, the fact that fundamental physics have not been making much progress in fifty years has been highlighted by several scientists. Hossenfelder (2018), for example, pointed out that "Nothing is moving in the foundations of physics. One experiment after the other is returning null results: No new particles, no new dimensions, no new symmetries."

Park et al. (2023, p. 138), using data on 45 million papers and 3.9 million patents from six large-scale datasets, " find that "papers and patents are increasingly less likely to break with the past in ways that push science and technology in new directions. This pattern holds universally across fields." It suggests indeed that "progress is slowing in several major fields."

More generally, in recent years scientific progress has been marked by hyper-specialization and hyper-authorship (Funk & Smith, 2022); reproducibility crises and false results (Baker, 2016; Ioannidis, 2005); retractions (Steen, 2011), and misconduct (Archer, 2020), an out- of-date peer review system (Dattani, 2022) where 90% of scientific papers are never cited (Meho, 2007).

6.3.3 Research Productivity

The declines in entrepreneurship, innovation, and science have been accompanied by a decline in research productivity—which in turn contributes to poorer entrepreneurship and innovation. Bloom et al. (2020), found that "Research productivity for the aggregate U.S. economy has declined by a factor of 41 since the 1930s, an average decrease of more than 5% per year." This has been despite a substantial and steady increase in the number of researchers in the country. The authors conclude that "ideas are getting harder to find."

It is not only that ideas are getting harder to find. Ideas are also getting harder to fund (Bhaskar, 2021). It is not possible to fund every new idea (there are basically infinite numbers of new ideas). In the competition for scarce funding, we may be selecting less- effective ideas—ideas that may promise more than they can deliver, which may be a problem pervasive in the ICT/digital industry where "gaming" R&D is common (Funk, 2019a, b).

The instability and crises in the global financial system—there has been more than 150 financial crises since the 1970s when the Bretton Woods system collapsed—is a feature of a stagnating economy in decline (Laeven & Valencia, 2020). It has contributed, through central banks pumping trillions of dollars and euros into economies as "quantitative easing" to prevent massive bank failure and recession, to excessive liquidity (Calcagnini et al., 2022)—real interest rates have by the late 2010s declined to their lowest levels in 5000 years (Holodny, 2016). In this environment, cash chases short-term returns, with little consideration for long-term investments in the types of technology and science that really matter.

6.4 The Zero-Sum Society

> *From now on, only relative growth is possible: the global economy is playing a zero-sum game, with an ever-shrinking pot to be divided amongst the winners* (Heinberg, 2011: 2).

The consequence of the decline in growth in the West, and the simultaneous decline in entrepreneurship, innovation, science, and research productivity has created a zero-sum society. With the size of the economic cake essentially fixed, or shrinking, the economy becomes a theater of conflict. One group, or one country, can only make itself better off at the expensive of another. Redistribution, instead of production, becomes the basis of the economy. In a zero-sum economy, higher and higher inequality is most often the outcome (Pikkety, 2013)—an outcome also acknowledged by proponents of degrowth—see Hartley et al. (2020).

For firms, in a zero-sum economy, defensive innovation (aimed at exploiting a fixed niche) becomes the default mode—to keep competitors out and extract more profits from existing markets. Hence, we have seen indicators of corporate dominance and industry concentration increase (Covarrubias et al., 2020), the share of labor in output decline (Autor et al., 2020), the rise of industrial policy nationalism (Johnston, 2023), de-globalization (Zeihan, 2023), poor quality, low-paying jobs (Graeber, 2018), and trade wars (Fetzer & Schwarz, 2021).

And in this degrowth, zero-sum economy, society is seemingly getting more risk-averse. Schrager (2022) observes that "the effort to stop growth misunderstand human nature, which thrives on the motivation to create and improve. Dooming people to stagnation deprives them of curiosity and purpose." And in the process, new ideas are not so welcome anymore.

According to Bhaskar (2021), "society has become more hostile to radical innovation, risk-averse, fractious, short-termist." Society has also become less tolerant toward migrants,[2] and have experienced personal rights decline and inclusiveness stagnate (Deloitte, 2022). Governments are less trusted: public trust in government in the United States has, for instance, fallen from 77% in 1964 in the economic growth golden age, to 17% in 2019.[3] Science used to be a "candle in the dark" (Sagan, 1997). In the zero-sum, degrowth economy of the West, it is not so anymore: moral relativism (Boudry, 2021), religious dogma (McPhetres & Zuckerman, 2018), and even outright anti-science sentiment (Kuntz, 2012) are eroding whatever is left of Europe's Enlightenment legacy.

6.5 The Degrowth Movement as the Outcome of Degrowth

It is in this context in which the Degrowth Movement has arisen. It is, like the rise in dogma, intolerance, and anti-science sentiment one of the outcomes—or symptoms—of degrowth in the West.[4] But paradoxically, the Degrowth Movement wants more of the same: more degrowth, not less (Fanning et al., 2022).[5]

It believes that not only will this prevent an ecological overshoot and environmental collapse, but that, contrary to the experience of the degrowth-West of the past fifty years, that this would lead to abundance and happiness. It is even claimed that limits and boundaries on consumption and resource use will stimulate innovation and creativity (Raworth, 2017; Kendrick, 2023).

The Degrowth Movement is not wrong in pointing to the limits of economic growth, or of its impacts on the ecological carrying capacity of the Earth. But they are hardly the first, or only one, to do so. Romer's Nobel Prize-winning contribution implies that economic growth cannot be maintained indefinitely if entrepreneurship, innovation, science, and

[2] See https://news.gallup.com/poll/320678/world-grows-less-accepting-migrants.aspx

[3] See https://www.pewresearch.org/politics/2022/06/06/public-trust-in-government-1958-2022/

[4] Demaria et al. (2016, p. 390) locates the "birth of degrowth as an international research agenda" to the first degrowth conference, in Paris in 2008: hence the Degrowth Movement was born during the Global Financial Crisis.

[5] See https://www.oneplanetnetwork.org/programmes/sustainable-lifestyles-education/about

research productivity are subject to decreasing returns—as the experience of the West suggests they are (Johansen & Sornette, 2001; Jones, 2022; Naudé, 2022; Nordhaus, 2020). And the empirical literature has noted the lack of absolute decoupling between economic growth and material use, and economic growth and carbon emissions on a global level (Haberl et al., 2020; Hannesson, 2021; Jackson & Victor, 2019; Ward et al., 2016; Wiedmann et al., 2015).

A blind spot of the Degrowth Movement is thinking we cannot decouple material use and carbon emissions from economic growth, but that we can indeed decouple innovation, happiness, social progress, tolerance, and twenty-first century values from economic growth. As Murphy (2015) warned, Degrowth may undo the social progress that has taken place in a growing, positive-sum economy:

> *In times of plenty, we can afford to be kind to those who are different. We are less threatened when we are comfortable. If our 21st Century standard of living peaks [...] then we may not have the luxury of viewing our social progress as an irreversible ratchet. Hard times revive old tribal instincts: different is not welcome.*

In a similar vein, Richard Heinberg, hardly a supporter of Green Growth, stresses that "societies in the midst of social crisis, and ones turning toward authoritarian regimes, are seldom able to muster efforts toward resource conservation, emissions reduction, and habitat preservation" (Heinberg, 2023).

The Degrowth Movement may also be mistaken in assuming that we can in centralized fashion, through the political process, dictate an orderly process of scaling down resource use consumption (and hence GDP), when redistribution, instead of production, becomes the basis of the economy. A similar fantasy did not play out well in the Soviet Union, indeed, the ecological damage from the degrowth period under communism turned the Soviet Union and its Eastern European satellites into one of the most polluted regions in the world (Brain, 2010; Shahgedanova & Burt, 1994; Schiermeier, 2019). The legacy endures to the present (Varieur et al., 2022).

Degrowth has been labeled as "dirty" (van den Bergh, 2011); as ecological iatrogenics (Naudé, 2023c); as a program of "ecological austerity for working-class people" (Chambers, 2021); and has been accused that it will "do more harm to the planet than good" (Nordhaus, 2020). When one realizes that we already live in a world resembling degrowth, and that we do not like it, these labels make sense.

6.6 Concluding Remarks

Perhaps the Degrowth Movement's most fundamental shortcoming is its shorttermism. The shorttermism of the Degrowth Movement partly reflects its lack of consequentialist ethics, which is in turn perhaps ideological, but can also reflect that most proponents of the movement are far removed from any of the potential bad outcomes of their advice (the majority live privileged lives in the Global North) and/or that they do not have any "skin in the game"—if their policy advice should work out well, they benefit; if not, they do not lose anything.

The development of technologies to prevent ecological overshoot, including a climate catastrophe, and the development of technologies to eventually reduce other existential risks will come to a screeching halt if the Degrowth Movement's shorttermist worldview is imposed. Loeb (2023) reminds us that "*[u]nrealistic illusions were the trademark of past civilizations that perished on Earth. Adaptation to reality based on evidence places a higher bar for our long-term survival.*" Perhaps, after all, while economic growth, driven by new ideas and energy, contains its own risks, perhaps it is the case that "the risks of stasis are far more troubling. Getting off the roller coaster mid-ride is not an option" (Mokyr, 2014). But what if the ride ends in a collapse?

References

Akcigit, U. and Ates, S. (2019). *Ten Facts on Declining Business Dynamism and Lessons from Endogenous Growth Theory* (CEPR Discussion Paper no. 13668). Centre for Economic Policy Research.

Archer, E. (2020). *The Intellectual and Moral Decline in Academic Research.* James G. Martin Center for Academic Renewal.

Autor, D., Dorn, D., Katz, L., Patterson, C., & Reenen, J. V. (2020). The Fall of the Labor Share and the Rise of Superstar Firms. *The Quarterly Journal of Economics, 135*(2), 645–709.

Baker, M. (2016). 1,500 Scientists Lift the Lid on Reproducibility. *Nature, 533*, 452–454.

Bhaskar, M. (2021). *Human Frontiers: The Future of Big Ideas in an Age of Small Thinking.* The Bridge Street Press.

Bijnens, G., & Konings, J. (2018). Declining Business Dynamism in Belgium. *Small Business Economics*, 1–39.

Bloom, N., Jones, C., van Reenen, J., & Webb, M. (2020). Are Ideas Getting Harder to Find? *American Economic Review, 110*(4), 1104–1144.

Boettcher, K. (2021). *Seeing Red over the Climate Crisis: Ecosocialism as Emergency Brake*. Thesis Presented to the Faculty of California State University, Stanislaus.

Bolt, J., & van Zanden, J. (2020). Maddison Style Estimates of the Evolution of the World Economy. A New 2020 Update. *Maddison-Project Working Paper WP-15*.

Bostrom, N. (2003). Astronomical Waste: The Opportunity Cost of Delayed Technological Development. *Utilitas, 15*(3), 308–314.

Boudry, M. (2021, July 29). Why Relativism Is the Worst Idea Ever. *Blog of the APA*.

Bradshaw, C., Ehrlich, P., Beattie, A., Ceballos, G., Crist, E., Diamond, J., Dirzo, R., Ehrlich, A., Harte, J., Pyke, G., Raven, P., Ripple, W., Saltré, F., Turnbull, C., Wackernagel, M., & Blumstein, D. (2021). Underestimating the Challenges of Avoiding a Ghastly Future. *Frontiers in Conservation Science, 1*, 615–641.

Brain, S. (2010). Stalin's Environmentalism. *The Russian Review, 69*(1), 93–118.

Bruers, S. (2021, December 30). The Case Against Degrowth. *Effective Altruism Forum Blog*.

Calcagnini, G., Gardini, L., Giombini, G., & Carrera, E. (2022). Does Too Much Liquidity Generate Instability? *Journal of Economic Interaction and Coordination, 17*, 191–208.

Chambers, C. (2021, July 20). *Degrowth: An Environmental Ideology with Good Intentions, Bad Politics*. Liberation School.

Cirkovic, M. (2002). Cosmological Forecast and Its Practical Significance. *Journal of Evolution and Technology, xii*.

Connor, D., & Storper, M. (2020). The Changing Geography of Social Mobility in the United States. *Proceedings of the National Academy of Sciences, 117*(48), 30309–30317.

Covarrubias, M., Gutiérrez, G., & Philippon, T. (2020). From Good to Bad Concentration? US Industries over the Past 30 Years. *NBER Macroeconomics Annual, 34*, 1–46.

Cowen, T. (2010). *The Great Stagnation*. Penguin (Dutton).

Coyne, J. (2019, January 31). Is the World Really Getting Poorer? A Response by Steve Pinker. *Why Evolution Is True Blog*.

Dattani, S. (2022). Real Peer Review Has Never Been Tried. *Works in Progress, 8*(21 July).

Decker, R., Haltiwanger, J., Jarmin, R., & Miranda, J. (2014). The Role of Entrepreneur- ship in US Job Creation and Dynamics. *Journal of Economic Perspectives, 28*(3), 3–24.

Deloitte. (2022). *2022 Social Progress Index*. https://www.socialprogress.org/global-index-2022-results/

Demaria, F., Schneider, F., Sekulova, F., & Martinez-Alier, J. (2016). What Is Degrowth? From an Activist Slogan to a Social Movement. In N. Haenn, A. Harnish, & R. Wilk (Eds.), *The Environment in Anthropology (Second Edition): A Reader in Ecology, Culture, and Sustainable Living* (pp. 390–400). New York University Press.

EC. (2011, September 20). *Analysis Associated with the Roadmap to a Resource Efficient Europe Part I*. European Commission Staff Working Paper SEC (2011) 1067 final.

Erixon, F., & Weigl, B. (2016). *The Innovation Illusion*. Yale University Press.

Fanning, A., O'Neill, D., Hickel, J., & Roux, N. (2022). The Social Shortfall and Ecological Overshoot of Nations. *Nature Sustainability, 5*, 26–36.

Fetzer, T., & Schwarz, C. (2021). Tariffs and Politics: Evidence from Trump's Trade Wars. *The Economic Journal, 131*(636), 1717–1741.

Funk, J. (2019a, October 23). Gaming the Systems of Venture Capital and R&D. *LinkedIn*.

Funk, J. (2019b). What's Behind Technological Hype? *Issues in Science and Technology, 36*(1), 36–42.

Funk, J., & Smith, G. (2022, October 4). The Hyper-Specialization of University Researchers. *Mind Matters*.

Gordon, R. (2018). *Why Has Economic Growth Slowed When Innovation Appears to Be Accelerating?* (NBER Working Paper 24554). National Bureau for Economic Research.

Graeber, D. (2018). *Bullshit Jobs: A Theory*. Simon & Schuster.

Haberl, H., Wiedenhofer, D., Virág, D., Kalt, G., Plank, B., Brockway, P., Fishman, T., Hausknost, D., Krausmann, F., Leon-Gruchalski, B., et al. (2020). A Systematic Review of the Evidence on Decoupling of GDP, Resource Use and GHG Emissions, Part II: Synthesizing the Insights. *Environmental Research Letters, 15*, 065003.

Haltiwanger, J. (2022). Entrepreneurship in the Twenty-First Century. *Small Business Economics, 58*, 27–40.

Hannesson, R. (2021). Are We Seeing Dematerialization of World GDP? *Biophysical Economics and Sustainability, 6*(4).

Hartley, T., van den Bergh, J., & Kallis, G. (2020). Policies for Equality Under Low or No Growth: A Model Inspired by Piketty. *Review of Political Economy, 32*(2), 243–258.

Heinberg, R. (2011). *The End of Growth: Adapting to Our New Economic Reality*. New Society Publishers.

Heinberg, R. (2023, June 15). Polycrisis, Unraveling, Simplification, or Collapse: Coming Soon to a Planet Near You? *Resilience*.

Hickel, J. (2015, September 23). Forget Developing Poor Countries, It's Time to De-develop Rich Countries. *The Guardian*.
Hickel, J. (2019). The Contradiction of the Sustainable Development Goals: Growth Versus Ecology on a Finite Planet. *Sustainable Development, 274*(5), 873–884.
Hickel, J. (2021). What Does Degrowth Mean? A Few Points of Clarification. *Globalizations, 18*(7), 1105–1111.
Hickel, J., & Hallegatte, S. (2022). Can we Live within Environmental Limits and Still Reduce Poverty? Degrowth or Decoupling? *Development Policy Review, 40*, e12584.
Holodny, E. (2016, December 14). The 5,000-year History of Interest Rates Shows Just How Historically Low US Rates Are Right Now. *Business Insider*.
Hopenhayn, H., Neira, J., & Singhania, R. (2018). From Population Growth to Firm Demographics: Implications from Concentration, Entrepreneurship and the Labor Share. *NBER Working Paper No. 25382*.
Hopenhayn, H., Neira, J., & Singhania, R. (2022). From Population Growth to Firm Demographics: Implications for Concentration, Entrepreneurship and the Labor Share. *Econometrica, 90*(4), 1879–1914.
Hossenfelder, S. (2018, November 23). The Present Phase of Stagnation in the Foundations of Physics Is Not Normal. *Nautilus*.
Huebner, J. (2005). A Possible Declining Trend for Worldwide Innovation. *Technological Forecasting and Social Change, 72*, 980–986.
Huggel, C., Bouwer, L., Juhola, S., et al. (2022). The Existential Risk Space of Climate Change. *Climatic Change, 174*(8).
Ioannidis, J. (2005). Why Most Published Research Findings Are False. *PLoSMed, 2*(8), e124.
Jackson, T., & Victor, P. (2019). Unraveling the Claims For (and Against) Green Growth. *Science, 366*(6468), 950–951.
Johansen, A., & Sornette, D. (2001). Finite-Time Singularity in the Dynamics of the World Population: Economic and Financial Indices. *Physica A, 294*(3–4), 465–502.
Johnston, R. (2023, February 7). Industrial Policy Nationalism: How Worried Should We Be? *Colombia SIPA*.
Jones, C. I. (2022). The End of Economic Growth? Unintended Consequences of a Declining Population. *American Economic Review, 112*(11), 3489–3527.
Kallis, G. (2011). In Defence of Degrowth. *Ecological Economics, 70*(5), 873–880.
Kallis, G., & March, H. (2015). Imaginaries of Hope: The Utopianism of Degrowth. *Annals of the Association of American Geographers, 105*(2), 360–336.
Kelly, B., Papanikolaou, D., Seru, A., & Taddy, M. (2021). Measuring Technological Innovation over the Long Run. *American Economic Review: Insights, 3*(3), 303–320.

Kendrick, J. (2023, May 10). Kate Raworth: Boundaries Unleash Creativity. *EU Observer.*

Konczal, M., & Steinbaum, M. (2016). *Declining Entrepreneurship, Labor Mobility and Business Dynamism.* Roosevelt Institute.

Kose, M. A., & Ohnsorge, F. (2023). *Falling Long-Term Growth Prospects: Trends, Expectations, and Policies.* The World Bank.

Kuntz, M. (2012). The Postmodern Assault on Science. *EMBO Report, 13*(10), 885–889.

Laeven, L., & Valencia, F. (2020). Systemic Banking Crises Database II. *IMF Economic Review, 68*(2), 307–361.

Lenton, T., Rockström, J., Gaffney, O., Rahmstorf, S., Richardson, K., Steffen, W., & Schellnhuber, H. (2019, November 27). Climate Tipping Points – Too Risky to Bet Against. *Nature.*

Loeb, A. (2023, May 23). Nothing Lasts Forever. *Medium.*

McPhetres, J., & Zuckerman, M. (2018). Religiosity Predicts Negative Attitudes Towards Science and Lower Levels of Science Literacy. *PLoS One, 13*(11), e0207125.

Meho, L. I. (2007). The Rise and Rise of Citation Analysis. *Physics World, 20*(1).

Mokyr, J. (2014, April 28). Growth and Technology: The Wild Ride Ahead. *Milken Institute Review.*

Morris, I. (2015). *Foragers, Farmers, and Fossil Fuels: How Human Values Evolve.* Princeton University Press.

Murphy, T. (2015, September 16). You Call this Progress? *Do the Math Blog.*

Naudé, W. (2008). *Entrepreneurship in Economic Development* (Working Paper 2008/20). UNU-WIDER.

Naudé, W. (2022). From the Entrepreneurial to the Ossified Economy. *Cambridge Journal of Economics, 46*(1), 105–131.

Naudé, W. (2023a). Melancholy Hues: The Futility of Green Growth and Degrowth, and the Inevitability of Societal Collapse. *IZA Discussion Paper No. 16139.*

Naudé, W. (2023b). Seven Reasons why Degrowth is No Solution to the Ecological Crisis. *Illuminem*, 23 Mar.

Naudé, W. & Nagler, P. (2018). *Technological Innovation, Entrepreneurship and Productivity in Germany, 1871–2015* (SPRU Working Paper Series (SWPS), 2018-02). Science Policy Research Unit, University of Sussex.

Nordhaus, T. (2020). Must Growth Doom the Planet? [Review of Growth: From Microorganisms to Megacities, by V. Smil]. *The New Atlantis, 61*, 76–86.

OECD. (2009). *Eco-Innovation in Industry: Enabling Green Growth.*

OECD. (2011). *Towards Green Growth* (OECD Green Growth Studies). OECD Publishing.

OECD. (2014). *Green Growth Indicators 2014* (OECD Green Growth Studies). OECD.

Park, M., Leahy, E., & Funk, R. (2023). Papers and Patents are Becoming Less Disruptive over Time. *Nature, 613*, 138–144.
Phillips, L. (2019, August 30). The Degrowth Delusion. *Open Democracy.*
Pikkety, T. (2013). *Capital in the 21st Century.* Harvard University Press.
Raworth, K. (2017). *Doughnut Economics: Seven Ways to Think Like a 21st-Century Economist.* Random House.
Romer, P. (1986). Increasing Returns and Long-Run Growth. *Journal of Political Economy, 94*(5), 1002–1037.
Romer, P. (1987). Growth Based on Increasing Returns Due to Specialization. *American Economic Review, 77*(2), 56–62.
Romer, P. (1990). Endogenous Technical Change. *Journal of Political Economy, 98*, S71–S102.
Romer, P. (1993). Idea Gaps and Object Gaps in Economic Development. *Journal of Monetary Economics, 32*(3), 543–573.
Romer, P. M. (1994). The Origins of Endogenous Growth. *Journal of Economic Perspectives, 8*(1), 3–22.
Romer, P. (2016, April 13). *The Deep Structure of Economic Growth.* Blog at https://paulromer.net/economic-growth/
Sagan, C. (1997). *The Demon-Haunted World: Science as a Candle in the Dark.* Ballantine Books.
Salgado, S. (2020). *Technical Change and Entrepreneurship.* Mimeo, Wharton School. Available at SSRN.
Schiermeier, Q. (2019, July 1). Soviet Union's Collapse Led to Massive Drop in Carbon Emissions. *Nature.*
Schrager, A. (2022, November 21). Growth Is Still Our Best Hope. *City Journal.*
Sequeira, T., Gil, P., & Alfonso, O. (2018). Endogenous Growth and Entropy. *Journal of Economic Behavior and Organization, 15*, 100–120.
Shahgedanova, M., & Burt, T. (1994). New Data on Air Pollution in the Former Soviet Union. *Global Environmental Change, 4*(3), 201–227.
Solow, R. M. (1956). A Contribution to the Theory of Economic Growth. *The Quarterly Journal of Economics, 70*(1), 65–94.
Steen, R. (2011). Retractions in the Scientific Literature: Is the Incidence of Research Fraud Increasing? *Journal of Medical Ethics, 37*, 249–253.
Steffen, W., Richardson, K., Rockström, J., Cornell, S., Fetzer, I., et al. (2015). Planetary Boundaries: Guiding Human Development on a Changing Planet. *Science, 347*(6223), 1259855.
Syvitski, J., Waters, C., Day, J., et al. (2020). Extraordinary Human Energy Consumption and Resultant Geological Impacts Beginning around 1950 CE Initiated the Proposed Anthropocene Epoch. *Communications Earth and Environment, 1*, 32.
Tenreyro, S. (2018). *The Fall in Productivity Growth: Causes and Implications.* Bank of England Preston Lecture Theatre, Queen Mary University of London.

Ugur, M., Trushin, E., & Solomon, E. (2016). A Firm-Level Dataset for Analyzing Entry, Exit, Employment and R&D Expenditures in the UK: 1997–2012. *Data in Brief, 8*, 153–157.

van den Bergh, J. (2011). Environment versus Growth – A Criticism of Degrowth and a Plea for A-growth. *Ecological Economics, 70*(5), 881–890.

Varieur, B., Fisher, S., & Landrigan, P. (2022). Air Pollution, Political Corruption, and Cardiovascular Disease in the Former Soviet Republics. *Annals of Global Health, 88*(1), 48.

Ward, J., Sutton, P., Werner, A., Costanza, R., Mohr, S., & Simmons, C. (2016). Is Decoupling GDP Growth from Environmental Impact Possible? *PLoS One, 11*(10), e0164733.

Wiedmann, T., Schandl, H., Lenzen, M., Moran, D., Suh, S., West, J., & Kanemoto, K. (2015). The Material Footprint of Nations. *Proceedings of the National Academy of Sciences, 112*(20), 6271–6276.

World Bank. (2012). *Inclusive Green Growth: The Pathway to Sustainable Development*. The World Bank.

Zeihan, P. (2023, February 2). Deglobalization: There's No Stopping It Now. *Zeihan on GeoPolitics.*

CHAPTER 7

Collapse, Unraveling, or Great Simplification?

Abstract This chapter outlines an approach beyond Green Growth and Degrowth: acceptance of an inevitable societal collapse (or unraveling) as a feature, and not a bug, of complexity, and managing such a collapse to minimize harm and get rid of obsolete structures. This may—and it is a big may—herald a phase-transition in economic growth and hence lay the foundation for *rebound growth*, and a transition to a new mode of "growth": which could be as qualitatively different from that characterizing the current global economy as the industrial world was different from the world of the hunter-gatherer economy. It was speculated at the end of this chapter that perhaps the only sustainable outcome, bar a catastrophic collapse, could be some sort of homeostatic awakening. Perhaps the very fact that our Dataome is buzzing with analysis of our ecological overshoot predicament is suggesting that humanity may be experiencing a homeostatic awakening in our collective intelligence.

Keywords Degrowth • Collapse • Unraveling • Great simplification • Phase-transition • Rebound growth • Artificial intelligence • Dataome

7.1 Introduction

What looks like a disaster may be nothing but a passage to a new condition which may be better than the old one—Udo Bardi (2020)

W. Naudé, *Economic Growth and Societal Collapse*,
https://doi.org/10.1007/978-3-031-45582-7_7

The question that remains is what to do about the detritovores if Green Growth and Degrowth are not effective solutions? Perhaps the answer lies in a third way: acceptance of a coming societal collapse, and preparation for a possible rebound that could take place. After all, as Steffen et al. (2015, p. 94) remind us "periods of growth, then collapse, followed by reorganisation is a common pattern in the human past." Is it time for another reorganization of human civilization?

A growing number of scholars have been engaging in this line of thinking, and some view societal collapse as "not a bug, but a feature" of complexity in the universe, arguing that unduly resisting it may only make matters worse (Bardi, 2017). Hagens (2018, 2020), somewhat in line with Tainter's view that collapse is a result of societies becoming too bureaucratic and inflexible because of growing complexity, recommends that the world prepare for a post-collapse, or *Great Simplification*. For Bardi (2017), collapse would offer the opportunity to "get rid of obsolete structures."

This chapter briefly, but critically, sets out the broad case for this view, noting at the outset that the scholarly and policy work on societal collapse is less established and less aligned than that of Green Growth and Degrowth. It is an emerging and diverse field that also touches on complex ethical issues—as among others the Longtermism movement has controversially raised (see e.g. MacAskill (2022) and Torres (2021))—of which a full analysis falls outside the scope of this book.

7.2 Trajectories of Civilization

The question that remains is what to do about the detritovores, if (exponential) growth, Green Growth, and Degrowth are fairy tales, that is, not effective solutions? One way to approach this is to ask what the long-term possible trajectories for human civilization may be. This is a question that Baum et al. (2019) tried to answer. Figure 7.1 is an adaptation of their exploration.

Figure 7.1 summarizes the key future trajectories that Baum et al. (2019) envisaged for human civilization, plus some elaborations. Baum et al. (2019) distinguishes between three possibilities: maintenance of the status quo, a positive technological transformation trajectory and/or an astronomical trajectory (where humans become spacefaring, and a catastrophe trajectory. The maintenance and technology/astronomical

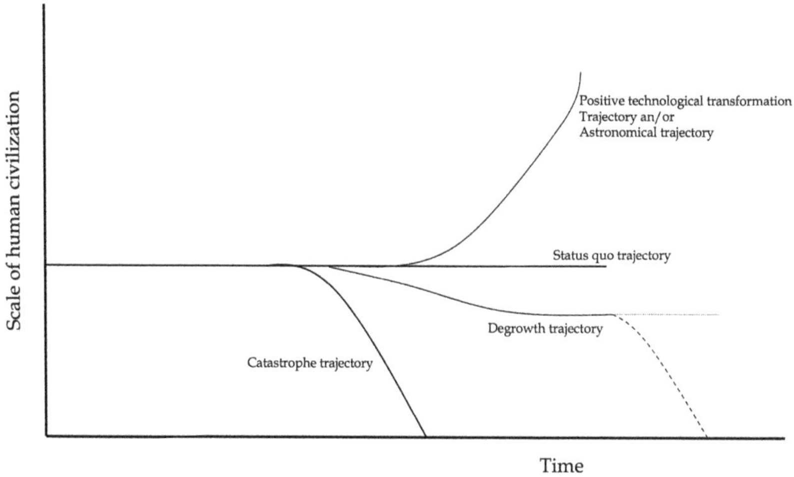

Fig. 7.1 Simple trajectories of human civilization. (Source: Author's adaptation of Fig. 1 of Baum et al., 2019, p. 55)

trajectories lean on Green Growth and the longtermism fantasies that drive the Silicon Valley Mindset.

To these I have added the Degrowth trajectory. It is shown as a lowering of the scale of human civilization compared to the status quo. Eventually though, the Degrowth trajectory turns into collapse/ catastrophe, as it robs a large population of the resources to solve problems.

The trajectories as set out in Fig. 7.1 are unsatisfactory. Clearly, from the content covered in this book, the status quo is not an option. Neither are Green Growth and its basis in the fantasies of Silicon Valley an option. Does the future trajectory of human civilization then boil down to a choice between a self-imposed (and likely totalitarian) downgrade and steered collapse, or an uncontrolled collapse? Or is there another way?

7.3 Collapse as the End of the World?

Easter Island (Rapa Nui), a remote Polynesian island in the southeastern Pacific, is one of the most studied historical cases of societal collapse following an ecological crisis. Between roughly 1200 AD and 1600 AD it had a complex, developing society, numbering around 15,000 by 1600. It then dramatically collapsed, to around 2000 inhabitants by 1700.

Diamond (2005), not uncontroversially,[1] ascribed this to the overshoot of the ecological system of the island. Decker and Reuveny (2005) asked "Could Simon and Boserup Have Saved Easter Island?" with reference to the view of Cornucopians like Julian Simon and Ester Boserup (see Chap. 2) that technological innovation (driven by population pressure) can prevent a civilization falling into a Malthusian trap as happened on Easter Island.

To try and answer this question, they construct a mathematical model to simulate a closed-system economy such as remote Easter Island, wherein technological innovation is endogenously determined by, among others, population growth and ecological pressures. From their model simulations they conclude that "endogenous innovation in the spirit of Simon and Boserup would not have saved Easter Island [...] It is questionable whether endogenous technological progress alone could save contemporary societies from a similar fate" (Decker & Reuveny, 2005, pp. 137, 138).

More than forty years before Decker and Reuveny (2005) simulated the collapse of Easter Island, the first mathematical, computer-based simulation model to study potential societal collapse was the *World*[3] model used to generate the predictions for the 1972 Club of Rome's Limits to Growth (LtG) study (Meadows et al., 1972). This study concluded that,

> *If the present growth trends in world population, industrialization, pollution, food production, and resource depletion continue unchanged, the limits to growth on this planet will be reached sometime within the next one hundred years* (Meadows et al., 1972, p. 23).

Its standard-run scenario, under business-as-usual conditions, predicted the limits to be reached, and the collapse of global society, around the middle of the twenty-first century (Turner, 2008). Updates of the LtG study by Turner (2014) and Herrington (2021) confirmed that the global economy was continuing to track the standard-run scenario well, implying that an Easter-Island-like fate may await global society in the near future.

The LtG study stimulated much scholarly work on environmental limits and their role in potential societal collapse. Subsequent contributions include Tainter (1988), Odum and Odum (2001), Weiss and Bradley

[1] An alternative to Diamond's (2005) theory of ecocide has been suggested by DiNapoli et al. (2020) who suggests that it was contact with Europeans, from the 1720s onwards, that led to the collapse of Rapa Nui's civilization.

(2001), Diamond (2005), Bardi (2020) Kemp et al. (2022), and Turchin (2023).

Tainter (1988, p. 4) defined societal collapse as having occurred when a society "displays a rapid, significant loss of an established level of socio-political complexity." He describes the immediate aftermath of collapse as follows (Tainter, 1988, p. 20):

> *The overarching structure that provides support services to the population loses capability or disappears entirely. No longer can the populace rely upon external defense and internal order, maintenance of public works, or delivery of food and material goods. Organization reduces to the lowest level that is economically sustainable, so that a variety of contending polities exist where there had been peace and unity. Remaining populations must become locally self-sufficient to a degree not seen for several generations. Groups that had formerly been economic and political partners now become strangers, even threatening competitors.*

There are several key causes of societal collapse discussed in the literature—it is not only ecological overshoot that poses a threat. For instance, existential hazards can cause a catastrophic (terminal end) collapse of society, and these hazards include nuclear war, artificial intelligence, a meteor impact, and a runaway pandemic (Ord, 2020). Societal collapse can also be the outcome of some sort of social overshoot or *social rot.*

Tainter (1988) explicitly linked collapse to complexity of civilization. Civilizations face never-ending problems, which rising complexity is an approach to solve. However, at some stage, rising complexity as problem-solving mechanism becomes subject to diminishing returns.

Burja (2020) argues that societal collapse is the eventual outcome of a succession problem, namely, how to ensure that the knowledge, expertise, and values required to manage a complex civilization gets adequately transferred to new generations. When societies fail in doing so, the slow erosion of knowledge—rot—leads to an intellectual Dark Age that precedes an actual collapse (Dark Age).

Turchin (2023) ascribes societal collapse to an overproduction of elites and immiseration of non-elites, which leads to a counter-elite revolt, which results in rising inequality, growing distrust and a breakdown of social resilience. The outcome is the eventual political disintegration of society. Using cliodynamics, Turchin (2023) finds that nations rise and fall through cycles of integration and disintegration each lasting around ~100 years on average.

Both Burja (2020) and Turchin (2023) see the writing on the wall as far as Western civilization is concerned. Turchin and Gavrilets (2009), for example, argue that as states attempt to control larger and larger populations, they construct larger and more complex hierarchies (bureaucracies) that at first have a politically and socially integrative result as they overcome the collective action problem. However, at some stage, due to various reasons, among them inter-elite conflict, these hierarchies start to unravel, and the collective action problem and its correlates reassert themselves. They consider the EU already as past this point, which is leading to a "reversal of the dynamic of integration" in the EU (Turchin & Gavrilets, 2009, p. 187).

Brozović (2023) surveys the literature on societal collapse brought about by an ecological overshoot.[2] He finds that among those who consider global societal collapse as inevitable, there is a tension between those who think that collapse will be irreversible, and bring about a dystopian future, and those who hope that it is but a painful, but necessary step, to a possibly better future.

Those who associate societal collapse with a dystopian future (i.e., as the end of the world), expect, in line with the LtG study's predictions, collapse to occur rapidly and to be irreversible.[3] The trajectory of human civilization (and of GDP, given the focus in this paper on GDP growth) will in this pessimistic view follow a Seneca curve (see Fig. 7.2), named after the Stoic philosopher Lucius Seneca who emphasized that "increases are of sluggish growth, but the way to ruin is rapid" (Bardi, 2020, p. 68).

The predictions of the LtG study follow the trajectory of Fig. 7.2—hence Turner (2014), in an update and review of the LtG study, concludes that "*it would appear that the global economy and population is on the cusp of collapse.*"

[2] It is related to the more recent literature that deals with the potential existential risks that humanity faces—a literature that largely dates to 2002 to Bostrom (2002) who coined the term "existential risk."

[3] An example is Clagston (2023), who argues that the "complete and permanent collapse of human industrialism" will occur around 2050.

Fig. 7.2 The Seneca Curve: The way to ruin is rapid. (Source: Author's compilation based on Bardi (2020))

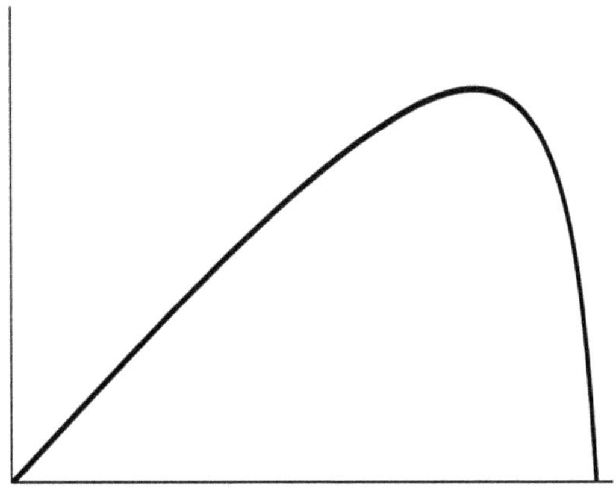

7.4 Collapse as the Beginning of a New World?

Others are, however, less pessimistic about the idea of societal collapse. Even Tainter (1988) who provided one of the earliest studies concluded that "whether collapse is *universally* a catastrophe, though, is an uncertain matter" (Tainter, 1988, p. 21). When it becomes too costly to maintain a complex civilization, in relation to the benefits that such complex bestows to solve problems, the solution is to de-complexify civilization.[4]

The idea that societal collapse should be acknowledged and even welcomed as the beginning of a new world, rather than the end of the world, has found expression in the work of, among others, Bardi (2020), Odum and Odum (2001), and Scranton (2015). Relatedly, Vollrath (2019) has argued that the stagnation in economic growth that has already set in in many economies, and which is expected to deepen as one would expect as the fossil fuel bonanza runs out, and these societies age, should be seen as a "sign of success."

McAnany and Yoffee (2010) questioned the very notion of "collapse," arguing that most previous societies that have been described as having

[4]Tainter's (1988) work implies that given the polycrisis facing civilization, the appearance of additional stressors that draw on its resources can tip it into collapse. It may thus be very likely that imposing the stressor to degrow—to starve society of its material and energy inputs—may be the stressor that accelerates collapse.

collapsed may rather have transformed and evolved,[5] indicating enduring resilience of human societies. For Ehrenreich (2020), like McAnany and Yoffee (2010), the notion of "collapse" underplays the nature of change, resilience, and adaptability of humans. He writes that,

> *If you close your eyes and open them again, the periodic disintegrations that punctuate our history — all those crumbling ruins — begin to fade, and something else comes into focus: wiliness, stubbornness and, perhaps the strongest and most essential human trait, adaptabilit […]. Perhaps it is what we do best. When one way doesn't work, we try another. When one system fails, we build another. We struggle to do things differently, and we push on. As always, we have no other choice.*

Bardi (2020, p. 4), like Tainter (1988), defines societal collapse with reference to complexity, stating that collapse is "a phase transition that leads to a state of reduced complexity, typically being rapid and abrupt." He argues (p. 53) that there can be six growth modes in principle characterizing the evolution of complex systems such as the economy.

These are (i) the *Solow mode* where, as many Cornucopians believe, the economy can continue to grow exponentially indefinitely; (ii) the *Malthus mode* where the economy grows until a certain size and then stop growing; (iii) the *Hubbert mode* where the economy grows to a certain size and then gradually declines following an inverted bell-shape trajectory; (iv) the *Seneca mode,* as discussed in Sect. 7.3, where the economy grows gradually over a long period and thereafter suddenly collapses; (v) the *Hokusai mode,* where the economy suddenly collapses as a result of an external existential impact, for instance, caused by a meteorite or catastrophic pandemic; and (vi) the *Seneca Rebound mode* (also described as the Lotka-Volterra mode), where the economy collapses but recovers and restarts growth following a series of cycles.

These potential six growth models of complex systems are depicted in Fig. 7.3.

[5] Greer (2005, pp. 11–12) prefers the term "succession" to collapse, arguing that the term collapse is associated only with negative connotations, while it may entail also opportunity for societal renewal and diversification, pointing out that the "Roman collapse enabled other societies to emerge from Rome's shadow, and launched major cultural initiatives such as vernacular literatures in the ancestors of today's Celtic, Germanic, and Romance languages." One could argue that modern Western Civilization and its Western Offshoots are the eventual succession to the Roman Empire.

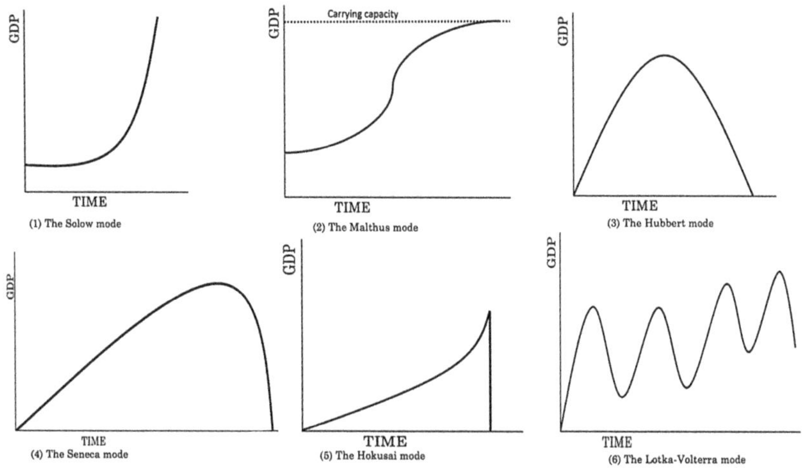

Fig. 7.3 Six growth modes of complex systems. (Source: Author's compilation based on Bardi (2020))

In terms of the modes depicted in Fig. 7.3, proponents of exponential and of Green Growth, implicitly if not explicitly at least, are under the illusion that the global economy is a complex system in the Solow Mode. The Degrowth Movement seems implicitly to labor under the illusion that the global economy follows either a Seneca or a Hubbert mode, or even that abrupt climate change could imply a *Hokusai mode*. They want to avoid this by a deliberate invoking of the *Hubbert mode* but forcing GDP (the complexity of the system) down to a level commensurate with the Malthus mode. It may, however, as has been remarked, trigger a faster collapse by putting further stressors on an overburdened system.

Put in this way, the difference between Green Growth and Degrowth is a difference between assumptions—or illusions—on the kind of growth mode that best characterizes the complex global economic system. Putting it this way also shows that there is another growth mode that neither Green Growth nor Degrowth has considered: that the global economic system is following a Lotka-Volterra (*Seneca Rebound*) mode.

One reason why perhaps neither Green Growth nor Degrowth consider this, is that analyzing such an economic system requires much deeper understanding of complexity and how complex systems' evolutionary paths are shaped. Bardi (2020, p. 181) quotes Meadows, one of the authors of the LtG study, as admitting that "The Limits of Growth cannot mimic the emergence of the industrial revolution from the agrarian age. Nor, admits Meadows, can it take the world from the industrial revolution to whatever follows next beyond that."

If indeed the global economic system would over time follow an oscillating pattern described by the Seneca Rebound mode, then societal collapse could be seen as "not a bug, but a feature" of complexity in the universe (Bardi, 2017).

Hagens (2020) seems to see collapse, if not as a feature, as inevitable, and, in line with Tainter's (1988) view that collapse is a result of societies becoming too bureaucratic and inflexible as a result of trying to assert control over its growing complexity, recommends[6] that the world prepare for a post-collapse, or "Great Simplification," inter alia by putting in place advance policies[7] that are "solutions that the political and economic world are not yet ready to implement but will be critically important to plan for."

Such a Great Simplification with *advance policies* is consistent with Bardi's (2020, pp. ix–xx) view that if collapse is not to be avoided, one should try to soften the blow (i.e., advance policies), but moreover that collapse—and a subsequent Great Stagnation—would offer the opportunity to "get rid of obsolete structures." This could lay the foundation for rebound growth and a transition to a new kind of economy—a kind of economy that we cannot now envisage, and that could be as qualitatively different from the current global economy as the industrial world was different from the world of the hunter-gatherer economy.

From a physics point of view, this is not ruled out. Physicists indeed consider rising and then falling complexity as a fundamental feature of the universe, given the Second Law of Thermodynamics that states that the entropy in a closed system (which the universe is) will always increase. Rising complexity can be seen as how the Universe accelerates from high order (low entropy) that marked the beginning of the universe (as a singularity before the Big Bang) to disorder (high entropy) that will mark the end of the universe.

[6] See for instance Nate Hagens' the *Great Simplification* Podcast at https://www.thegreatsimplification.com/

[7] For the case for advance policy, See Nate Hagens at https://vimeo.com/520475641. An example of a proposed advance policy is to put systems in place to "untax" human labor and tax nonrenewable inputs at source.

Aaronson et al. (2014, p. 1) explains that "our universe lacked complex structures at the Big Bang and will also lack them after black holes evaporate and particles are dispersed." They use the example of milk being poured into a cup of black coffee: at first, the black coffee has low complexity and high entropy. Once the milk is poured and its molecules interact with the coffee, it creates highly complex patterns, until the milk is fully dissipated and the coffee assumes an equal brown color—a state of low complexity and higher entropy (Aaronson et al., 2014).

Olson (2015, p. 1) points out that in the universe, "the appearance of aggressively expanding advanced life is geometrically similar to the process of nucleation and bubble growth in a first-order cosmological phase transition" and provides a model that describes how an intelligent complex civilization could arise and expand (i.e., increase its complexity and material footprint over time). Over time, such civilizations arise throughout the universe (not only on planet Earth) and utilize such amounts of energy that this and the resultant radiation eventually change the very physical structure of the universe.

This has been taken to imply that "we have completely misjudged the significance of life to the universe. Intelligent life may be the universe's large-scale, general-purpose tool for seeking out and minimizing deeply hidden reserves of free energy" (Fullarton, 2016). In other words, such as humans have been doing with the energy bolus. In Olson's (2015) model, while the universe is a closed system, the Earth and other planets are not—the Earth will continue to receive energy from its sun for another roughly 5 billion years.

The Second Law of Thermodynamics and its implications for whether economic growth could resemble a Seneca Rebound mode, therefore raises the question: Is the Earth really, for all intents and purposes, an open system, or is it a closed system?

The Earth is not a closed system because it is clearly, in a thermodynamic sense, out of equilibrium—and this makes the planet habitable (Kleidon, 2012). Boulding (1966), in making the argument that the planet is a "Spaceship Earth," acknowledged that this is because the Earth is an open system with respect to energy from the sun but stressed that it is a closed system with respect to materials. The belief in a Solow Mode of growth depends on humans obtaining more material-use efficiency, for example, through recycling, and continued value-added growth through recombination of ideas and materials, and that the energy that will be needed to enable this recycling and recombinatory growth can be obtained from more efficiently harnessing renewable energy from the sun. After all, "our total energy use is approximately 17 TW, which is roughly 10,000 times less than the power of the radiant solar energy arriving at the upper atmosphere" (Buchanan, 2017, p. 106).

Given the timescales that better harnessing the power of radiant solar energy would require against the timescales of peak oil, it seems unlikely that the global economy would follow a Solow mode of growth. Some collapse—unraveling—may be inevitable. Whether this will eventually rebound, perhaps characterized by qualitatively different growth as discussed, thus depends on whether humans can manage the transition from being Detritovores and manage the innovation to generate the technology to harness sufficient energy.[8] If so, and these may be big ifs, a Seneca Rebound may be the relevant growth mode, and humanity will be able to continue to fulfill its speculative destiny as the universe's tool to seek out and minimize "deeply hidden reserves of free energy." Or not. There is one other puzzle to consider, which may help shift our prior probabilities for a Seneca Rebound in either one or the other direction.

7.5 Homeostatic Awakening

7.5.1 *The Eerie Silence*

In 1950, reputedly during lunch, the Nobel laureate physicist Enrico Fermi posed the question "*where is everybody?*" referring to the lack of evidence for any other civilization in the universe (Gray, 2015). Fermi's question has been turned into Fermi's Paradox (Hart, 1975), which is a paradox since, given the age of the universe (13.8 billion years) and the potential number of habitable planets, there should have been enough time for an advanced civilization to arise and become spacefaring and colonize the galaxy.

How can an advanced civilization, once it has arisen, colonize the galaxy? It has been calculated that an advanced civilization uses self-reproducing intelligent starprobes, known as Von Neumann Probes, and only travelling at 1/10th the speed of light, the entire Milky Way Galaxy could

[8] Not all scientists are convinced that seeking to harness renewable solar energy in this way would be appropriate. Murphy (2022) is concerned that "if every jackass on the planet has access to cheap and abundant energy, what do you think they'll do with it? Will they use it to restore ecosystems, or hack more of it down for their own short-term gain?"

be covered in 500,000 years (Valdes and Freitas Jr., 1980). According to Matloff (2022, p. 206), "From a technological point of view, there seems to be no obstacle to the ultimate terrestrial construction of Von Neumann probes."

Even if we do not meet any Von Neumann Probes, the techno-signatures of advanced alien civilizations ought to have been observed by now. This is especially the case since the more advanced and complex a civilization becomes, the greater is its energy consumption. Kardashev (1964) proposed that civilizations can be classified in terms of their technological ability to utilize energy. The Earth is almost a Type I civilization.[9] A Type II civilization would utilize all the energy from its sun, for example, through construction of a Dyson sphere—which we should be able to observe; and a Type III civilization would utilize all the energy from all the stars in its galaxy.

The rise and spread of civilization need only have happened once for us to have been aware of their presence by now. But despite all efforts, and the Search for Extraterrestrial Intelligence (SETI), there is until now no evidence of any other civilization in the universe. Instead of extraterrestrials (ET), we have been met by a Great Silence, or an *Eerie Silence*, according to Davies (2010).

7.5.2 The Great Filter

The *Eerie Silence* has been taken to possibly suggest that there is a "Great Filter" that prevents the rise and/or survival of technologically advanced civilizations (Hanson, 1998). The Great Filter should be understood as several very unlikely steps that need to be taken for life to originate and develop into a spacefaring civilization. If any one of these steps cannot be accomplished, civilizations' possibilities may be truncated. It has for instance been suggested that catastrophic climate change due to ecological overshoot (driven by energy and technologies) may act as a Great Filter in future to truncate human civilization. Perhaps similar mechanisms operate throughout the universe—those civilizations cannot arise beyond the

[9] Between 1800 and 2019, human energy consumption grew twenty-eight times, resulting in human civilization moving from a Kardashev Civilization of degree 0.58 to one of degree 0.725. At current trends, it is predicted to become a Kardashev Type I Civilization by the year 2406 (±16 years) (Re, 2022).

ecological overshoot point. This may explain the Eerie Silence and Fermi's Paradox.

Understanding more about the nature of life and how likely it can arise in the universe is of cardinal importance in settling this. For instance, let the number of civilizations in the universe be determined by Npq, where N = the number of planets that are habitable; p is the probability that on one of these a civilization develops and q is the conditional probability that it becomes a spacefaring, galaxy-colonizing civilization (following the astronomical trajectory—see Fig. 7.1). Current estimates are that there are a very large number of potentially habitable planets with $\approx 2 \times 10^{19}$ terrestrial planets around Sun-like stars and $\approx 7 \times 10^{20}$ around M-dwarf like stars (Zackrisson et al., 2016). The lack of any evidence for any other civilization in the universe suggests that p is very small (Bostrom, 2008).

Therefore, the importance of the SETI is that it may help us pin down whether the Great Filter is ahead of human civilization, or whether we may have passed it. If SETI would discover evidence of life outside of planet Earth—such as microbes on Mars—it may indicate that p is large, and hence that the absence of other civilizations means that q is very small. This would mean the Great Filter is ahead of humanity (Bostrom, 2008). This would imply that growth and subsequent collapse may be following a *Seneca Mode*, after all. The search for extraterrestrial intelligence (SETI) has therefore great value in potentially resolving uncertainty about the possibility of a Seneca Rebound.

7.5.3 *Asymptotic Burnout*

It takes all the running you can do just to stay in the same place—Lewis Carroll, in *Alice in Wonderland*.

There is one solution or answer to the Fermi Paradox that is consistent with the Seneca Rebound mode (Lotka-Volterra) of civilizational development, as well as with the Malthus mode. This is that civilizations follow, as a fundamental scaling law, a growth trajectory that leads to "asymptotic burnout"—when economic scale increases to such an extent that planetary systems are overshot. Either such civilizations collapse—which is why there is no evidence (so far) in the Universe of them—or they achieve what Wong and Bartlett (2022) call "homeostatic awakening"—when the civilization becomes aware of its own trajectory and succeeds in adjusting it to be consistent with planetary boundaries. Thus, "civilizations either collapse from burnout or redirect themselves to prioritizing homeostasis, a state where cosmic expansion is no longer a goal, making them difficult to detect remotely" (Wong and Bartlett, 2022).

Figure 7.4 summarizes the asymptotic burnout argument depicting a trajectory that is virtually identical to the Lotka-Volterra (Seneca Rebound) mode as shown in Fig. 7.3. It depicts a metacycle of collapse (Wong and Bartlett, 2022) and successive super-exponential growth trajectories (West, 2017). The scale of human civilization grows super-exponentially (as in Fig. 2.1). At some stage, it approaches a "singularity"—or what in present terms is ecological overshoot. Johansen and Sornette (2001) had previously raised this notion of a singularity (a "finite-time singularity") in terms of super-exponential growth, which refers to a phase-transition of sorts (like water becoming steam at high temperatures) since mathematically, the "acceleration of the growth rate contains endogenously its limit in the shape of a finite-time singularity to be interpreted as a transition to a qualitatively new behaviour" (Johansen & Sornette, 2001, p. 1). They

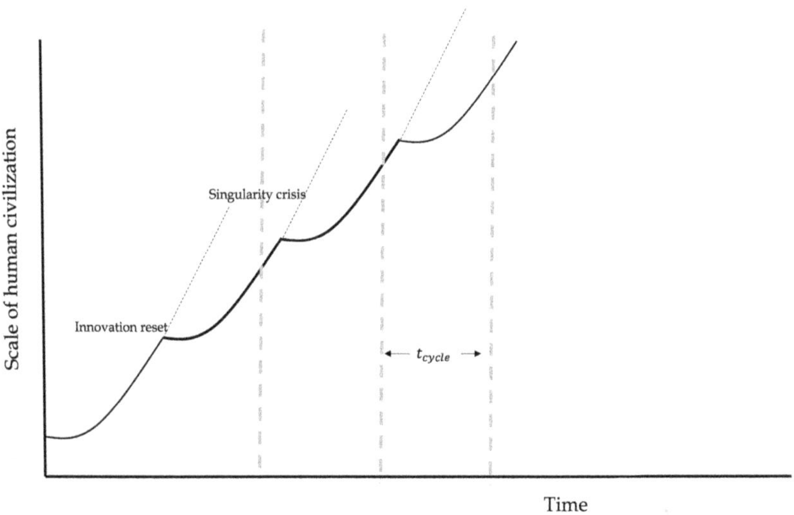

Fig. 7.4 Red Queen Effect and asymptotic burnout. (Source: Author's compilation based on Wong and Bartlett (2022), Bettencourt et al. (2007) and West, 2017))

predicted that this singularity will occur around the year 2052 ± 10 years[10]—incidentally not far off from the 2040 predicted for peak oil.[11]

This "singularity crisis," caused by overshoot through growth approaching "infinity" and demanding more and more resources, can be avoided through an *innovation reset*: adoption of some technology that allows growth to continue. For instance, human civilization has seen different growth modes through its history, from that characterizing forager societies to that underlying industrial societies, and in each successive new growth mode, growth accelerated.

But this only postpones the final reckoning—kicking the proverbial can down the road. Wong and Bartlett (2022) define the t_{cycle} as the time interval between innovation resets. As the scale of human civilization increases, the t_{cycle} becomes shorter. It means that society must innovate at a faster and faster rate (West, 2017). It is a *Red Queen Effect*, after the character of the Red Queen in *Alice in Wonderland* who exclaimed that "it takes all the running you can do just to stay in the same place."

Eventually, the t_{cycle} will become too short for civilization to come up with another innovation reset. Indeed, in the case of current human civilization, as Chap. 6 (Sect. 6.3) has shown, innovation is not getting faster and faster, but seems to be slowing down.

At this point, civilization may realize that it has no choice but to break the Red Queen cycle and try to achieve homeostasis with the Earth System on which it depends. In this "homeostatic awakening," civilization may reprioritize away from an economic system that creates EGOs, winner-take-all outcomes, political and environmental disintegration, and terminate any ambitions it could have to colonize the galaxy.

Perhaps human civilization has entered, or is approaching, a state of homeostatic awakening. The Dataome may be playing a potentially central role in this. Wong and Bartlett (2022) explain that the Dataome is facilitating the emergence of a planetary mind by removing physical limitations in communication and increasingly driving not only human-to-human information sharing, but computer-to-computer information sharing, and the emergence of AI that represents a new phase in planetary collective

[10] Jorgen Randers, a coauthor of the 1973 LtG study, published a book in 2012 called "2052: A Global Forecast for the Next 40 years," wherein he concludes that by the year 2052 things will be "getting worse" (Randers, 2012,p. 15).

[11] As mentioned, Sequeira et al. (2018) developed an endogenous economic growth model with a "complexity index'" in which economic growth is finite. Their model dynamics predict that the current economic slowdown (also reflected in the slowdown in TFP—see Chap. 6) will continue until economic growth collapses completely around the year 2450.

intelligence. Maybe it is indeed the case the technology evolves, and as the saying goes that a scholar is a library's way of multiplying, so human civilization may ultimately be the way that technology and its representation as the Dataome evolve. Matt Ridley, among others, has argued that technology indeed seems to evolve in this way, that "technology is driving its own progress" (Ridley, 2015, p. 125). And as Cesar Hidalgo has pointed out "the universe is made of energy, matter and information, and while energy and matter are here by default, information needs to find ways to emerge" (Hidalgo, 2015, p. 175). Through the Dataome, technology seems to be driving the emergence of information, and through its channeling of energy and matter, it is "getting its from bits" as John Wheeler termed it[12] (Wheeler, 1989; Wilczek, 1999).

The Dataome seems to be constructing a model of reality that "reveals the trajectory" humanity is on (Wong and Bartlett, 2022), and at the same time questioning the very trajectory that the industrial revolution has put the planet on. It seems to be sharing information and directing the search for further information on how to deal with the potential of ecological overshoot. This book, which the reader is likely to read in electronic format, and which is disseminated across the planet at the speed of light through the Internet and emails, is part of this internal conversation that the Dataome is having on its future. The debates between Green Growth and Degrowth are indeed largely conducted in the Dataome. The Dataome is conversing with itself.

Whether the Dataome will be able to guide the identification, selection, and application of actions that will result in planetary homeostasis is the question. The Dataome, like a human brain, may be infected with bad memes, mis- and disinformation, and cancerous-like growth of useless information. Social media for example may be amplifying extreme views—including extreme views and biased online journalism on climate change (Lim & Bentley, 2022; Pielke, 2023). The prospect of a digital dystopia must be taken seriously (Tirole, 2021). But it may also be that our homeostatic awakening is taking place too late—that we will not have enough time to correct for our ecological overshoot trajectory.

[12] As Wheeler (1989, p. 311) argued, "all things physical are information-theoretic in origin." Hidalgo (2015) refers to physical objects produced by humans as "crystallized imagination," giving the example that "iPhones and iPads are mental exports rather than imports, since they are products that were begotten in our minds before they became part of the world" (Hidalgo, 2015, p. 50).

7.6 Concluding Remarks

This chapter asked what to do about the detritovores, if (exponential) growth, Green Growth, and Degrowth are not effective solutions? Two possibilities for humanity beyond Degrowth and Green Growth were discussed in this closing chapter of the book.

The first was that societal collapse may be inevitable—and the end. Collapse could result in humanity ending up in a dystopian future—with a fate like that of the inhabitants of Easter Island (Diamond, 2005).

The second is that collapse could, as an increasing number of scholars have been arguing, be necessary to make a new mode of economic growth—rebound growth—possible (Bardi, 2017; Beard & Torres, 2020; Odum & Odum, 2001; Scranton, 2015). Phoenix-like, a new and better society may arise.[13] In this view, collapse may be a feature, not a bug, of universal patterns characterizing growth from the smallest to the grandest scale (Bardi, 2017; West, 2017).

The interest in societal collapse rose noticeably following the slowdown in Western growth rates in the 1970s and 1980s, starting with the Club of Rome's *Limits to Growth* (LtG) report in 1972 Meadows et al. (1972). The tone was further set by Joseph Tainter, in his 1988 book *The Collapse of Complex Societies* (Tainter, 1988) and John Leslie's 1996 book *The End of the World* (Leslie, 1996). More recently, Hagens (2018, 2020), somewhat reflecting Tainter's view that collapse is a result of societies becoming too bureaucratic and inflexible because of growing complexity, recommended that the world prepare for a post-collapse, or *Great Simplification*.[14] For Bardi (2017), collapse would offer the opportunity to "get rid of obsolete structures."

In the next and final chapter, we will consider what some of these obsolete structures could be.

[13] The question is whether collapse will entail the extinction of humanity. Ord (2020), in his study of existential risks facing humanity, concludes that while the risks from climate change and environmental damage are serious, and higher than the risks of extinction from natural risks (which he puts at a probability of less than 0.05% per century), there is nevertheless a significant probability that humanity will survive. Collapse indeed needs not be fatal.

[14] See https://www.thegreatsimplification.com/

References

Aaronson, S., Carroll, S., & Ouellette, L. (2014). Quantifying the Rise and Fall of Complexity in Closed Systems: The Coffee Automaton. *arXiv:1405.6903* [cond-mat.stat-mech].

Bardi, U. (2017). *The Seneca Effect: Why Growth Is Slow, But Collapse Is Rapid*. Springer.

Bardi, U. (2020). *Before the Collapse: A Guide to the Other Side of Growth*. Springer.

Baum, S. D., Armstrong, S., Ekenstedt, T., Häggström, O., Hanson, R., Kuhlemann, K., Maas, M. M., Miller, J. D., Salmela, M., Sandberg, A., Sotala, K., Torres, P., Turchin, A., & Yampolskiy, R. V. (2019). Long-Term Trajectories of Human Civilization. *Foresight, 21*(1), 53–83.

Beard, S., & Torres, E. (2020, March 12). *Ripples on the Great Sea of Life: A Brief History of Existential Risk Studies*. Mimeo. SSRN.

Bettencourt, L. M., Lobo, J., Helbing, D., Kühnert, C., & West, G. B. (2007). Growth, Innovation, Scaling, and the Pace of Life in Cities. *Proceedings of the National Academy of Sciences, 104*, 7301–7306.

Bostrom, N. (2002). Existential Risks: Analyzing Human Extinction Scenarios and Related Hazards. *Journal of Evolution and Technology, 9*(1).

Bostrom, N. (2008). Where Are They? Why I Hope the Search for Extraterrestrial Life Find Nothing. *MIT Technology Review*, May/June:72–77.

Boulding, K. (1966). The Economics of the Coming Spaceship Earth. In H. Jarrett (Ed.), *Environmental Quality in a Growing Economy* (pp. 3–14). Resources for the Future/Johns Hopkins University Press.

Brozović, D. (2023). Societal Collapse: A Literature Review. *Futures, 145*, 103–175.

Buchanan, M. (2017). The Thermodynamics of Earth. *Nature Physics, 13*, 106.

Burja, S. (2020, August 19). Why Civilizations Collapse. *The Side View*.

Clugston, C. O. (2023). *Industrialism – Our Commitment to Impermanence*. Booklocker.

Davies, P. (2010). *The Eerie Silence: Renewing Our Search for Alien Intelligence*. Houghton Mifflin.

Decker, C. S., & Reuveny, R. (2005). Endogenous Technological Progress and the Malthusian Trap: Could Simon and Boserup Have Saved Easter Island? *Human Ecology, 33*(1), 119–140.

Diamond, J. (2005). *Collapse: How Societies Choose to Fail or Succeed*. Viking Press.

DiNapoli, R., Rieth, T., Lipo, C., & Hunt, T. (2020). A Model-Based Approach to the Tempo of Collapse: The Case of Rapa Nui (Easter Island). *Journal of Archaeological Science, 116*, 105094.

Ehrenreich, B. (2020, November 4). How Do You Know When Society Is About to Fall Apart? *New York Times Magazine*.

Fullarton, C. (2016, January 27). Life-Altered Cosmologies. *CQG+*.

Gray, R. (2015). The Fermi Paradox Is Neither Fermi's Nor a Paradox. *Astrobiology, 15*(3), 195–199.
Greer, J. M. (2005). *How Civilizations Fall: A Theory Of Catabolic Collapse.* At https://www.ecoshock.org/transcripts/greer_on_collapse.pdf
Hagens, N. (2018, April 23). Where are We Going? *Resilience.*
Hagens, N. (2020). Economics for the Future – Beyond the Superorganism. *Ecological Economics, 169*, 106520.
Hanson, R. (1998, September 15). *The Great Filter – Are We Almost Past It?* Mimeo.
Hart, M. (1975). An Explanation for the Absence of Extraterrestrials on Earth. *Quarterly Journal of the Royal Astronomical Society, 16*, 128–135.
Herrington, G. (2021). Update to Limits to Growth: Comparing the World3 Model with Empirical Data. *Journal of Industrial Ecology, 25*(3), 614–626.
Hidalgo, C. (2015). *Why Information Grows: The Evolution of Order, from Atoms to Economies.* Penguin.
Johansen, A., & Sornette, D. (2001). Finite-Time Singularity in the Dynamics of the World Population: Economic and Financial Indices. *Physica A, 294*(3–4), 465–502.
Kardashev, N. (1964). Transmission of Information by extraterrestrial Civilizations. *Soviet Astronomy.*
Kemp, L., Xu, C., Depledge, J., Ebi, K., Gibbins, G., Kohler, T., Rockström, J., Scheffer, M., Schellnhuber, H., Steffen, W., & Lenton, T. (2022). Climate Endgame: Exploring Catastrophic Climate Change Scenarios. *Proceedings of the National Academy of Sciences, 119*(34), e2108146119.
Kleidon, A. (2012). How Does the Earth System Generate and Maintain Thermodynamic Disequilibrium and What does It Imply for the Future of the Planet? *Philosophical Transactions A: Mathematical, Physical and Engineering Sciences, 370*(1962), 1012–1040.
Leslie, J. (1996). *The End of the World: The Science and Ethics of Human Extinction.* Routledge.
Lim, S., & Bentley, P. J. (2022). Opinion Amplification Causes Extreme Polarization in Social Networks. *Scientific Reports, 12*, 18131.
MacAskill, W. (2022). *What We Owe the Future.* Basic Books.
Matloff, G. (2022). Von Neumann Probes: Rationale, Propulsion, Interstellar Transfer Timing. *International Journal of Astrobiology, 21*(4), 205–211.
McAnany, P. A., & Yoffee, N. (2010). *Questioning Collapse: Human Resilience, Ecological Vulnerability, and the Aftermath of Empire.* Cambridge University Press.
Meadows, D., Meadows, D., Randers, J., & Behrens, W., III. (1972). *The Limits to Growth; A Report for the Club of Rome's Project on the Predicament of Mankind.* Universe Books.
Murphy, T. (2022, February 16). Human Exceptionalism. *Do the Math Blog.*

Odum, H., & Odum, E. (2001). *A Prosperous Way Down: Principles and Policies.* University Press of Colorado.

Olson, S. J. (2015). Homogeneous Cosmology with Aggressively Expanding Civilizations. *Classical and Quantum Gravity, 32*, 215–225.

Ord, T. (2020). *The Precipice: Existential Risk and the Future of Humanity.* Hachette Books.

Pielke, R. (2023, June 26). Climate Journalism in Broken. *The Honest Broker.*

Randers, J. (2012). *2052: A Global Forecast for the Next Forty Years.* Chelsea Green Publishing Co.

Re, F. (2022). *Can the Theory of Everything Be the Great Filter?* University di Milano Bicocca.

Ridley, M. (2015). *The Evolution of Everything: How Small Changes Transform Our World.* 4th Estate Books.

Scranton, R. (2015). *Learning to Die in the Anthropocene: Reflections on the End of a Civilization.* City Lights Publishers.

Sequeira, T., Gil, P., & Alfonso, O. (2018). Endogenous Growth and Entropy. *Journal of Economic Behavior and Organization, 15*, 100–120.

Steffen, W., Broadgate, W., Deutsch, L., Gaffney, O., & Ludwig, C. (2015). The Trajectory of the Anthropocene: The Great Acceleration. *The Anthropocene Review, 2*(1), 81–98.

Tainter, J. (1988). *The Collapse of Complex Societies.* Cambridge University Press.

Tirole, J. (2021). Digital Dystopia. *American Economic Review, 111*(6), 2007–2048.

Torres, E. (2021, July 28). The Dangerous Ideas of Longtermism and Existential Risk. *Current Affairs.*

Turchin, P. (2023). *End Times: Elites, Counter-Elites, and the Path of Political Disintegration.* Penguin.

Turchin, P., & Gavrilets, S. (2009). Evolution of Complex Hierarchical Societies. *Social Evolution & History, 8*(2), 167–198.

Turner, G. (2008). A Comparison of the Limits to Growth with 30 Years of Reality. *Global Environmental Change, 18*(3), 397–411.

Turner, G. (2014). Is Global Collapse Imminent? An Updated Comparison of the Limits to Growth with Historical Data. *Melbourne Sustainable Society Institute, Research Paper No. 4.*

Valdes, F., & Freitas, R. A., Jr. (1980). Comparison of Reproducing and Nonreproducing Starprobe Strategies for Galactic Exploration. *Journal of the British Interplanetary Society, 33*, 402–408.

Vollrath, D. (2019). *Fully Grown: Why a Stagnant Economy Is a Sign of Success.* University of Chicago Press.

Weiss, H., & Bradley, R. S. (2001). What Drives Societal Collapse? *Science, 291*(5504), 609–610.

West, G. (2017). *Scale: The Universal Laws of Life and Death in Organisms, Cities and Companies*. Weidenfeld and Nicolson.

Wheeler, J. B. (1989). Information, physics, quantum: The search for links. In W. H. Zurek (Ed.), *Complexity, Entropy, and the Physics of Information*. Addison-Wesley.

Wilczek, F. (1999). Getting Its from Bits. *Nature, 397*, 303–306.

Wong, M. L., & Bartlett, S. (2022). Asymptotic Burnout and Homeostatic Awakening: A Possible Solution to the Fermi Paradox? *Journal of the Royal Society Interface, 19*, 20220029.

Zackrisson, E., Calissendor, P., González, J., Benson, A., Johansen, A., & Janson, M. (2016). Terrestrial Planets Across Space and Time. *The Astrophysical Journal, 833*(2), 1–12.

CHAPTER 8

Toward a Humpty Dumpty Economics

Abstract This chapter contains a summary and cautionary remarks. It argues for a Humpty Dumpty economics, that is, economic growth theory that takes into consideration the Second Law of Thermodynamics and hence accords fundamental importance to energy. This provides a fitting conclusion to a book that has considered two distinct positions to achieve the Great Decoupling: Green Growth and Degrowth. It was found that neither Green Growth nor Degrowth will be able to achieve the Great Decoupling. Neither will prevent "Humpty Dumpty"—a metaphor for the Second Law, from falling off the wall. This left the reader with the prospect of a Great Collapse. The question a Great Collapse raises is whether it spells the end—as an existential threat—or whether it is another phase in the cycle of integration and disintegration of civilizations over time? Whether a homeostatic awakening as discussed in Chap. 7 has come in time for us to manage our relationship with planetary systems better, is however unknown. As our collective intelligence continues to crunch on this problem, it may do us all good not to fall into doomerism and apocalyptic anxiety and panic, since as the rhyme extolls us "*don't Cry for Humpty or Humpty's Big Spill—He's Just Gone Where the Rest of the Universe Will.*"

Keywords Summary • Second Law of Thermodynamic • Homeostatic awakening • Humpty Dumpty • Collective intelligence • Dataome

W. Naudé, *Economic Growth and Societal Collapse*,
https://doi.org/10.1007/978-3-031-45582-7_8

8.1 Summary

Against the span of 300,000 years that modern humans have been around, the economic growth achieved in the last 0.08% of its history is anomalous. It has been compared to living on a "rocket ship that took off five seconds ago, and nobody knows where it's going" (Wiblin & Harris, 2021). This book tried to provide some answers to the broad question where this "rocket ship" that is modern civilization, is headed, and to the more specific questions: Has the world economy ecologically overshot planetary systems critical to our survival? What does this mean for the future trajectory of society? How can we best fix it—by stopping and reversing overshoot through technology (Green Growth) or by purposefully reducing the size of the economy (Degrowth)? Or is it best to prepare for societal collapse and a possible rebound afterwards?

To answer these questions succinctly, it is useful to recap the contents of this book.

In **Chap. 2** it was pointed out that this question has been a topic of intense debate, at least since 1798, when the Reverend Thomas Malthus published *Essay on the Principle of Population*, warning that progress is inherently limited by land. Subsequently, other "Malthusians" and "neo-Malthusians" similarly stressed the limits to growth; however, the failure of their predictions that food and other resources will run out and that overpopulation will lead to famine, gave fuel to the "Cornucopians." They trust that technological innovation will continue to turn scarcity into abundance, and that economic growth can be continued indefinitely.

In **Chap. 3** it was argued that the Cornucopian belief in continued growth is based on assumption of no fundamental material resource scarcity, but that this belief is difficult to convincingly substantiate. Two problems were discussed in this regard: the first was the growing evidence that economic growth is overshooting planetary boundaries, and that this poses an existential threat. The second was the idea of a carbon pulse as being the main mechanism that has been driving exponential economic growth—a stock of resources that has been largely ignored, or assumed away, by Cornucopians. Section 8.3 concluded that if the Cornucopians are to convincingly argue for unlimited economic growth, they need to be able to provide a case that technological innovations will be able to (i) mitigate climate change, (ii) steer around possible existential threats from ecological overshoot, and (iii) make up for the energy loss implied by the end of the carbon pulse (cheap and abundant fossil fuels).

In **Chap. 4** the Cornucopians's response to these challenges was set out—which can broadly be described as a response that is built around the promotion of what can be labeled "Green Growth." Through Green Growth, the hope is that economic growth can be decoupled from the environment—that economic growth can continue without exhausting resources or contributing to global warming, and that alternative, renewable and non-carbon energy sources can be found to substitute for the phasing out of fossil fuels. Green Growth is today the mainstream paradigm toward economic growth.

It was argued that although green growth can result in many beneficial outcomes on the environment, through for example enabling greater resource efficiency and allowing for decoupling between economic growth and some environmental outcomes—all of this potentially good, barring unintended consequences such as re-materialization, human rights abuses and new wars—it may not be able to result in complete dematerialization and absolute decoupling. Green Growth may therefore not be able to stop an ecological overshoot and the risks that this will pose to human civilization.

In **Chap. 5** the Neo-Malthusians's rejection of Green Growth was outlined. This entailed discussion of the Degrowth Movement that argues that the only way to avoid resource depletion and an existential climate crisis is to make a concerted effort to scale down GDP—to "Degrow" the economy. The Degrowth Agenda is Malthusian. It attempts to provide an agenda—with a basis in Marxism—for enabling this, and to provide for high levels of human welfare within planetary boundaries. It was argued that Degrowth will not be likely to stop an ecological overshoot. Particularly, it was argued that degrowth would not only be ineffective, but it would be likely to worsen the environment; that it is a very expensive method to reduce carbon emissions; that it can be seen as a form of austerity for the working class; and that it is redundant. For these reasons, among others, degrowth as policy agenda is politically infeasible. The only example of a country where something like degrowth was ever maintained for a limited period, was in seventeenth- and eighteenth-century Japan in the Edo period, but under a brutal dictatorship.

Chapter 6 argued that Degrowthers miss that in the West, we already live in a degrowth-type world, and that there is much about it that we do not like. Chapter 6 described the degrowth world—the Great

Stagnation—that the West has been in since the 1970s, and its correlates: declining entrepreneurship, innovation and science, and research productivity. The declines in these suggest that the hope that a degrowth economy can generate the technological progress, creativity and social cohesion necessary to tackle ecological and social crises is far-fetched. Moreover, as recent decades of economic stagnation have illustrated, the consequence of degrowth is a zero-sum society. With the size of the economic cake essentially fixed or shrinking, the economy is a theatre of conflict. One group, or one country, can only make itself better off at the expense of another. Redistribution, instead of production, is the basis of the economy.

Chapter 7 asked the question, what to do about the detritovores, if green growth and degrowth are not effective solutions? It was speculated that perhaps the answer lies in acceptance of a coming societal collapse, and preparation for a possible rebound that could take place. A growing number of scholars have been engaging in this line of thinking, and some view societal collapse as "not a bug, but a feature" of complexity in the universe. Such societal collapse could turn out to the irreversible—a veritable "end of the world." However, it may also be the case that a societal collapse could be followed by a rebound—meaning that societal collapse could amount to a *phase-transition* in the mode of economic growth. In this view, a societal collapse could be an opportunity to get rid of obsolete structures, laying the foundation for rebound growth and a transition to a new kind of economy—a kind of economy that we cannot now envisage, and that could be as qualitatively different from the current global economy as the industrial world was different from the world of the hunter-gatherer economy.

What are the conclusions that we can draw from this for the key questions that were raised in the introduction?

8.2 Humpty Dumpty Economics

In the introduction to this book, its central questions were posed using the old nursery rhyme of Humpty Dumpty as metaphor, and it was stated that the questions this book explore are whether Humpty Dumpty (our outsized economy) can be prevented from falling off the (overshoot) wall, and how? Or whether after its fall, it can be put together again (perhaps better)?

Humpty Dumpty is also a metaphor for the Second Law of Thermodynamics, which was discussed in Chap. 7. The Second Law states that the entropy in a closed system (which the universe is) will always increase. Rising complexity on planet Earth—including our civilization with its Dataome as recent manifestation of this—can be seen as how the Universe accelerates from high order (low entropy) that marked the beginning of the universe (as a singularity before the Big Bang) to disorder (high entropy) that will mark the end of the universe—just like black coffee with cream poured in will change from low entropy (all black before the cream is poured) to high entropy and complexity (swirls of cream and coffee not fully mixed) to low entropy again (evenly brown).

Zach Weinersmith has drawn a delightful cartoon wherein he reformulates the Humpty Dumpty rhyme to illustrate the Second Law (see Weinersmith, 2014).

Humpty Dumpty sat on a Wall
His Height was at Υ and his Mass wasn't Small.
Off of the Wall he Unhappily Fell
And Diminished his Υ in the Gravity Well.
All the King's Thermodynamicists Saw
That Humpty was Screwed by their Second Great Law.
All the King's Horses and All the King's Men
Lacked the E to put Humpty Together Again.
But don't Cry for Humpty of Humpty's Big Spill
He's Just Gone Where the Rest of the Universe Will.

Humpty Dumpty economics is economic growth theory that takes into consideration the Second Law of Thermodynamics, and hence accords fundamental importance to energy. From this perspective, this book's answers to the questions it explored are as follows.

First, the fall of Humpty Dumpty from the wall that is ecological overshoot will not be prevented. Green Growth, and the Silicon Valley Mindset of its Technofeudalists who advocate technology as the uber-solution to human civilization's challenges, was argued to be a fairy tale. Not even the Tech-elite billionaires seem to believe in it and, on the back of an ethics program called Longtermism, are justifying the neglect of current global challenges to further their escape from the planet and the impending fall off the wall of Humpty Dumpty.

The Degrowth Movement likewise has no solution to prevent Humpty Dumpty from falling off the wall. In fact, the Degrowth Movement wants to proactively push Humpty Dumpty down to a lower rung on the wall. This book has argued that this push may make his fall more likely—and possibly even harder. It is a fairy tale to believe that we can, through decentralized democratic political systems inhabited by status quo biased politicians and loss-averse voters, collectively agree to shrink our economies and, in the case of the West, abandon its geopolitical position in the process.

Second, can Humpty Dumpty be put together after they do fall? In Chap. 7 it was asked whether the fall would be “the end of the world” (i.e., catastrophic) or whether it could be a new beginning—of a phase-transition toward rebound economic growth and development? The answer, from the Second Law of Thermodynamics seems to be that eventually this would not be possible.

Al previous forms of human civilization and “empires” collapsed, but were followed by new civilizations and empires that arose out of their dust. None of these were, however, global, planetary civilizations like the present. And even if our planetary civilization would rebound after collapsing, the number of such rebounds could be limited.

8.3 Conclusion: Don’t Cry for Humpty

It has been said that, in the light of ecological overshoot, that human civilization faces two future possibilities: a Great Decoupling or a Great Collapse (Steffen et al., 2015). In this book, two distinct positions to achieve the Great Decoupling were critically evaluated: Green Growth and Degrowth. Green Growth wants to achieve the Great Decoupling through a climate technology revolution. Degrowth wants to achieve that through a planned down-scaling of economic activity (GDP and material throughput). The conclusion was that neither Green Growth nor Degrowth will be able to achieve the Great Decoupling. Neither will prevent Humpty Dumpty from falling off the wall.

This leaves us with the prospect of a Great Collapse. Is this the end—an existential threat—or merely another phase in the cycle of integration and disintegration of civilizations over time? Is it a feature and not a bug of the changing complexity on planet Earth? Should our planning be aimed at a soft landing and aim for a rebound? And if so, how do we identify and change obsolete structures? The challenge is that obsolete structures are not only closely aligned and in many ways outcomes of the dynamics of ecological overshoot, but also implicated in social overshoot, social rot, and a Great Stagnation. This, and the political disintegration with accompanying loss of societal trust will make any attempt at a soft landing and rebound extremely difficult. Unlikely, some would say.

Perhaps the possibility for rebound growth, like Green Growth and Degrowth, may turn out to be an illusion—even though perhaps an illusion worth holding to. As *Nassim Nicholas Taleb pointed out, "Never rid anyone of an illusion unless you can replace it in his mind with another illusion."*

It was speculated at the end of Chap. 7 that perhaps the only sustainable outcome, bar a catastrophic collapse, could be some sort of homeostatic awakening. This would be consistent with the Fermi Paradox—the puzzle why we do not have evidence (yet) of any other civilizations in the universe. Energy-guzzling super-exponentially scaling civilizations with a complex emerging Dataome like ours elsewhere in the Universe seems to have, like ours now, to have experienced asymptotic burnout and either went extinct, or managed to change their relationship with the biophysical foundations and limits of their planetary systems, and abandoned ideas of further civilizational scaling and galactic expansion. Perhaps the very fact that our Dataome is buzzing with analysis of our ecological overshoot predicament is suggesting that we are experiencing a homeostatic awakening in our collective intelligence.

Whether this homeostatic awakening has come in time for us to manage our relationship with planetary systems better, is however unknown—if it is possible at all. As our collective intelligence continues to crunch on this problem, it may do us all good not to fall into doomerism and apocalyptic anxiety and panic, since, as the rhyme extolls us, "*don't Cry for Humpty or Humpty's Big Spill – He's Just Gone Where the Rest of the Universe Will.*"

References

Steffen, W., Broadgate, W., Deutsch, L., Gaffney, O., & Ludwig, C. (2015). The Trajectory of the Anthropocene: The Great Acceleration. *The Anthropocene Review, 2*(1), 81–98.

Weinersmith, Z. (2014, June 4). Humpty Dumpty and the Great Second Law: A Physics Fable. *Medium*.
Wiblin, R., & Harris, K. (2021, August 19). Holden Karnofsky on the Most Important Century. *80,000 Hours Podcast*.

References

Aaronson, S., Carroll, S., & Ouellette, L. (2014). Quantifying the Rise and Fall of Complexity in Closed Systems: The Coffee Automaton. *arXiv:1405.6903* [cond-mat.stat-mech].

Acemoglu, D. (2009). *Introduction to Modern Economic Growth*. Princeton University Press.

Acemoglu, D. (2023). Distorted Innovation: Does the Market Get the Direction of Technology Right? *AEA Papers and Proceedings, 113*, 1–28.

Agrawal, A., McHale, J., & Oettl, A. (2018). *Finding Needles in Haystacks: Artificial Intelligence and Recombinant Growth* (NBER Working Paper no. 24541). National Bureau for Economic Research.

Agrawal, A., McHale, J., & Oettl, A. (2019). *Artificial Intelligence, Scientific Discovery, and Commercial Innovation*. Mimeo.

Akbulut, B. (2021). Degrowth. *Rethinking Marxism, 33*(1), 98–110.

Akcigit, U. and Ates, S. (2019). *Ten Facts on Declining Business Dynamism and Lessons from Endogenous Growth Theory* (CEPR Discussion Paper no. 13668). Centre for Economic Policy Research.

Aleksander, S. (2019, April 22). 1960: The Year the Singularity Was Cancelled. *Slate Star Codex Blog*.

Alexander, S. (2016, May 28). Book Review: Age of EM. *Slate Star Codex Blog*.

Alexander, S. (2022, August 23). Book Review: What We Owe the Future. *Astral Codex Ten*.

Aligica, P. (2009). Julian Simon and the Limits to Growth Neo-Malthusianism. *The Electronic Journal of Sustainable Development, 1*(3), 73–84.

W. Naudé, *Economic Growth and Societal Collapse*,
https://doi.org/10.1007/978-3-031-45582-7

Alkire, S., Nogales, R., Quinn, N. N., & Suppa, N. (2023). On Track or Not? Projecting the Global Multidimensional Poverty Index. *Journal of Development Economics*, 103150.

Archer, E. (2020). *The Intellectual and Moral Decline in Academic Research.* James G. Martin Center for Academic Renewal.

Armstrong McKay, D., Staal, A., Abrams, J., Winkelmann, R., Sakschewski, B., Loriani, S., Fetzer, I., Cornell, S., Rockström, J., & Lenton, T. (2022). Exceeding 1.5°C Global Warming Could Trigger Multiple Climate Tipping Points. *Science, 377*(6611), eabn7950.

Arrhenius, S. (1896). On the Influence of Carbonic Acid in the Air upon the Temperature of the Ground. *Philosophical Magazine and Journal of Science, 5*(41), 237–276.

Aschenbrenner, L. (2020). *Existential Risk and Growth* (GPI Working Paper No. 6-2020). Global Priorities Institute, University of Oxford.

Auffhammer, M. (2018). Quantifying Economic Damages from Climate Change. *Journal of Economic Perspectives, 32*(4), 33–52.

Autor, D., Dorn, D., Katz, L., Patterson, C., & Reenen, J. V. (2020). The Fall of the Labor Share and the Rise of Superstar Firms. *The Quarterly Journal of Economics, 135*(2), 645–709.

Baker, M. (2016). 1,500 Scientists Lift the Lid on Reproducibility. *Nature, 533*, 452–454.

Bardi, U. (2017). *The Seneca Effect: Why Growth Is Slow, But Collapse Is Rapid.* Springer.

Bardi, U. (2020). *Before the Collapse: A Guide to the Other Side of Growth.* Springer.

Bardi, U., & Lavacchi, A. (2009). A Simple Interpretation of Hubbert's Model of Resource Exploitation. *Energies, 2*, 646–661.

Barnosky, A., Matzke, N., Tomiya, S., et al. (2011). Has the Earth's Sixth Mass Extinction Already Arrived? *Nature, 471*, 51–57.

Bauer, A. M., Edgeworth, M., Edwards, L. E., Ellis, E. C., Gibbard, P., & Merritts, D. J. (2021). Anthropocene: Event or Epoch? *Nature, 597*, 332.

Baum, S. D., Armstrong, S., Ekenstedt, T., Häggström, O., Hanson, R., Kuhlemann, K., Maas, M. M., Miller, J. D., Salmela, M., Sandberg, A., Sotala, K., Torres, P., Turchin, A., & Yampolskiy, R. V. (2019). Long-Term Trajectories of Human Civilization. *Foresight, 21*(1), 53–83.

Beard, S., & Torres, E. (2020, March 12). *Ripples on the Great Sea of Life: A Brief History of Existential Risk Studies.* Mimeo. SSRN.

Benanav, A. (2020). *Automation and the Future of Work.* Verso.

Beek, L. v., Hajer, M., Pelzer, P., van Vuuren, D., & Cassen, C. (2020). Anticipating Futures Through Models: The Rise of Integrated Assessment Modelling in the Climate Science-Policy Interface Since 1970. *Global Environmental Change, 65*, 102191.

Bergström, A., Stringer, C., Hajdinjak, M., Scerri, E., & Skoglund, P. (2021). Origins of Modern Human Ancestry. *Nature, 590*, 229–237.

Berman, A. (2023, May 27). Does Renewable Energy Have a Higher EROI than Fossil Fuels? *The Petroleum Truth Report.*

Bettencourt, L. M., Lobo, J., Helbing, D., Kühnert, C., & West, G. B. (2007). Growth, Innovation, Scaling, and the Pace of Life in Cities. *Proceedings of the National Academy of Sciences, 104*, 7301–7306.

Bhaskar, M. (2021). *Human Frontiers: The Future of Big Ideas in an Age of Small Thinking*. The Bridge Street Press.

Bijnens, G., & Konings, J. (2018). Declining Business Dynamism in Belgium. *Small Business Economics*, 1–39.

Bleischwitz, R. (2010). International Economics of Resource Productivity Relevance, Measurement, Empirical Trends, Innovation, Resource Policies. *International Economics and Economic Policy, 7*, 227–244.

Bloom, N., Bunn, P., Chen, S., Mizen, P., & Smietanka, P. (2020a, March 27). The Economic Impact of Coronavirus on UK Businesses: Early Evidence from the Decision Maker Panel. *VOX CEPR Policy Portal.*

Bloom, N., Jones, C., van Reenen, J., & Webb, M. (2020b). Are Ideas Getting Harder to Find? *American Economic Review, 110*(4), 1104–1144.

Boettcher, K. (2021). *Seeing Red over the Climate Crisis: Ecosocialism as Emergency Brake*. Thesis Presented to the Faculty of California State University, Stanislaus.

Bolt, J., & van Zanden, J. (2020). Maddison Style Estimates of the Evolution of the World Economy. A New 2020 Update. *Maddison-Project Working Paper WP-15.*

Bos, F. (1992). *The History of National Accounting* (*MPRA Paper*). University Library of Munich. https://doi.org/10.2139/ssrn.1032598

Boserup, E. (1965). *The Conditions of Agricultural Growth: The Economics of Agrarian Change Under Population Pressure*. Routledge.

Boserup, E. (1981). *Population and Technological Change: A Study of Long-Term Trends.* Chicago University Press.

Bostrom, N. (2002). Existential Risks: Analyzing Human Extinction Scenarios and Related Hazards. *Journal of Evolution and Technology, 9*(1).

Bostrom, N. (2003). Astronomical Waste: The Opportunity Cost of Delayed Technological Development. *Utilitas, 15*(3), 308–314.

Bostrom, N. (2008). Where Are They? Why I Hope the Search for Extraterrestrial Life Find Nothing. *MIT Technology Review*, May/June:72–77.

Bostrom, N. (2009). The Future of Humanity. *Geopolitics, History, and International Relations, 1*(2), 41–78.

Bostrom, N. (2013). Existential Risk Prevention as Global Priority. *Global Policy, 4*, 15–31.

Bostrom, N. (2014). *Superintelligence: Paths, Dangers, Strategies.* Oxford University Press.

Boudry, M. (2021, July 29). Why Relativism Is the Worst Idea Ever. *Blog of the APA*.
Boulding, K. (1966). The Economics of the Coming Spaceship Earth. In H. Jarrett (Ed.), *Environmental Quality in a Growing Economy* (pp. 3–14). Resources for the Future/Johns Hopkins University Press.
Bowen, A., & Hepburn, C. (2014). Green Growth: An Assessment. *Oxford Review of Economic Policy, 30*(3), 407–422.
Bradshaw, C., Ehrlich, P., Beattie, A., Ceballos, G., Crist, E., Diamond, J., Dirzo, R., Ehrlich, A., Harte, J., Pyke, G., Raven, P., Ripple, W., Saltré, F., Turnbull, C., Wackernagel, M., & Blumstein, D. (2021). Underestimating the Challenges of Avoiding a Ghastly Future. *Frontiers in Conservation Science, 1*, 615–641.
Brain, S. (2010). Stalin's Environmentalism. *The Russian Review, 69*(1), 93–118.
Brazeau, M. (2018, April 4). *Remember the Guano Wars: A Response to Breakthrough's Essay on the Hidden Footprint of Making All Farms Organic*. The Breakthrough Institute.
Bretschger, L. (2021). Getting the Costs of Environmental Protection Right: Why Climate Policy Is Inexpensive in the End. *Ecological Economics, 188*, 10711.
Brewer, A. (1987). Turgot: Founder of Classical Economics. *Economica, 54*(216), 417–428.
Bricker, D., & Ibbitson, J. (2020). *Empty Planet: The Shock of Global Population Decline*. Little, Brown Book Group.
Brockway, P., Owen, A., Brand-Correa, L., & Hardt, L. (2019). Estimation of Global Final-Stage Energy-Return-On-Investment for Fossil Fuels with Comparison to Renewable Energy Sources. *Nature Energy, 4*, 612–621.
Brown, P. (2022, December 1). *Human Deaths from Hot and Cold Temperatures and Implications for Climate Change*. The Breakthrough Institute.
Brozović, D. (2023). Societal Collapse: A Literature Review. *Futures, 145*, 103–175.
Bruers, S. (2021, December 30). The Case Against Degrowth. *Effective Altruism Forum Blog*.
Bryan K. (2018, October 11). How We Create and Destroy Growth: The 2018 Nobel Laureates. *VoxEU CEPR*.
Buchanan, M. (2017). The Thermodynamics of Earth. *Nature Physics, 13*, 106.
Burja, S. (2020, August 19). Why Civilizations Collapse. *The Side View*.
Burkart, K. G., Brauer, M., Aravkin, A. Y., et al. (2021). Estimating the Cause-Specific Relative Risks of Non-optimal Temperature on Daily Mortality: A Two-Part Modelling Approach Applied to the Global Burden of Disease Study. *Lancet, 398*, 685–697.
Calcagnini, G., Gardini, L., Giombini, G., & Carrera, E. (2022). Does Too Much Liquidity Generate Instability? *Journal of Economic Interaction and Coordination, 17*, 191–208.
Caldwell, R. R., & Stebbins, A. (2008). A Test of the Copernican Principle. *Physical Review Letters, 100*, 191302.

Campbell, C., & Laherrere, J. (1998). The End of Cheap Oil. *Scientific American, 278*(3), 80–86.

Capasso, M., Hansen, T., Heiberg, J., Klitkou, A., & Steen, M. (2019). Green Growth – A Synthesis of Scientific Findings. *Technological Forecasting and Social Change, 146*, 390–402.

Caplan, M. E. (2020). Black dwarf supernova in the far future. *Monthly Notices of the Royal Astronomical Society, 497*(4), 4357–4362.

Catton, W. (1982). *Overshoot: The Ecological Basis of Revolutionary Change.* University of Illinois Press.

Catton, W. (1998). What If Malthus Were Writing Today? *Organization & Environment, 11*(4), 434–437.

Chambers, C. (2021, July 20). *Degrowth: An Environmental Ideology with Good Intentions, Bad Politics.* Liberation School.

Chaplin-Kramer, R., Neugarten, R. A., Sharp, R. P., et al. (2023). Mapping the Planet's Critical Natural Assets. *Nature Ecology and Evolution, 7*, 51–61.

Christian, D. (2017). *The Noösphere. Edge: What Scientific Term or Concept Ought to Be More Widely Known?* Edge.Org.

Cirkovic, M. (2002). Cosmological Forecast and Its Practical Significance. *Journal of Evolution and Technology, xii.*

Clancy, M. (2021, June 18). Combinatorial Innovation and Technological Progress in the Very Long Run. *New Things Under the Sun.*

Clark, G., & Jacks, D. (2007). Coal and the Industrial Revolution, 1700–1869. *European Review of Economic History, 11*(1), 39–72.

Clugston, C. O. (2023). *Industrialism – Our Commitment to Impermanence.* Booklocker.

Cobb, K. (2015, February 15). William Catton's Warning. *Resource Insights.*

Cobb, C. W., & Douglas, P. H. (1928). A Theory of Production. *American Economic Review, 18*, 139–165.

Cockburn, I. M., Henderson, R., & Stern, S. (2019). The Impact of Artificial Intelligence on Innovation: An Exploratory Analysis. In A. Agrawal, J. Gans, & A. Goldfarb (Eds.), *The Economics of Artificial Intelligence: An Agenda* (pp. 115–148). University of Chicago Press.

Connor, D., & Storper, M. (2020). The Changing Geography of Social Mobility in the United States. *Proceedings of the National Academy of Sciences, 117*(48), 30309–30317.

Cook, G. (2018, February 15). The Secret Behind One of the Greatest Success Stories in All of History. *Scientific American.*

Court, V., & Fizaine, F. (2017). Long-Term Estimates of the Energy-Return-On-Investment (EROI) of Coal, Oil, and Gas Global Productions. *Ecological Economics, 138*, 145–159.

Covarrubias, M., Gutiérrez, G., & Philippon, T. (2020). From Good to Bad Concentration? US Industries over the Past 30 Years. *NBER Macroeconomics Annual, 34*, 1–46.

Cowen, T. (2010). *The Great Stagnation*. Penguin (Dutton).
Cowie, R. H., Bouchet, P., & Fontaine, B. (2022). The Sixth Mass Extinction: Fact, Fiction or Speculation? *Biological Reviews, 97*(April 2022), 640–663.
Coyne, J. (2019, January 31). Is the World Really Getting Poorer? A Response by Steve Pinker. *Why Evolution Is True Blog*.
Crary, A. (2023). The Toxic Ideology of Longtermism. *Radical Philosophy, 214*, 49–57.
Crawford, J. (2022, October 7). Can Economic Growth Continue over the Long-Term? *Longnow*.
Cremer, C. Z., & Kemp, L. (2021). *Democratising Risk: In Search of a Methodology to Study Existential Risk*. The Future of Humanity Institute (FHI), University of Oxford.
Curtis, B. (2015, December 23). The Life and Death of King Coal. *The Conversation*.
D'Alessandro, S., Cieplinski, A., Distefano, T., et al. (2020). Feasible Alternatives to Green Growth. *Nature Sustainability, 3*, 329–335.
Daly, H. (1992). *Steady- State Economics* (2nd ed.). Earthscan.
Dattani, S. (2022). Real Peer Review Has Never Been Tried. *Works in Progress, 8*(21 July).
Davidson, T. (2021, June 17). Report on Whether AI Could Drive Explosive Economic Growth. *Open Philanthropy*.
Davies, P. (2010). *The Eerie Silence: Renewing Our Search for Alien Intelligence*. Houghton Mifflin.
Dawkins, R. (1998). *Unweaving the Rainbow: Science, Delusion, and the Appetite for Wonder*. Houghton Mifflin.
Dearing, J., Cooper, G., & Willcock, S. (2023, June 25). Ecological Doom-Loops: Why Ecosystem Collapses may Occur Much Sooner than Expected, *The Conversation*.
Decker, C. S., & Reuveny, R. (2005). Endogenous Technological Progress and the Malthusian Trap: Could Simon and Boserup Have Saved Easter Island? *Human Ecology, 33*(1), 119–140.
Decker, R., Haltiwanger, J., Jarmin, R., & Miranda, J. (2014). The Role of Entrepreneur- ship in US Job Creation and Dynamics. *Journal of Economic Perspectives, 28*(3), 3–24.
Dell, M., Jones, B., & Olken, B. (2012). Climate Change and Economic Growth: Evidence from the Last Half Century. *American Economic Journal: Macroeconomics, 4*(3), 66–95.
Deloitte. (2022). *2022 Social Progress Index*. https://www.socialprogress.org/global-index-2022-results/
DeLong, J. B. (1998). *Estimates of World GDP, One Million B.C. – Present*. Department of Economics, U.C. Berkeley at http://econ161.berkeley.edu/

Demaria, F., Schneider, F., Sekulova, F., & Martinez-Alier, J. (2016). What Is Degrowth? From an Activist Slogan to a Social Movement. In N. Haenn, A. Harnish, & R. Wilk (Eds.), *The Environment in Anthropology (Second Edition): A Reader in Ecology, Culture, and Sustainable Living* (pp. 390–400). New York University Press.

Dercon, S. (2014). Is Green Growth Good for the Poor? *World Bank Research Observer, 29*(2), 163–185.

Deutsch, D. (1998). *The Fabric of Reality: The Science of Parallel Universes – And Its Implications.* Penguin Books.

Diamond, J. (2005). *Collapse: How Societies Choose to Fail or Succeed.* Viking Press.

Diffenbaugh, N., & Burke, M. (2019). Global Warming has Increased Global Economic Inequality. *Proceedings of the National Academy of Sciences, 116*(20), 9808–9813.

DiNapoli, R., Rieth, T., Lipo, C., & Hunt, T. (2020). A Model-Based Approach to the Tempo of Collapse: The Case of Rapa Nui (Easter Island). *Journal of Archaeological Science, 116*, 105094.

Dirzo, R., Ceballos, G., & Ehrlich, P. (2022). Circling the Drain: The Extinction Crisis and the Future of Humanity. *Philosophical Transactions of the Royal Society of London Biological Sciences, 377*(1857), 20210378.

Domingos, P. (2015). *The Master Algorithm: How the Quest for the Ultimate Learning Machine Will Remake Our World.* Penguin Books.

Easterlin, R., & O'Connor, K. J. (2020). The Easterlin Paradox. *IZA DP No. 13923.*

Easterlin, R., McVey, L., Switek, M., Sawangfa, O., & Zweig, J. (2010). The Happiness- Income Paradox Revisited. *Proceedings of the National Academy of Sciences, 107*, 2246322468.

EC. (2011, September 20). *Analysis Associated with the Roadmap to a Resource Efficient Europe Part I.* European Commission Staff Working Paper SEC (2011) 1067 final.

Eden, M., & Kuruc, K. (2023). *The Long-Run Relationship Between Per Capita Incomes and Population Size.* Mimeo.

Ehrenreich, B. (2020, November 4). How Do You Know When Society Is About to Fall Apart? *New York Times Magazine.*

Ehresman, T., & Okereke, C. (2015). Environmental Justice and Conceptions of the Green Economy. *International Environmental Agreements: Politics, Law and Economics, 15*, 13–27.

Ehrlich, P. (1968). *The Population Bomb.* Ballantine Books.

Epstein, A. (2022). *Fossil Future: Why Global Human Flourishing Requires More Oil, Coal, and Natural Gas – Not Less.* Penguin Books.

Erisman, J., Sutton, M., Galloway, J., Klimont, Z., & Winiwarter, W. (2008). How a Century of Ammonia Synthesis Changed the World. *Nature Geoscience, 1*, 636–639.

Erixon, F., & Weigl, B. (2016). *The Innovation Illusion*. Yale University Press.
Fanning, A. L., & Hickel, J. (2023, June 5). Compensation for Atmospheric Appropriation. *Nature Sustainability*.
Fanning, A., O'Neill, D., Hickel, J., & Roux, N. (2022). The Social Shortfall and Ecological Overshoot of Nations. *Nature Sustainability, 5*, 26–36.
Ferguson, N., Kornejew, M., Schmelzing, P., & Schularick, M. (2023). *The Safety Net: Central Bank Balance Sheets and Financial Crises, 1587-2020* (Economics Working Paper 23102). Hoover Institution.
Fetzer, T., & Schwarz, C. (2021). Tariffs and Politics: Evidence from Trump's Trade Wars. *The Economic Journal, 131*(636), 1717–1741.
Fichtner, J., Heemskerk, E., & Garcia-Bernardo, J. (2017, May 10). These Three Firms Own Corporate America. *The Conversation*.
Fix, B. (2015). Putting Power Back into Growth Theory. *Review of Capital as Power, 1*(2), 1–37.
Fix, B. (2020a). *Can the World Get Along Without Natural Resources?* (Working Papers on Capital as Power, No. 2020/05). Forum on Capital as Power – Toward a New Cosmology of Capitalism.
Fix, B. (2020b, November 16). Peak Oil Never Went Away. *Economics from the Top Down*.
Fix, B. (2020c, July 11). Why America Won't Be 'Great' Again. *Economics from the Top Down*.
Fizaine, F., & Court, V. (2016). Energy Expenditure, Economic Growth, and the Minimum EROI of Society. *Energy Policy, 95*, 172–186.
Floyd, J., Alexander, S., Lenzen, M., Moriarty, P., Palmer, G., Chandra-Shekeran, S., Foran, B., & Keysser, L. (2020). Energy Descent as a Post-Carbon Transition Scenario: How 'Knowledge Humility' Reshapes Energy Futures for Post-normal Times. *Futures, 122*, 102565.
Fraumeni, B. (2022). Gross Domestic Product: Are Other Measures Needed? *IZA World of Labor*, 368v2. https://doi.org/10.15185/izawol.368.v2
Friedemann, A. J. (2021). *Life After Fossil Fuels: A Reality Check on Alternative Energy*. Springer.
Fuchs, R., Herold, M., Verburg, P., & Clevers, J. (2013). A High-Resolution and Harmonized Model Approach for Reconstructing and Analysing Historic Land Changes in Europe. *Biogeosciences, Biogeosciences, 10*, 15431559.
Fullarton, C. (2016, January 27). Life-Altered Cosmologies. *CQG+*.
Funk, J. (2019a, October 23). Gaming the Systems of Venture Capital and R&D. *LinkedIn*.
Funk, J. (2019b). What's Behind Technological Hype? *Issues in Science and Technology, 36*(1), 36–42.
Funk, J., & Smith, G. (2022, October 4). The Hyper-Specialization of University Researchers. *Mind Matters*.

Georgescu-Roegen, M. (1971). *The Entropy Law and the Economic process.* Harvard University Press.

Georgescu-Roegen, N. (1975). Energy and Economic Myths. *Southern Economic Journal, 41*(3), 347–381.

Giljum, S., Bruckner, M., & Martinez, A. (2015). Material Footprint Assessment in a Global Input-Output Framework. *Journal of Industrial Ecology, 19,* 792–804.

GIS. (2022, August 1). *The ECB: Broken Rules, Frivolous Policy.* Comment by Prince Michael of Liechtenstein.

Gleick, P. (2020, July 15). Book Review: Bad Science and Bad Arguments Abound in Apocalypse Never by Michael Shellenberger. *Yale Climate Connections.*

Gollin, D. (2002). Getting Income Shares Right. *Journal of Political Economy, 110,* 458–474.

Goodman, P. S. (2022). *Davos Man: How the Billionaires Devoured the World.* Custom House.

Gordon, R. (2018). *Why Has Economic Growth Slowed When Innovation Appears to Be Accelerating?* (NBER Working Paper 24554). National Bureau for Economic Research.

Gowdy, J. (2020). Our Hunter-Gatherer Future: Climate Change, Agriculture and Uncivilization. *Futures, 115,* 102488.

Graeber, D. (2018). *Bullshit Jobs: A Theory.* Simon & Schuster.

Grasso, M., & Heede, R. (2023). Time to Pay the Piper: Fossil Fuel Companies' Reparations for Climate Damages. *One Earth, 6*(5), 459–463.

Gray, R. (2015). The Fermi Paradox Is Neither Fermi's Nor a Paradox. *Astrobiology, 15*(3), 195–199.

Greaves, H., & MacAskill, W. (2021). *The Case for Strong Longtermism* (GPI Working Paper No. 5-2021). Global Priorities Institute, University of Oxford.

Greer, J. M. (2005). *How Civilizations Fall: A Theory Of Catabolic Collapse.* At https://www.ecoshock.org/transcripts/greer_on_collapse.pdf

Gros, F. (2011). *A Philosophy of Walking.* Verso.

Gupta, R. (2023). JWST Early Universe Observations and ΛCDM Cosmology. *Monthly Notices of the Royal Astronomical Society*: stad2032.

Habashi, F. (2000). The First Oil Well in the World. *Bulletin for History of Chemistry, 25*(1), 64–66.

Haberl, H., Wiedenhofer, D., Virág, D., Kalt, G., Plank, B., Brockway, P., Fishman, T., Hausknost, D., Krausmann, F., Leon-Gruchalski, B., et al. (2020). A Systematic Review of the Evidence on Decoupling of GDP, Resource Use and GHG Emissions, Part II: Synthesizing the Insights. *Environmental Research Letters, 15,* 065003.

Hagens, N. (2018, April 23). Where are We Going? *Resilience.*

Hagens, N. (2020). Economics for the Future – Beyond the Superorganism. *Ecological Economics, 169,* 106520.

Hagens, N., & White, D. (2021). *Reality Blind: Integrating the Systems Science Under- pinning Our Collective Futures Vol. 1.* Independently Published.
Hall, C. (2017). Will EROI Be the Primary Determinant of Our Economic Future? The View of the Natural Scientist Versus the Economist. *Joule, 1*, 635–638.
Hallock, J. L., Wu, W., Hall, C. A. S., & Jefferson, M. (2014). Forecasting the Limits to the Availability and Diversity of Global Conventional Oil Supply: Validation. *Energy, 64*, 130–153.
Haltiwanger, J. (2022). Entrepreneurship in the Twenty-First Century. *Small Business Economics, 58*, 27–40.
Hannesson, R. (2021). Are We Seeing Dematerialization of World GDP? *Biophysical Economics and Sustainability, 6*(4).
Hansen, J., Sato, M., Kharecha, P., Beerling, D., Berner, R., Masson-Delmotte, V., Pagani, M., Raymo, M., Royer, D. L., & Zachos, J. C. (2008). Target Atmospheric CO_2: Where Should Humanity Aim? *The Open Atmospheric Science Journal, 2*, 217–231.
Hanson, R. (1998, September 15). *The Great Filter – Are We Almost Past It?* Mimeo.
Hanson, R. (2000). *Long-Term Growth as a Sequence of Exponential Modes.* Mimeo/George Mason University.
Hanson, R. (2001). *Economic Growth Given Machine Intelligence.* Mimeo.
Hanson, R. (2009). Limits to Growth. *Overcoming Bias Blog.*
Hanson, R. (2018). *The Age of EM: Work, Love, and Life when Robots Rule the Earth.* Oxford University Press.
Hanson, R. (2020, December 21). How Far to Grabby Aliens? Part 1. *Overcoming Bias Blog.*
Harford, T. (2017, January 2). How Fertilizer Helped Feed the World. *BBC News.*
Hart, M. (1975). An Explanation for the Absence of Extraterrestrials on Earth. *Quarterly Journal of the Royal Astronomical Society, 16*, 128–135.
Hartley, T., van den Bergh, J., & Kallis, G. (2020). Policies for Equality Under Low or No Growth: A Model Inspired by Piketty. *Review of Political Economy, 32*(2), 243–258.
Hausfather, Z., Drake, H. F., Abbott, T., & Schmidt, G. A. (2020). Evaluating the Performance of Past Climate Model Projections. *Geophysical Research Letters, 47*, e2019GL085378.
Hausfather, Z., Marvel, K., Schmidt, G. A., Nielsen-Gammon, J. W., & Zelinka, M. (2022). Climate Simulations: Recognize the 'Hot Model' Problem. *Nature, 605*, 26–20.
Head, M. J., Steffen, W., Fagerlind, D., Waters, C. N., Poirier, C., et al. (2021). The Great Acceleration Is Real and Provides a Quantitative Basis for the Proposed Anthropocene. *Journal of International Geoscience.* https://doi.org/10.18814/epiiugs/2021/021031

Heinberg, R. (2011). *The End of Growth: Adapting to Our New Economic Reality*. New Society Publishers.

Heinberg, R. (2023, June 15). Polycrisis, Unraveling, Simplification, or Collapse: Coming Soon to a Planet Near You? *Resilience*.

Heinberg, R., & Miller, A. (2023). *Welcome to the Great Unraveling: Navigating the Polycrisis of Environmental and Social Breakdown*. Post Carbon Institute.

Herrington, G. (2021). Update to Limits to Growth: Comparing the World3 Model with Empirical Data. *Journal of Industrial Ecology, 25*(3), 614–626.

Herz, J. (2019, October 11). *The Fairy Tale of Eternal Economic Growth: Swedish Activist Greta Thunberg Brings Attention to the Need to Steward our Planet*. EESI (Environmental and Energy Studies Institute).

Hickel, J. (2015, September 23). Forget Developing Poor Countries, It's Time to De-develop Rich Countries. *The Guardian*.

Hickel, J. (2019). The Contradiction of the Sustainable Development Goals: Growth Versus Ecology on a Finite Planet. *Sustainable Development, 274*(5), 873–884.

Hickel, J. (2020). Quantifying National Responsibility for Climate Breakdown: An Equality-Based Attribution Approach for Carbon Dioxide Emissions in Excess of the Planetary Boundary. *Lancet Planet Health, 4*, e399–e404.

Hickel, J. (2021). What Does Degrowth Mean? A Few Points of Clarification. *Globalizations, 18*(7), 1105–1111.

Hickel, J., & Hallegatte, S. (2022). Can we Live within Environmental Limits and Still Reduce Poverty? Degrowth or Decoupling? *Development Policy Review, 40*, e12584.

Hickel, J., Kallis, G., Jackson, T., O'Neill, D. W., Schor, J., Steinberger, J. K., Victor, P., & Ürge-Vorsatz, D. (2022). Degrowth Can Work – Here's How Science Can Help. *Nature, 612*, 400–403.

Hidalgo, C. (2015). *Why Information Grows: The Evolution of Order, from Atoms to Economies*. Penguin.

Hoekstra, A., & Wiedmann, T. (2014). Humanity's Unsustainable Environmental Foot- print. *Science, 344*(6188), 1114–1117.

Holden, N., White, E., Lange, M., et al. (2018). Review of the Sustainability of Food Systems and Transition Using the Internet of Food. *npj Science of Food, 2*, 18.

Holdren, J. (1993, September 7). A Brief History of IPAT (Impact= Population x Affluence x Technology). *MAHB*.

Holodny, E. (2016, December 14). The 5,000-year History of Interest Rates Shows Just How Historically Low US Rates Are Right Now. *Business Insider*.

Hopenhayn, H., Neira, J., & Singhania, R. (2018). From Population Growth to Firm Demographics: Implications from Concentration, Entrepreneurship and the Labor Share. *NBER Working Paper No. 25382*.

Hopenhayn, H., Neira, J., & Singhania, R. (2022). From Population Growth to Firm Demographics: Implications for Concentration, Entrepreneurship and the Labor Share. *Econometrica, 90*(4), 1879–1914.
Horowitz, J. (2022, November 15). Degrowth: A Dangerous Idea or the Answer to the World's Biggest Crisis? *CNN Business.*
Hossenfelder, S. (2018, November 23). The Present Phase of Stagnation in the Foundations of Physics Is Not Normal. *Nautilus.*
Hubbert, M. (1956). *Nuclear Energy and the Fossil Fuels.* Presented before the Spring Meeting of the Southern District, American Petroleum Institute, Plaza Hotel, San Antonio, Texas, March 7–9.
Huebner, J. (2005). A Possible Declining Trend for Worldwide Innovation. *Technological Forecasting and Social Change, 72*, 980–986.
Huggel, C., Bouwer, L., Juhola, S., et al. (2022). The Existential Risk Space of Climate Change. *Climatic Change, 174*(8).
Hyatt, J. (2022, November 17). Sam Bankman-Fried's Donations to Effective Altruism Nonprofits Tied to An Oxford Professor Are at Risk Of Being Clawed Back. *Forbes.*
Ioannidis, J. (2005). Why Most Published Research Findings Are False. *PLoSMed, 2*(8), e124.
IPCC. (2018). Global *Warming of 1.5°C.* Intergovernmental Panel on Climate Change.
Jackson, T. (2009). *Prosperity Without Growth? The Transition to a Sustainable Economy.* Sustainable Development Commission.
Jackson, N. (2011, May 17). Infographic: How Big Is a Yottabyte? *The Atlantic.*
Jackson, T. (2021). *Post Growth – Life After Capitalism.* Policy Press.
Jackson, T., & Victor, P. (2019). Unraveling the Claims For (and Against) Green Growth. *Science, 366*(6468), 950–951.
Jacobson, M., & Occhino, F. (2012). Labor's Declining Share of Income and Rising Inequality. *Federal Reserve Bank of Cleveland Economic Commentary*, pp. 1–5.
Jakob, M., & Edenhofer, O. (2014). Green Growth, Degrowth, and the Commons. *Oxford Review of Economic Policy, 30*(3), 447–468.
Jefferson, M. (2016). A Global Energy Assessment. *WIREs Energy and Environment, 5*(1), 7–15.
Jevons, W. (1866). *The Coal Question* (2nd ed.). Macmillan.
Johansen, A., & Sornette, D. (2001). Finite-Time Singularity in the Dynamics of the World Population: Economic and Financial Indices. *Physica A, 294*(3–4), 465–502.
Johnson, S., & Kwak, J. (2011). *13 Bankers: The Wall Street Takeover and the Next Financial Meltdown.* Random House.
Johnston, R. (2023, February 7). Industrial Policy Nationalism: How Worried Should We Be? *Colombia SIPA.*

Jones, C. (1995). R&D – Based models of Economic Growth. *Journal of Political Economy, 103*(4), 759–783.
Jones, C. I. (2001). Was an Industrial Revolution Inevitable? Economic Growth over the Very Long Run. *Advances in Macroeconomics, 1*(2), article 1.
Jones, B. (2009). The Burden of Knowledge and the Death of Renaissance Man: Is Innovation Getting Harder? *Review of Economic Studies, 76*(1), 283–317.
Jones, C. I. (2016). The Facts of Economic Growth. In J. B. Taylor & H. Uhlig (Eds.), *Handbook of Macroeconomics* (Vol. 2, pp. 3–69).
Jones, C. I. (2022). The End of Economic Growth? Unintended Consequences of a Declining Population. *American Economic Review, 112*(11), 3489–3527.
Kaag, J. (2021, October 20). Thoreau's Economics: The Truly Precious Costs Precious Little. *Psyche.*
Kaiho, K. (2022). Relationship Between Extinction Magnitude and Climate Change During Major Marine and Terrestrial Animal Crises. *Biogeosciences, 19*(14), 3369–2022.
Kaldor, N. (1961). Capital Accumulation and Economic Growth. In F. A. Lutz & D. C. Hague (Eds.), *The Theory of Capital* (pp. 177–222). St. Martin's Press.
Kallis, G. (2011). In Defence of Degrowth. *Ecological Economics, 70*(5), 873–880.
Kallis, G. (2021). Limits, Ecomodernism and Degrowth. *Political Geography, 87*, 102367.
Kallis, G., & March, H. (2015). Imaginaries of Hope: The Utopianism of Degrowth. *Annals of the Association of American Geographers, 105*(2), 360–336.
Kapoor, R., & Murmann, J. P. (2023). The Organizational and Technological Origins of the U.S. Shale Gas Revolution, 1947 to 2012. *Industrial and Corporate Change*, dtad021.
Kara, S. (2023). *Cobalt Red: How the Blood of the Congo Powers Our Lives.* Macmillan.
Karabarbounis, L., & Neiman, B. (2013). The Global Decline of the Labor Share. *Quarterly Journal of Economics, 129*, 61–103.
Kardashev, N. (1964). Transmission of Information by extraterrestrial Civilizations. *Soviet Astronomy.*
Karnofsky, H. (2021a, July 13). All Possible Views About Humanity's Future Are Wild. *Cold Takes Blog.*
Karnofsky, H. (2021b, July 27). Digital People Would Be an Even Bigger Deal. *Cold Takes Blog.*
Karnofsky, H. (2021c, August 3). This Can't Go On. *Effective Altruism Forum.*
Karpf. D. (2022, August 13). Against Jackpot-Longtermism: Examining the Stories Tech Billionaires Tell Themselves. *The Future, Then and Now.*
Kauppi, P. E., Ausubel, J., Fang, J., Mather, A., Sedjo, R., & Waggoner, P. (2006). Returning Forests Analyzed with the Forest Identity. *Proceedings of the National Academy of Sciences, 103*(46), 17574–17579.

Kelly, B., Papanikolaou, D., Seru, A., & Taddy, M. (2021). Measuring Technological Innovation over the Long Run. *American Economic Review: Insights, 3*(3), 303–320.

Kemp, L., Xu, C., Depledge, J., Ebi, K., Gibbins, G., Kohler, T., Rockström, J., Scheffer, M., Schellnhuber, H., Steffen, W., & Lenton, T. (2022). Climate Endgame: Exploring Catastrophic Climate Change Scenarios. *Proceedings of the National Academy of Sciences, 119*(34), e2108146119.

Kendrick, J. (2023, May 10). Kate Raworth: Boundaries Unleash Creativity. *EU Observer*.

Ketcham, C. (2023, April 4). The Green Growth Delusion. *TruthDig*.

King, C. W. (2015). Comparing World Economic and Net Energy Metrics, Part 3: Macroeconomic Historical and Future Perspectives. *Energies, 8*, 12997–13020.

Kissinger, M., & Rees, W. (2009). Assessing Sustainability in a Globalizing World: Toward Interregional Industrial Ecology. *Journal of Industrial Ecology, 13*(3), 357–360.

Kleidon, A. (2012). How Does the Earth System Generate and Maintain Thermodynamic Disequilibrium and What does It Imply for the Future of the Planet? *Philosophical Transactions A: Mathematical, Physical and Engineering Sciences, 370*(1962), 1012–1040.

Klinger, B. A., & Ryan, S. J. (2022). Population Distribution within the Human Climate Niche. *PLOS Climate, 1*(11), e0000086.

Knox, J. (2022). The Metaverse, or the Serious Business of Tech Frontiers. *Postdigital Science Education, 4*, 207–215.

Kolbert, E. (2014). *The Sixth Extinction: An Unnatural History*. Henry Holt and Company.

Konczal, M., & Steinbaum, M. (2016). *Declining Entrepreneurship, Labor Mobility and Business Dynamism*. Roosevelt Institute.

Koppl, R., Deveraux, A., Herriot, J., & Kauffman, S. (2019). *The Industrial Revolution as a Combinatorial Explosion*. Mimeo.

Kose, M. A., & Ohnsorge, F. (2023). *Falling Long-Term Growth Prospects: Trends, Expectations, and Policies*. The World Bank.

Kotchen, M. (2021). The Producer Benefits of Implicit Fossil Fuel Subsidies in the United States. *Proceedings of the National Academy of Sciences of the USA, 118*(14), e2011969118.

Kotkin, J. (2020). *The Coming of Neo Feudalism: A Warning to the Global Middle Class*. Encounter Books.

Kremer, M. (1993). The O-Ring Theory of Economic Development. *The Quarterly Journal of Economics, 108*, 551–575.

Kuntz, M. (2012). The Postmodern Assault on Science. *EMBO Report, 13*(10), 885–889.

Kurzweil, R. (2005). *The Singularity Is Near: When Humans Transcend Biology*. Viking Press.

Kuznets, S. (1971, December 11). *Prize Lecture*. Available at: https://www.nobelprize.org/prizes/economic-sciences/1971/kuznets/lecture/

Laeven, L., & Valencia, F. (2020). Systemic Banking Crises Database II. *IMF Economic Review, 68*(2), 307–361.

Landes, D. (1999). *The Wealth and Poverty of Nations: Why Some Are So Rich and Some So Poor*. Norton & Co.

Lanier, J. (2023, April 20). There is no A.I. *The New Yorker*.

Lazonick, W. (2014, September). Profits without prosperity. *Harvard Business Review*.

Lee, R. (1988). Induced Population Growth and Induced Technological Progress: Their Interaction in the Accelerating Stage. *Mathematical Population Studies, 1*(3), 265–288.

Lehto, K., Lehto, H., Brozinski, A., Gardner, E., Eklund, O., Rajala, K., & Vuorisalo, T. (2013). Time Trek: A 13.7 km Long Nature Trail Leading Through the History of the Universe and the Earth. *International Journal of Astrobiology, 12*(1), 1–7.

Lent, J. (2018, May 21). Steven Pinker's Ideas Are Fatally Flawed. These Eight Graphs Show Why. *Open Democracy*.

Lenton, T. M., Held, H., Kriegler, E., & Schellnhuber, H. (2008). Tipping Elements in the Earth's Climate System. *Proceedings of the National Academy of Sciences, 105*(6), 1786–1793.

Lenton, T., Rockström, J., Gaffney, O., Rahmstorf, S., Richardson, K., Steffen, W., & Schellnhuber, H. (2019, November 27). Climate Tipping Points – Too Risky to Bet Against. *Nature*.

Lenton, T.M., Xu, C., Abrams, J.F. et al. (2023, May 22). Quantifying the Human Cost of Global Warming. *Nature Sustainability*.

Lepenies, P., & Gaines, J. (2016). *The Power of a Single Number: A Political History of GDP*. Columbia University Press.

Lequiller, F., & Blades, D. (2014). *Understanding National Accounts* (2nd ed.). OECD Publishing.

Leslie, J. (1996). *The End of the World: The Science and Ethics of Human Extinction*. Routledge.

Ligozat, A., Lefévre, J., Bugeau, A., & Combaz, J. (2022). Unraveling the Hidden Environmental Impacts of AI Solutions for Environment. *arXiv:2110.11822* [cs.AI].

Lim, S., & Bentley, P. J. (2022). Opinion Amplification Causes Extreme Polarization in Social Networks. *Scientific Reports, 12*, 18131.

Loeb, A. (2023, May 23). Nothing Lasts Forever. *Medium*.

Lomborg, B. (2019, January 16). Making Every Development Dollar Count. *Project Syndicate*.

Lomborg, B. (2020). Welfare in the 21st Century: Increasing Development, Reducing Inequality, the Impact of Climate Change, and the Cost of Climate Policies. *Technological Forecasting and Social Change, 156.*

López, L., & Rodó, X. (2020). The End of Social Confinement and COVID-19 Re-Emergence Risk. *Nature Human Behaviour, 4,* 746–755.

Löwy, M. (1987). The Romantic and the Marxist Critique of Modern Civilization. *Theory and Society, 16*(6), 891–904.

MacAskill, W. (2022). *What We Owe the Future.* Basic Books.

Magee, C., & Devezas, T. C. (2017). A Simple Extension of Dematerialization Theory: Incorporation of Technical Progress and the Rebound Effect. *Technological Forecasting and Social Change, 117,* 196–205.

Malthus, T. (1798). *An Essay on the Principle of Population.* Printed for J. Johnson, in St. Paul's Churchyard.

Mann, A. (2020, August 11). This Is the Way the Universe Ends: Not with a Whimper, But a Bang. *Science.org.*

Masselot, P., Mistry, M., Vanoli, J., Schneider, R., Iungman, T., Garcia-Leon, D., Ciscar, J. C., Feyen, L., Orru, H., Urban, A., et al. (2023). Excess Mortality Attributed to Heat and Cold: A Health Impact Assessment Study in 854 Cities in Europe. *Lancet Planet Health, 7*(4), e271–e281.

Matloff, G. (2022). Von Neumann Probes: Rationale, Propulsion, Interstellar Transfer Timing. *International Journal of Astrobiology, 21*(4), 205–211.

Maxwell, S. (2017, April 24). Review of Kate Raworth's Doughnut Economics. *Simon Maxwell Blog.*

Mazzucato, M. (2018). Mission-Oriented Innovation Policies: Challenges and Opportunities. *Industrial and Corporate Change, 27*(5), 803–815.

McAfee, A. (2019). *More from Less: The Surprising Story of How We Learned to Prosper Using Fewer Resources – And What Happens Next.* Scribner.

McAnany, P. A., & Yoffee, N. (2010). *Questioning Collapse: Human Resilience, Ecological Vulnerability, and the Aftermath of Empire.* Cambridge University Press.

McCallum, M. (2015). Vertebrate Biodiversity Losses Point to a Sixth Mass Extinction. *Biodiversity and Conservation, 24,* 2497–2519.

McGlade, C. (2012). A Review of the Uncertainties in Estimates of Global Oil Resources. *Energy, 47*(1), 262–270.

McPhetres, J., & Zuckerman, M. (2018). Religiosity Predicts Negative Attitudes Towards Science and Lower Levels of Science Literacy. *PLoS One, 13*(11), e0207125.

Meadows, D., Meadows, D., Randers, J., & Behrens, W., III. (1972). *The Limits to Growth; A Report for the Club of Rome's Project on the Predicament of Mankind.* Universe Books.

Mearns, E. (2016, May 25). ERoEI for Beginners. *Energy Matters.*

Meho, L. I. (2007). The Rise and Rise of Citation Analysis. *Physics World, 20*(1).

Mitchell, J. (2004). Petroleum Reserves in Question. *Chatham House Paper SDP BP 04/03.*
Mohr, S., Wang, J., Ellem, G., Ward, J., & Giurco, D. (2015). Projection of World Fossil Fuels by Country. *Fuel, 1*, 120–135.
Mokyr, J. (2007). The Power of Ideas. *World Economics, 8*(3), 53–110.
Mokyr, J. (2014, April 28). Growth and Technology: The Wild Ride Ahead. *Milken Institute Review.*
Mokyr, J. (2016). *A Culture of Growth: The Origins of the Modern Economy.* Princeton University Press.
Moloney, E. (2022, March 10). Call to Restart Irish Peat Harvesting Amid Energy Crisis and Russia's War on Ukraine. *Independent.Ie.*
Monbiot, G. (2022, May 19). The Banks Collapsed in 2008 – And Our Food System Is About to Do the Same. *The Guardian.*
Morris, I. (2015). *Foragers, Farmers, and Fossil Fuels: How Human Values Evolve.* Princeton University Press.
Murphy, T. (2015, September 16). You Call this Progress? *Do the Math Blog.*
Murphy, T. (2022a, February 16). Human Exceptionalism. *Do the Math Blog.*
Murphy, T. (2022b). Limits to Economic Growth. *Nature Physics, 18*, 844–847.
Murphy, D. J., & Hall, C. A. (2011). Energy Return on Investment, Peak Oil, and the End of Economic Growth. *Annals of the New York Academy of Sciences, 1219*, 52–72.
Murphy, T., Murphy, D., Love, T., LeHew, M., & McCall, B. (2021). Modernity is Incompatible with Planetary Limits: Developing a PLAN for the Future. *Energy Research & Social Science, 81*, 102239.
Murphy, D. J., Raugei, M., Carbajales-Dale, M., & Rubio Estrada, B. (2022). Energy Return on Investment of Major Energy Carriers: Review and Harmonization. *Sustainability, 14*(12), 7098.
Murray, J., & King, D. (2012). Oil's Tipping Point Has Passed. *Nature, 481*, 433–435.
Naudé, W. (2008). *Entrepreneurship in Economic Development* (Working Paper 2008/20). UNU-WIDER.
Naudé, W. (2021). Artificial Intelligence: Neither Utopian Nor Apocalyptic Impacts Soon. *Economics of Innovation and New Technology, 30*(1), 1–24.
Naudé, W. (2022a). From the Entrepreneurial to the Ossified Economy. *Cambridge Journal of Economics, 46*(1), 105–131.
Naudé, W. (2022b). The Future Economics of Artificial Intelligence: Mythical Agents, a Singleton and the Dark Forest. *IZA Discussion Paper No. 15713.*
Naudé, W. (2023a). Melancholy Hues: The Futility of Green Growth and Degrowth, and the Inevitability of Societal Collapse. *IZA Discussion Paper No. 16139.*
Naudé, W. (2023b). Seven Reasons why Degrowth is No Solution to the Ecological Crisis. *Illuminem*, 23 Mar.

Naudé, W., & Nagler, P. (2015). *Industrialisation, Innovation, Inclusion* (UNU-MERIT Working Paper 2015-043). United Nations University.

Naudé, W. & Nagler, P. (2018). *Technological Innovation, Entrepreneurship and Productivity in Germany, 1871–2015* (SPRU Working Paper Series (SWPS), 2018-02). Science Policy Research Unit, University of Sussex.

Nisbet, R. (1975). Turgot and the Contexts of Progress. *Proceedings of the American Philosophical Society, 119*(3), 214–222.

Nordhaus, T. (2020). Must Growth Doom the Planet? [Review of Growth: From Microorganisms to Megacities, by V. Smil]. *The New Atlantis, 61*, 76–86.

Nordhaus, W. (2021). Are We Approaching an Economic Singularity? Information Technology and the Future of Economic Growth. *American Economic Journal: Macroeconomics, 13*(1), 299–332.

Noy, I. (2009). The Macroeconomic Consequences of Disasters. *Journal of Development Economics, 88*, 221–231.

Obama, B. (2016, October 12). Barack Obama: Now Is the Greatest Time to Be Alive. *Wired.*

Odum, H. (1973). Energy, Ecology, and Economics. *Ambio, 2*(6), 220–227.

Odum, H., & Odum, E. (2001). *A Prosperous Way Down: Principles and Policies.* University Press of Colorado.

OECD. (2009). *Eco-Innovation in Industry: Enabling Green Growth.*

OECD. (2011). *Towards Green Growth* (OECD Green Growth Studies). OECD Publishing.

OECD. (2014). *Green Growth Indicators 2014* (OECD Green Growth Studies). OECD.

Olson, S. J. (2015). Homogeneous Cosmology with Aggressively Expanding Civilizations. *Classical and Quantum Gravity, 32*, 215–225.

Olson, B., Elliott, R., & Matthews, C. M. (2019, January 2). Fracking's Secret Problem – Oil Wells Aren't Producing as Much as Forecast. *The Wall Street Journal.*

Ord, T. (2020). *The Precipice: Existential Risk and the Future of Humanity.* Hachette Books.

Oreskes, N. (2004). The Scientific Consensus on Climate Change. *Science, 30*, 1686–1686.

Osman, M. B., Tierney, J., Zhu, J., Tardif, R., Hakim, G. J., King, J., & Poulsen, C. J. (2021). Globally Resolved Surface Temperatures Since the Last Glacial Maximum. *Nature, 599*(7884), 239–244.

Owen, D. (2011). *The Conundrum: How Scientific Innovation, Increased Efficiency, and Good Intentions Can Make Our Energy and Climate Problems Worse.* Riverhead Books.

Oxfam. (2022, January). Inequality Kills. *Oxfam Briefing Paper.*

Oxfam. (2023, January 16). Richest 1% Bag Nearly Twice as Much Wealth as the Rest of the World Put Together over the Past Two Years. *Press Briefing.*

Park, M., Leahy, E., & Funk, R. (2023). Papers and Patents are Becoming Less Disruptive over Time. *Nature, 613*, 138–144.

Perry, M. (2016, April 21). 18 Spectacularly Wrong Predictions Made Around the Time of the First Earth Day in 1970, Expect More This Year. *AEIdeas.*

Peters, L. (2015). *Sovereignty: The UN and the Westphalian Legacy.* The United Nations/Palgrave Macmillan.

Petigura, E. A., Howard, A., & Marcya, G. (2013). Prevalence of Earth-Size Planets Orbiting Sun-Like Stars. *Proceedings of the National Academy of Sciences, 110*(48), 19273–19278.

Phillips, L. (2019, August 30). The Degrowth Delusion. *Open Democracy.*

Pielke, R. (2023, June 26). Climate Journalism in Broken. *The Honest Broker.*

Pielke, R., & Ritchie. (2021). How Climate Scenarios Lost Touch with Reality. *Issues in Science and Technology, 37*(4).

Pielke, R., Burgess, M. G., & Ritchie, J. (2022). Plausible 2005–2050 Emissions Scenarios Project Between 2 °C and 3 °C of Warming by 2100. *Environmental Research Letters, 17*, 024027.

Pikkety, T. (2013). *Capital in the 21st Century.* Harvard University Press.

Pikkety, T., & Zucman, G. (2014). Capital is Back: Wealth-Income Ratios in Rich Countries 1700–2010. *The Quarterly Journal of Economics, 129*(3), 1255–1310.

Pinker, S. (2018). *Enlightenment Now: The Case for Reason, Science, Humanism, and Progress.* Viking.

Piper, K. (2021, August 3). Can We Save the Planet by Shrinking the Economy? *Vox.*

Pomeranz, K. (2000). *The Great Divergence: China, Europe, and the Making of the Modern World Economy.* Princeton University Press.

Pooley, G., & Tupy, M. L. (2018). *The Simon Abundance Index: A New Way to Measure Availability of Resources* (Policy Analysis No. 857). Cato Institute.

Raddatz, C. (2009). *The Wrath of God: Macroeconomic Costs of Natural Disasters* (Policy Research Working Paper Series WPS 5039). World Bank, Policy Research Department.

Randers, J. (2012). *2052: A Global Forecast for the Next Forty Years.* Chelsea Green Publishing Co.

Rankin, J. (2021, July 16). Enough with the Burning: EU Executive Accused of Sacrificing Forests. *The Guardian.*

Raworth, K. (2017). *Doughnut Economics: Seven Ways to Think Like a 21st-Century Economist.* Random House.

Re, F. (2022). *Can the Theory of Everything Be the Great Filter?* University di Milano Bicocca.

Rees, W. E. (2021). A Note of Climate Change and Cultural Denial. *Population Matters.*

Rees, W. E. (2022). Why Large Cities Won't Survive the Twenty-First Century. In R. Brears (Ed.), *The Palgrave Encyclopedia of Urban and Regional Futures.* Palgrave Macmillan.

Reinsel, D., Gantz, J., & Rydning, J. (2018, November). The Digitization of the World from Edge to Core. *IDC White Paper.*

Rennert, K., Errickson, F., Prest, B., Rennels, L., Newell, R., Pizer, W., Kingdon, C., et al. (2022). Comprehensive Evidence Implies a Higher Social Cost of CO2. *Nature, 610*(7933), 687–692.

Resnick, D., Tarp, F., & Thurlow, J. (2012). The Political Economy of Green Growth: Cases from Southern Africa. *Public Administration & Development, 32*(3), 215–228.

Richards, C., Lupton, R., & Allwood, J. (2021). Re-Framing the Threat of Global Warming: An Empirical Causal Loop Diagram of Climate Change, Food Insecurity and Societal Collapse. *Climatic Change, 164*(49).

Ridley, M. (2011). *The Rational Optimist: How Prosperity Evolves.* Fourth Estate.

Ridley, M. (2015). *The Evolution of Everything: How Small Changes Transform Our World.* 4th Estate Books.

Ridley, M. (2020). *How Innovation Works: And Why It Flourishes in Freedom.* HarperCollins.

Ritchie, P., Clarke, J., Cox, P., & Huntingford, C. (2021). Overshooting Tipping Point Thresholds in a Changing Climate. *Nature, 592*, 517–523.

Robinson, N. (2019, May 29). The World's Most Annoying Man. *Current Affairs.*

Robinson, M., & Shine, T. (2018). Achieving a Climate Justice Pathway to 1.5 °C. *Nature Climate Change, 8*, 564–569.

Rockström, J., Steffen, W., Noone, K., Persson, A., Chapin, F., Lambin, E., Lenton, T., et al. (2009). Planetary Boundaries: Exploring the Safe Operating Space for Humanity. *Ecology and Society, 14*(2).

Rockström, J., Gupta, J., Qin, D., et al. (2023). Safe and Just Earth System Boundaries. *Nature, 619*, 102–111.

Rogoff, K. (2019, May 4). Modern Monetary Nonsense. *Project Syndicate.*

Romer, P. (1986). Increasing Returns and Long-Run Growth. *Journal of Political Economy, 94*(5), 1002–1037.

Romer, P. (1987). Growth Based on Increasing Returns Due to Specialization. *American Economic Review, 77*(2), 56–62.

Romer, P. (1990). Endogenous Technical Change. *Journal of Political Economy, 98*, S71–S102.

Romer, P. (1993). Idea Gaps and Object Gaps in Economic Development. *Journal of Monetary Economics, 32*(3), 543–573.

Romer, P. M. (1994). The Origins of Endogenous Growth. *Journal of Economic Perspectives, 8*(1), 3–22.

Romer, P. (2016, April 13). *The Deep Structure of Economic Growth.* Blog at https://paulromer.net/economic-growth/

Romer, P. (2019, February 5). *The Deep Structure of Economic Growth.* Blog: https://paulromer.net

Roodman, D. (2020, June 15). Modelling the Human Trajectory. *Open Philanthropy.*

Rushkoff, D. (2022). *Survival of the Richest: Escape Fantasies of the Tech Billionaires.* W.W. Norton.

Russell, S. (2019). *Human Compatible: Artificial Intelligence and the Problem of Control.* Viking Books.

Sabin, P. (2013). *The Bet: Paul Ehrlich, Julian Simon, and Our Gamble over Earth's Future.* Yale University Press.

Sagan, C. (1994). *Pale Blue Dot: A Vision of the Human Future in Space.* Ballantyne Books.

Sagan, C. (1997). *The Demon-Haunted World: Science as a Candle in the Dark.* Ballantine Books.

Salgado, S. (2020). *Technical Change and Entrepreneurship.* Mimeo, Wharton School. Available at SSRN.

Sandberg, A. (2013). An Overview of Models of Technological Singularity. In M. More & N. Vita-More (Eds.), *The Transhumanist Reader.* Wiley.

Scharf, C. (2021a). *The Ascent of Information: Books, Bits, Genes, Machines and Life's Unending Algorithm.* Riverhead Books.

Scharf, C. (2021b, October 24). The Selfish Dataome: Does the Data We Produce Serve Us, or Vice Versa? *Nautilus.*

Schiermeier, Q. (2019, July 1). Soviet Union's Collapse Led to Massive Drop in Carbon Emissions. *Nature.*

Schmelzer, M., & Nowshin, T. (2023, June 27). Ecological Reparations and Degrowth: Towards a Convergence of Alternatives Around World-making After Growth. *Development.*

Schokkaert, E. (2019). Review of Kate Raworth's Doughnut Economics. London: Random House. *Erasmus Journal for Philosophy and Economics, 12*(1), 125–132.

Schrager, A. (2022, November 21). Growth Is Still Our Best Hope. *City Journal.*

Schwartzman, D. (2012). A Critique of Degrowth and Its Politics. *Capitalism Nature Socialism, 23*(1), 119–125.

Scranton, R. (2015). *Learning to Die in the Anthropocene: Reflections on the End of a Civilization.* City Lights Publishers.

Sequeira, T., Gil, P., & Alfonso, O. (2018). Endogenous Growth and Entropy. *Journal of Economic Behavior and Organization, 15*, 100–120.

Shahgedanova, M., & Burt, T. (1994). New Data on Air Pollution in the Former Soviet Union. *Global Environmental Change, 4*(3), 201–227.

Shannon, C. (1948). A Mathematical Theory of Communication. *The Bell System Technical Journal, 27*, 379–423.

Shulman, C., & Bostrom, N. (2021). Sharing the World with Digital Minds. In S. Clarke, H. Zohny, & J. Savulescu (Eds.), *Rethinking Moral Status.* Oxford University Press.

Simon, J. (1982). Paul Ehrlich Saying It Is So Doesn't Make It So. *Social Science Quarterly, 63*(2), 381–385.

Simon, J. L. (1996). *The Ultimate Resource 2*. Princeton University Press.

Singer, K. (2023, June 7). Policies for More Ecologically-Sound Tech. *Katie Singer's Substack*.

Smil, V. (2004). *Enriching the Earth: Fritz Haber, Carl Bosch, and the Transformation of World Food Production*. MIT Press.

Smil, V. (2022). *How the World Really Works*. Penguin Books.

Solow, R. M. (1956). A Contribution to the Theory of Economic Growth. *The Quarterly Journal of Economics, 70*(1), 65–94.

Song, H., Kemp, D., Tian, L., Chu, D., Song, H., & Dai, X. (2021). Thresholds of Temperature Change for Mass Extinctions. *Nature Communications, 12*(4694).

Speight, J. (2020). Chapter 5 – Hydraulic Fracturing. In J. Speight (Ed.), *Shale Oil and Gas Production Processes*. Gulf Professional Publishing.

Steel, D., DesRoches, T., & Mintz-Woo, K. (2022). Climate Change and the Threat to Civilization. *Proceedings of the National Academy of Sciences, 119*(42), e2210525119.

Steen, R. (2011). Retractions in the Scientific Literature: Is the Incidence of Research Fraud Increasing? *Journal of Medical Ethics, 37*, 249–253.

Steffen, W., Richardson, K., Rockström, J., Cornell, S., Fetzer, I., et al. (2015a). Planetary Boundaries: Guiding Human Development on a Changing Planet. *Science, 347*(6223), 1259855.

Steffen, W., Broadgate, W., Deutsch, L., Gaffney, O., & Ludwig, C. (2015b). The Trajectory of the Anthropocene: The Great Acceleration. *The Anthropocene Review, 2*(1), 81–98.

Stern, N., Stiglitz, J., & Taylor, C. (2022). The Economics of Immense Risk, Urgent Action and Radical Change: Towards New Approaches to the Economics of Climate Change. *Journal of Economic Methodology, 29*(3), 181–216.

Stevenson, B., & Wolfers, J. (2013). Subjective Well-Being and Income: Is There Any Evidence of Satiation? *The American Economic Review, 103*(3), 598–604.

Stiglitz, J. E., Sen, A., & Fitoussi, J.-P. (2009). *Report by the Commission on the Measurement of Economic Performance and Social Progress*. Commission on the Measurement of Economic Performance and Social Progress.

Supran, G., & Hickey, C. (2022). *Three Shades of Green (washing): Content Analysis of Social Media Discourse by European Oil, Car, and Airline Companies*. Available at https://ati.io/three-shades-of-greenwashing/

Syvitski, J., Waters, C., Day, J., et al. (2020). Extraordinary Human Energy Consumption and Resultant Geological Impacts Beginning around 1950 CE Initiated the Proposed Anthropocene Epoch. *Communications Earth and Environment, 1*, 32.

Tainter, J. (1988). *The Collapse of Complex Societies*. Cambridge University Press.

Tansley, A. (1935). The Use and Abuse of Vegetational Concepts. *Ecology, 16*, 284–307.

Tenreyro, S. (2018). *The Fall in Productivity Growth: Causes and Implications.* Bank of England Preston Lecture Theatre, Queen Mary University of London.

Timperley, J. (2021). The Broken $100-Billion Promise of Climate Finance – And How to Fix It. *Nature, 5982*, 400–402.

Tirole, J. (2021). Digital Dystopia. *American Economic Review, 111*(6), 2007–2048.

Torres, E. (2021, July 28). The Dangerous Ideas of Longtermism and Existential Risk. *Current Affairs.*

Truscello, M. (2018). Catastrophism and Its Critics: On the New Genre of Environmentalist Documentary Film. In J. Jagodzinski (Ed.), *Interrogating the Anthropocene* (Palgrave Studies in Educational Futures). Palgrave Macmillan.

Turchin, P. (2003). *Historical Dynamics: Why States Rise and Fall.* Princeton University Press.

Turchin, P. (2023). *End Times: Elites, Counter-Elites, and the Path of Political Disintegration.* Penguin.

Turchin, P., & Gavrilets, S. (2009). Evolution of Complex Hierarchical Societies. *Social Evolution & History, 8*(2), 167–198.

Turner, G. (2008). A Comparison of the Limits to Growth with 30 Years of Reality. *Global Environmental Change, 18*(3), 397–411.

Turner, G. (2014). Is Global Collapse Imminent? An Updated Comparison of the Limits to Growth with Historical Data. *Melbourne Sustainable Society Institute, Research Paper No. 4.*

Tverberg, G. E. (2012). Oil Supply Limits and the Continuing Financial Crisis. *Energy, 37*, 27–34.

Ugur, M., Trushin, E., & Solomon, E. (2016). A Firm-Level Dataset for Analyzing Entry, Exit, Employment and R&D Expenditures in the UK: 1997–2012. *Data in Brief, 8*, 153–157.

UNEP. (2022). *The Closing Window: Emissions Gap Report 2022.* United Nations Environmental Programme.

Valdes, F., & Freitas, R. A., Jr. (1980). Comparison of Reproducing and Nonreproducing Starprobe Strategies for Galactic Exploration. *Journal of the British Interplanetary Society, 33*, 402–408.

van den Bergh, J. (2011). Environment versus Growth – A Criticism of Degrowth and a Plea for A-growth. *Ecological Economics, 70*(5), 881–890.

van der Leeuw, S. (2020). *Social Sustainability, Past and Future: Undoing Unintended Consequences for the Earth's Survival.* Cambridge University Press.

Varieur, B., Fisher, S., & Landrigan, P. (2022). Air Pollution, Political Corruption, and Cardiovascular Disease in the Former Soviet Republics. *Annals of Global Health, 88*(1), 48.

Varoufakis, Y. (2021, June 28). Techno-Feudalism Is Taking Over. *Project Syndicate.*

Varoufakis, Y. (2023). *Technofeudalism: What Killed Capitalism.* Penguin.

Vollrath, D. (2019). *Fully Grown: Why a Stagnant Economy Is a Sign of Success.* University of Chicago Press.

Von Foerster, H., Mora, P. M., & Amio, L. (1960). Doomsday: Friday, 13 November A.D. 2026. *Science, 132*(3436), 1291–1295.

Wackernagel, M., & Rees, W. (1996). *Our Ecological Footprint: Reducing Human Impact on the Earth.* New Society Publishers.

Wallace-Wells, D. (2019, February 2). 'The Devastation of Human Life Is in View': What a Burning World Tells Us About Climate Change. *The Guardian.*

Ward, P., & Brownlee, D. (2000). *Rare Earth: Why Complex Life Is Uncommon in the Universe.* Copernicus Books.

Ward, J., Sutton, P., Werner, A., Costanza, R., Mohr, S., & Simmons, C. (2016). Is Decoupling GDP Growth from Environmental Impact Possible? *PLoS One, 11*(10), e0164733.

Waters, C., & Turner, S. (2022). Defining the Onset of the Anthropocene. *Science, 378*(6621), 706–708.

WEC. (2013). *World Energy Resources: Survey 2013.* World Energy Council.

Weinersmith, Z. (2014, June 4). Humpty Dumpty and the Great Second Law: A Physics Fable. *Medium.*

Weinstein, E. (2021). *Embedded Growth Obligations.* The Portal Group.

Weiss, H., & Bradley, R. S. (2001). What Drives Societal Collapse? *Science, 291*(5504), 609–610.

Weiss, M., & Claudio Cattaneo, C. (2017). Degrowth – Taking Stock and Reviewing an Emerging Academic Paradigm. *Ecological Economics, 137*, 220–230.

Weitzman, M. (1998). Recombinant Growth. *Quarterly Journal of Economics, 113*(2), 331–360.

West, G. (2017). *Scale: The Universal Laws of Life and Death in Organisms, Cities and Companies.* Weidenfeld and Nicolson.

Wheeler, J. B. (1989). Information, physics, quantum: The search for links. In W. H. Zurek (Ed.), *Complexity, Entropy, and the Physics of Information.* Addison-Wesley.

Wiblin, R., & Harris, K. (2021, August 19). Holden Karnofsky on the Most Important Century. *80,000 Hours Podcast.*

Wiedmann, T., Schandl, H., Lenzen, M., Moran, D., Suh, S., West, J., & Kanemoto, K. (2015). The Material Footprint of Nations. *Proceedings of the National Academy of Sciences, 112*(20), 6271–6276.

Wilczek, F. (1999). Getting Its from Bits. *Nature, 397*, 303–306.

Willcock, S., Cooper, G. S., Addy, J., & Dearing, J. A. (2023, June). Earlier Collapse of Anthropocene Ecosystems driven by Multiple Faster and Noisier Drivers. *Nature Sustainability.*

Willett, W., Rockström, J., Loken, B., Springmann, M., et al. (2019). Food in the Anthropocene: the EAT-Lancet Commission on Healthy Diets from Sustainable Food Systems. *The Lancet, 393*(10170), 447–492.

WMO (2023). *WMO Global Annual to Decadal Climate Update (Target years: 2023–2027)*. World Meteorological Society.

Wong, M. L., & Bartlett, S. (2022). Asymptotic Burnout and Homeostatic Awakening: A Possible Solution to the Fermi Paradox? *Journal of the Royal Society Interface, 19*, 20220029.

World Bank. (2012). *Inclusive Green Growth: The Pathway to Sustainable Development.* The World Bank.

World Bank. (2021). *The Changing Wealth of Nations 2021: Managing Assets for the Future.* World Bank.

Wright, R. (2023, June 29). Artificial Intelligence and the Noosphere: Seeing the age of AI in cosmic perspective can help us navigate it. *Nonzero Newsletter.*

Wrigley, E. (2010). *Energy and the English Industrial Revolution.* Cambridge University Press.

Wrigley, E. (2011, July 22). Opening Pandoras Box: A New Look at the Industrial Revolution. *VOXEU.*

Wunderling, N., Donges, J., Kurths, J., & Winkelmann, R. (2020). Interacting Tipping Elements Increase Risk of Climate Domino Effects Under Global Warming. *Earth Systems Dynamics, 18*, 1–21.

Zackrisson, E., Calissendor, P., González, J., Benson, A., Johansen, A., & Janson, M. (2016). Terrestrial Planets Across Space and Time. *The Astrophysical Journal, 833*(2), 1–12.

Zeihan, P. (2022, April 27). Greentech and the End of the World. *Zeihan on Geopolitics* (Blog).

Zeihan, P. (2023, February 2). Deglobalization: There's No Stopping It Now. *Zeihan on GeoPolitics.*

Zysman, J., & Huberty, M. (2012). Religion and Reality in the Search for Green Growth. *Intereconomics, 3*, 140–163.

Index[1]

[1] Note: Page numbers followed by 'n' refer to notes.

W. Naudé, *Economic Growth and Societal Collapse*,
https://doi.org/10.1007/978-3-031-45582-7

www.ingramcontent.com/pod-product-compliance
Ingram Content Group UK Ltd.
Pitfield, Milton Keynes, MK11 3LW, UK
UKHW020835290926
15470UKWH00004B/1370

* 9 7 8 3 0 3 1 4 5 5 8 1 0 *